The Splendid Years

The Splendid Years

The Memoirs of an Abbey Actress and 1916 Rebel

Maire Nic Shiubhlaigh with
Edward Kenny

Edited By David Kenny

NEW ISLAND

THE SPLENDID YEARS
First published in 1955 by James Duffy.
This edition published in 2016 by
New Island Books,
16 Priory Hall Office Park,
Stillorgan,
County Dublin.
Republic of Ireland.

www.newisland.ie

PRINT ISBN: 978-1-84840-509-7
EPUB ISBN: 978-1-84840-510-3
MOBI ISBN: 978-1-84840-511-0

British Library Cataloguing Data.
A CIP catalogue record for this book is available from the British Library.

Typeset by JVR Creative India
Cover design by Karen Vaughan
Printed by ScandBook AB, Sweden

In memory of my father,
Edward 'Ted' Kenny,
and my friend Paul Drury.
The two greatest journalists I have known.

– D.K. (2016)

'I have squandered the splendid years that the Lord God gave to my youth ... Lord, if I had the years, I would squander them over again.'

— 'The Fool', P. H. Pearse

Contents

PART FOUR – THE RISING

Introduction

by David Kenny

I

THE FOLLOWING is a story about the Abbey and Yeats that has never been told before.

It's a cold, crisp December afternoon in the fourth year of the new century, and the curtain has just fallen on Kathleen Ni Houlihan (not literally). Yeats's silver mane trails like a will-o'-the-wisp up the aisle towards the bar area. A member of the Walker/ Nic Shiubhlaigh family spots him and points him out to his companion. 'Get up there and say hello,' the companion orders. 'He'll be glad to meet you.'

The Yeats who is being observed is Michael Yeats—son of W. B.—and the Walker is me. My mother, Gráinne Kenny, in between rib-nudges, has pointed out that Yeats and I are the only two people at the centenary celebrations who have blood ties to the founding of the Abbey Theatre. Five members of my father's family were either on the stage or working behind the scenes on its opening night in 1904. My grand-aunt, Maire Nic Shiubhlaigh, was the first leading lady, playing Kathleen; grand-uncle Frank was the young man in *On Baile's Strand*; great-grandmother Mary Anne was the wardrobe mistress; and my grandmother 'Gipsy' and grand-aunt Annie were selling programmes. The latter were also actresses, appearing under the names 'Betty King' and 'Eileen O'Doherty'.

It is entirely probable too that my great grandfather, Matthew, printed the bills and programmes. He was a master printer and had his own publishing company, the Tower Press. He also printed the *War News* for Pearse and the 1917 edition of the Proclamation.

Michael Yeats only had his father there on the opening night, so I outnumbered him in terms of ghosts of thespians past. I tried to focus on this utterly ridiculous piece of logic as I nervously followed him through the bar, past the John B. Yeats portrait of my grandaunt … and into the gents.

I waited by the door, my cheeks glowing redder than a Sellafield fish. I have never been in the habit of hanging around toilet doors. I collared Mr Yeats as he left. He was in his eighties and the spitting image of his father, whose poetry I have always loved. I said something along the lines of: 'Mr Yeats … portrait … bar area … grand-aunt … mumble … mumble.'

He stared at me, relatively benignly for a man being accosted in a public toilet.

'I beg your pardon?'

I composed myself, remembering that, according to my dad, John B. Yeats was in love with Maire and had proposed to her with the words: 'How would you like to be the stepmother of an internationally famous poet?' I made a mental note not to repeat those uncorroborated words to Michael Yeats.

'Your grandad, John B. Yeats, was very good friends with my grand-aunt, Maire Nic Shiubhlaigh.'

If octogenarian eyes can dance, his did a rumba.

'Maire was your grand-aunt? Beautiful woman. I have a sketch of her in my hallway at home in Dalkey.'

I couldn't have been more nervous if I had been speaking to Willie Yeats himself. My brain crashed, and I heard myself saying: 'I live in Dalkey too.'

His subsequent look reflected the idiocy of this pointless statement. He must have felt sorry for me, as he ignored it and continued.

'Maire and my father had a dreadful row,' he said. I was stunned. History concertinaed. Here was Yeats's son describing the schism at the heart of the Abbey in 1905 over professionalism versus patriotism that led to my grand-aunt walking out, with several other leading players. It wasn't just a 'row': it rocked the Abbey to its foundations, and led to the founding of the Theatre of Ireland with MacDonagh and Plunkett among other 1916 notables. Again, I was stuck for words.

'Oh well,' I stammered, 'that's water under the bridge now.'

Before he had time to reflect on the astonishing banality of this comment, the toilet door was thrown open by a large rustic gentleman in desperate need of the loo. In my memory's half-blind eye I can see Michael Yeats being flung across the floor by the force of the blow.

He wasn't of course, but it seemed like a natural end to our conversation. As he rubbed his shoulder, I mumbled 'bye' and legged it. While I in no way advocate violence (intentional or otherwise) against the elderly, I like to think that this was Maire giving Yeats a dead arm, by proxy, from the beyond the grave.

Willie Yeats richly deserved it, certainly in the eyes of my father. He spent his entire life raging against the misconception that Yeats alone had 'founded' our national theatre.

The above anecdote may seem like an odd way to open an introduction to my grand-aunt's personal recollections of the Abbey's foundation and the fight in Jacob's. It is certainly a bit crude, but that's the way it happened. Life is seldom 'neat'. The call I received from Michael Yeats a few months later was equally embarrassing. I was in work at the *Herald* and thought the voice on the other end of the phone was my publisher, Ed Higel, playing a trick on me. I used some choice Dublin expletives, joining in on the 'joke'. Michael Yeats must have thought I was an utter fruitcake. Again, he was polite and told me he hadn't any new information for me about the Abbey spat. I still cringe thinking about that call.

Both encounters illustrate, for me, how close we still are to the pivotal events in Irish history. Michael Yeats remembered the Abbey 'split' of 1905 as a 'terrible row' between his father and my grand-aunt. It was as though we were discussing a recent family spat.

History is all around us. It's still tangible. Walk through the GPO and you are retracing the steps of Pearse and Connolly. There are still Irish people alive who were children during the Civil War. The over-forties in Ireland remember the Troubles that were brought about by the partitioning of our island—a direct result of the actions of the brave people who rose up against the British Empire between 1916 and 1922. Search your attic and you may find a letter or a medal or a mildewed souvenir kept by a dead relative. These may lead you back to the Repeal Movement or the Parnell era or the cultural revival or 1916. Talk to someone in their late seventies or eighties and you may be rewarded with childhood memories of their aunts or uncles who played a part in securing freedom for the greater part of this island.

That is how close 1916 and the War of Independence are. They are two generations, or less, away.

Michael Yeats grew up in the shadow of our greatest poet. My father, who wrote this book, grew up in the shadow of the Abbey and 1916. I grew up in the shadow of my father, knowing, in broad terms, that our family had been involved in some of the most momentous events in Irish history, and knowing also that he had written a book when he was in his late teens. The book had not been available to the wider public since 1955 because he had taken it out of print soon after its publication. He was unhappy with his publishers, James Duffy, for omissions and stylistic oversights. I also knew that Ted was working on a much bigger narrative incorporating *The Splendid Years*. He intended it to be an Irish *Roots* (Alex Haley's book was enjoying huge success at the time).

And that is just about the sum of what I knew. Dad and I spoke, but we didn't always communicate. I listened, but only half-listened. I was young and I loved him, but he carried his family's sense of injustice, of being forgotten, on his shoulders all his life. This made communication about the subject with him quite difficult for me. He was a product of his upbringing: raised by his widowed mother, his 1916-veteran aunt and her husband, who was a former Director of Intelligence of the IRA.

When dad died in 1999, aged seventy-two, he took his store of family lore and memories with him — or so I believed. I thought that I would never corroborate any of the outlandish tales that managed to get through to me: the story of how one of his forebears had split with his Ascendancy family, converted and married a nun; how my great-grandad had been a firm friend of Parnell's, and had walked the eight miles, from Glasthule, into the GPO on Easter Monday (at the age of seventy) to fight for Ireland; how his auntie Maire had co-founded the Abbey Theatre; and how much of a pretentious tosspot W. B. Yeats really was.

Twelve years after his death, I finally began sifting through his remaining papers and the mildewed 'junk' in his office at my mother's house. He had given the most important papers and memorabilia to the National Library and Northwest University Illinois in 1966. What I found was considered 'ephemera' fifty years ago. There was an old battered sea chest stuffed with torn and bruised fragments: a masonic passport dated 1811, love letters to my granny from a dead poet, Victorian photographs taken in Vance's on Stephen's Green, small circular headshots of the 1916 signatories, printed samples of Pearse's handwriting, Cuala prints....

There was a copy of a nicotine-dyed portrait of Maire as Lavarcham, painted by A.E., which hung in our sitting room when I was a child. It had spooked me and I always used to sit with my back to it while watching *Zorro* and *Swap Shop* on the black-and-white PYE TV. In my mother's kitchen there was a blue steel tray that had been a wedding gift from an old friend of my granny's. And, above all, there was dad's treasured collection of dusty books, including two copies of *The Splendid Years*. Next to these was a signed edition of Tom Barry's *Guerilla Days in Ireland*. The inscription read: 'Major General Eamonn Price, IRA, Dublin. To Bob—my brother-in-law. As a token of friendship and as a reminder of the guerilla days when you served as one of the senior officers of the Army of the Republic. Tom Barry, Cork, 28.10.1949'.

Naturally, this grabbed my attention. I read Barry's book before *The Splendid Years*, and was hooked on the period. The next book I picked up was *Somewhere to the Sea* by Kenneth Reddin (again, before *The Splendid Years*). It's a love story set against the backdrop of the War of Independence. I nearly dropped it when Maire and Granny Gip appeared as talking characters on Bloody Sunday, and in the former's case described as a 1916 veteran.

I wanted to know more. The fog of childhood memories condensed. I recalled our holiday home in Laytown where I spent the first ten summers of my life. On a bedroom wall there was a wedding photo showing Michael Collins as best man. In the annex there was a glass case of stuffed birds, a painted wardrobe and a pristine but ancient typewriter (said to have belonged to James Joyce). I slowly put the pieces together. Last century's ephemera was pushing and prompting my curiosity. It was tugging at the hem of my conscience. I found a black-bordered letter addressed to Maire from a man called Rónán. He was asking her if he had ever lived up to the expectations of his mother, Áine. Was she disappointed that he had not become the man his father had been? He had cared for Áine all his life, and was clearly in a state of deep depression.

I found out who that man was, and wrote an article about him for the *Irish Examiner* in 2013. I'll deviate briefly from this narrative now to share that story with you.

MAY 2013. My mother was watching us from the sink, through the steam rising from her potato pot. 'Come in for your tea and bring my good blue tray with you.' Her 'good blue tray' had been discarded and was leaning against the blackened anthracite bunker.

It was bearing up remarkably well, considering it had spent the morning being used as a sleigh. It was an expensive tray, bought as a wedding present in Switzer's by a friend of my father's family, the Walkers. A man named Rónán. He was a 'sad figure', my mother said.

I grew up surrounded by 1916 memorabilia. Not holsters or bayonets, but minutiae: buttons, photographs, books. A blue tray. History exists in both the heroic and the mundane. My dad's family was steeped in 1916. My great-grandad, Matthew Walker, printed the *Irish War News* for Pearse and delivered his farewell letter to his mother. My Abbey actress grandmother (Gipsy Kenny) carried despatches for Charlie Burgess—you know him as Cathal Brugha. My grand-aunt, Maire nic Shiubhlaigh, led Cumann na mBan at Jacob's during the Rising.

Seven years ago I was rustling through grand-aunt Maire's papers when a letter fluttered to the floor. It was from a man who had lost his mother. It was signed, simply, 'Rónán'. I had an inkling whom he might be, so I searched my father's books and took down Piaras F. Mac Lochlainn's *Last Words: Letters and Statements of the Leaders Executed after the Rising at Easter 1916*. I found the entry I was looking for and returned to the letter. I saw a ten-year-old boy holding a watch chain outside Kilmainham Gaol. The boy is Éamonn Ceannt's son, Rónán. He is the man who gave us the blue tray. His mother is Áine Ceannt. Maire had spent the day before the Rising at their house.

The tragically modest tone of Rónán's letter gives the impression of a man who feels that life has passed him by:

> Maire, from time to time, for years past, I have wondered if mamy [*sic*] was, in a way, disappointed in me for not having shown myself to have been as fine a man as my father was.
>
> I never had the courage to ask mamy, and she never gave me any special reason for my idea, but, yet, she may, deep down, have felt I was a bit of a failure. I'd rather know the answer to that question than be kept in ignorance, so if mamy ever spoke of the matter, will you please tell me what she said, even if it's hard to hear? Please remember, I'm not just looking for words of praise and suchlike but just to be told the truth. Whilst I haven't exactly got an 'inferiority complex', at the same time I have no great sense of my own importance, and it won't do me any harm to know the truth.
>
> Mamy loved my father until death parted them, and until she died she loved and honoured his memory and felt hurt when he appeared to be forgotten by those who owed him, equally with his companions, the freedom and good life which 1916 ushered in.
>
> Therefore, it might have seemed to her that my lack of forcefulness etc. as compared with my father's courage

was a bit of a 'let-down', shall we say. Anyhow, tell me, if you know.

Rónán had never recovered from the death of his father. His words contrast starkly with Éamonn's as he awaited his fate. He calmly bequeaths a watch chain to Rónán and writes that everyone is cheerful and resigned to their fates. 'Tell Rónán to be a good boy and remember Easter 1916 forever.'

A few hours before dawn, at 2.30 a.m., Éamonn lets his emotional mask slip and writes to Áine:

> Not wife but widow before these lines reach you. I am here without hope of this world [...] My poor little sweetheart [...] Ever my comforter [...] What can I say? I die a noble death for Ireland. My sweetheart of the hawthorn hedges and Summer's eves....

An hour later, he is blindfolded and put sitting on a soapbox before being executed. His son's letter shows the tragic effect the executions of the 1916 leaders had on their families. Áine became an anti-Treaty 'diehard' during the Civil War, and suffered for it.

Rónán suffered too. Try to imagine being ten, knowing that your father is about to be shot. Try to imagine then living in the shadow of a colossus you could never hope to emulate. Ceannt's death was no sterile 'blood sacrifice'; it was a tragedy for his family. He was a man, not an icon. He was one of us.

As Éamonn was preparing to die, another comrade was penning his final words. Michael Mallin wrote to his baby son: 'Joseph, my little man, be a priest if you can.' Father Joseph is still alive today. That's how near 1916 is.

Éamonn's last words to his son were: 'My little son, Rónán. Take care of your mother.' Rónán fulfilled his father's wishes. He never married, and looked after his mother until her death. He never realised it, but he too was a hero. He gave up his own life for the care of another. Éamonn and Rónán Ceannt showed that ordinary people are capable of extraordinary selflessness. That's the true legacy of 1916. Revolutions are fought by ordinary people hoping to build an ordinary world.

Our Ireland needs heroes. We can draw on the memory of their courage to rebuild our country, post-Troika. We're still the same race that produced men like Éamonn Ceannt. 1916 is only a fingernail's breadth away. It's in the mundane. It's in an old letter. It's in a tray skittering down a snow-clad garden. It's in all of us.

II

My father must have felt the same way as Rónán to some extent. How could he ever hope to emulate the heroism of his aunt, uncle and mother? It is an extraordinary compliment to Maire that Rónán was so intimate with her, sharing his deep sense of self-doubt. Áine had been shunned, Maire had been 'airbrushed'. They had that feeling of being forgotten in common.

I continued to look for more clues about the family with which Ted was so besotted. Every now and then I would receive emails from historians wanting to know more about Maire Nic Shiubhlaigh. I, in turn, learned snippets from these people. I didn't put very much effort into it. As a veteran hack, I should have researched and written the family history in a matter of months, not years. Perhaps some psychologist can explain why I, and my father, dithered. Could it be something to do with not wanting to let go of the past?

The advent of 2016 finally prompted me to make my father's corrections to *The Splendid Years*; to republish the book that meant so much to him as it wrote Maire back into the narrative of the Abbey's history. Yeats had claimed the credit for founding the theatre and training the actors. In his Nobel speech he praised Sara Allgood, her acting 'rival', and didn't mention Maire.

Dad would point out, on the rare occasions when we would talk about the Abbey, 'Yeats founded the Irish Literary Theatre, which was a failure. The Fay brothers, my aunt and uncle and others, founded the national theatre. They were the visionaries who gave him bodies and voices to get his work across.'

That may sound simplistic, but the truth is that Yeats and Lady Gregory had been waiting for Irish actors to emerge and create a movement that would lead to the Abbey. Yeats and Gregory were generals without an army. The Fays and the Walkers were troops awaiting ammunition and leadership. Together they rebelled against the conventions of the day and created a new dramatic voice.

The Splendid Years recounts those early days from the perspective of Maire Nic Shiubhlaigh. It is *not* a biography; it is her personal recollections of two periods: the national theatre movement and 1916, as told to my father. It's a modest account in many ways. She didn't want to stoke up old rows, and underplays the sacrifices she and her family made for Irish nationalism.

Her personal writings in the National Library of Ireland are a little less discreet, and reveal her sense of humour. She raises the curtain just enough for us to see how she truly felt about certain individuals: poseur Yeats was horrible to her; Sara Allgood could be a bit of a monster; Pearse's worship of Yeats was on one occasion 'disgusting'. In *The Splendid Years*, however, she is kindness personified.

That is not to say that this is a PC account of a theatre's birth and a rebellion. (How could any account of either of these things be bland?) It is far from it. It bristles and fizzes with vignettes and cameos from Joyce, Synge, Marcievicz.... Its pace and voice are contemporary. This is my father's influence. He was a phenomenally gifted journalist.

So who was Maire Nic Shiubhlaigh?

Mary Elizabeth Walker was born on 8 May 1883 (died 9 November 1958) in Charlemont Street, Dublin, into a prominent nationalist *Gaelgoiri* family. Her father was Matthew Walker, who published a Parnellite paper in Carlow, the *Vindicator*, and was a member of the IRB. He printed the *War News* for Pearse in 1916 (and the 1917 version of the Proclamation, among other periodicals and seditious IRB material).

Maire started acting in her late teens and was a founder-member of the Abbey Theatre, and its first leading lady on its opening night in 1904 when she appeared as Kathleen Ni

Houlihan. After splitting with the Abbey in 1905 in a row over W. B. Yeats's move to make the theatre professional, she went on to help found the Theatre of Ireland, and led Cumann na mBan in Jacob's in 1916.

That's the overview. Maire did an awful lot more than that. She was always destined to do her bit for the cause of national freedom. To understand her nationalist idealism we must look at her family background, and in particular her extraordinary father, Matt.

While researching the Walker family history for this introduction, I stumbled across an old manuscript in my mother's home. To my absolute astonishment and delight it was the skeleton of the 'greater' book my dad had been working on before his death. It's called *The Walkers and The Splendid Years*. He was interspersing the family story with sections of Maire's text from this book. It is unfinished, except for one part: the story of the Walkers' life in Carlow during the last momentous period in Irish political life before the Rising: the Parnell split.

Without this, I would never have fully understood how Maire came to be such a committed nationalist. It is published here for the first time.

III

The Renegade Walkers

— by Edward Kenny

MARY ANNE WALKER was the well-dressed young matron who used to walk down Tullow Street in Carlow town in the early 1890s, performing her weekly shopping with an air that caused plenty of comment—and some hidden envy of the way she carried it off.

On these expeditions she would always be accompanied by at least two of her six children. Sometimes it would be the eldest boy, Frank, aged about thirteen, and the second boy, Charlie, both in immaculately cut sailor blouses and neat knickerbockers. Or it might be the eldest girl, Daisy, and the second girl, Maire—slender, with shoulder-length blondish hair and strange, attractive golden-brown eyes.

It was characteristic of Mary Anne that the girls were always dressed the same as her, apart from one or two minor technical differences. Their skirts would, of course, be folded elegantly five or six inches above their buttoned ankle-boots, and while Mary Anne always wore a large, well-endowed hat, they would sometimes go bare-headed or wear ribboned headgear on warm summer days.

Otherwise, their outfits would duplicate hers, down to the square-crocheted panel on their bosoms, their narrow, pinched-in waistlines, and sometimes even a knitted shawl or short cape in shiny, rustling material.

By all accounts, this weekly trip was quite a sight, moving from shop to shop behind Mary Anne, the cherries on her hat clinking defiantly when she nodded to acquaintances or tried to ignore those who pointedly passed her by. There was a constant undercurrent about these encounters. The public image she projected was of a well-organised, slightly dehumanised woman who knew what she wanted and minded her own business. On her shopping trips she seldom carried anything heavier than a pair of gloves, and she never brought her purchases home with her. The amount of food she bought was never particularly large, and it was surprising that she was never refused when she ordered that it be delivered to her door.

It would have been natural for her to avoid certain shops where the well-to-do did their business, and whose owners' politics differed so violently from her husband's. But she had the ability to invest everything she did with an air of elegant significance that made all her gestures, however small, seem important. When she went shopping with her little entourage, the comments would vary between 'There's the Dublin dressmaker from the Athy Road,' to, more maliciously, 'That Parnellite woman is ordering people around again.'

About five years later, when the time came for Mary Anne and her family to leave Carlow, she allowed herself the luxury of reflection as she locked up the little Walker home. One of her greatest attributes was her objectivity, and she was able to conclude, rightly, that she was leaving with a mixture of regret and relief. She had loved the town, with its heaving market days, narrow sloping streets and busy, barge-filled river. She would miss the friends she had made, but in her mind politics and Carlow would always go together. It was not so long ago that a stone had crashed through one of her upstairs windows, narrowly missing a sleeping child. She knew that old bitterness dies hard.

Essentially, Mary Anne Walker was a warm-hearted, impulsively generous woman, and the image she projected when she first went to Carlow was assumed. She called it her 'armour', and the fact that she felt she had to assume it was as good as any commentary on conditions in Ireland at the time, and the controversy in which she and her husband were involved.

In 1891, when Matt Walker went to Carlow with his young family, Parnell's hitherto unassailable position as head of the Parliamentary Party was already badly eroded. His spectacular career was about to crash in even more sensational fashion. A whole era in Irish political history was ending, and the Walkers, typically, were caught up in the most unprofitable aspect of it.

Matt was an unsuccessful businessman. He was a printer, and his political affiliations had brought him back from Dublin to his native Carlow to manage an unprofitable local newspaper, the Parnellite *Vindicator*, at the height of the Irish Party split. The paper was new, vocal, and doomed to failure even before Matt arrived. Parnell, already involved in the O'Shea divorce suit, had not even tried to defend himself, had lost the case, and public opinion was outraged.

It was a time when past work was forgotten. Parnell's rise to power and his extraordinary political achievements in less than ten years, and the personality and eloquence that had welded the diverse elements of the party together, dumbfounded Westminster and made Home Rule a probability. The final blow was the opposition of the Irish bishops. Its effect on a Catholic electorate ended Parnell's chances of a return to political power. In Carlow it established Matt, Mary and their children, if not as apostates, then at least as Parnellite outsiders, which was nearly as bad.

In 1891, the biggest political controversy in decades was raging in Ireland. Carlow is a town about sixty miles from Dublin, in a region split, as everywhere was, on the Parnell issue. It would be unfair to assess its attitudes only through Mary Anne's eyes. If the Walkers felt they were cold-shouldered by elements in the town, it was as much their own fault as anyone else's: they were taking a rigid political stand. The effect of the Parnell–O'Shea scandal was devastating, and the bitterness that followed it was intense.

It isn't easy at this distance in time to realise the effect produced by the divorce action without knowing the place Parnell had held in Irish minds. He was, or had been, a national idol. Someone had called him the Tribune of Ireland: the enigmatic political leader who forced his will and the Irish case on the blasé British Parliament. He had just emerged triumphantly from the Pigott forgeries scandal, making him even more popular. In London, *The Times* had published facsimiles of letters allegedly by Parnell condoning the murder in the Phoenix Park of the new Chief Secretary for Ireland, Lord Cavendish, and the permanent Undersecretary, Burke.

Pigott, who had forged the letters, confessed under cross-examination, escaped to Spain and shot himself. The effect on Parnell's image was tremendous. British public opinion, outraged at the deception, swung violently in his favour. His prestige was never greater. In the Commons, his opponents had risen alongside his supporters to applaud his return after the forgeries were exposed. Into the middle of all this, the divorce petition by O'Shea, a former Parnellite, had dropped like a bomb. It certainly looked like another conspiracy, and the surprise that followed Parnell's decision not to contest the charge threw the country into confusion. Incredibly, it seemed that he could not foresee the danger and believed that his political ability and his reputation as a leader would prevail over the moral issue. He also believed that his marriage to Kitty O'Shea after the divorce settlement would settle it once and for all.

However, outraged Catholic sensibilities, combined with the political implications of the situation after Gladstone virtually demanded Parnell's removal, was enough to demolish his popularity irredeemably. The Irish Party split in two. The issue was swamped in a storm of recrimination, accusation and counter-accusation.

It was against this background of blind, sometimes bigoted, bickering, of disappointment and despair, that Walker and his younger brother, Ned, tried to publish a newspaper vindicating Parnell, and Mary Anne tried to rear a young family. Inevitably, the emotion that was to prevail among the Walker children was one of rigid self-sacrificial nationalism, and it was a feeling that was to persist in every member of the family for the rest of their lives.

The *Vindicator*, published weekly for a penny, stumbled out every Thursday, sustained by the Walkers' hard work, the remains of the finance voted to it by the pro-Parnell elements in the Irish Party, and a lot of faith and hope, to say nothing of charity. It frequently ranted unreasonably, and just as frequently it sustained body blows from the clergy, who had a captive audience at Mass on Sundays.

Public opinion varied as the controversy continued, and there were breaks in both camps. One *Vindicator* employee left indignantly after a talk with his confessor, on the grounds that Parnellites were anti-Christs. On the other hand, two Catholic curates from a parish across the River Barrow in Kilkenny used to arrive on printing nights, muffled in topcoats, minus canonical leave and Roman collars, to take turns at winding the Wharfedale press that turned out the ever-diminishing copies.

The paper was an informative product of its time, but not for the general news that it carried, which was slight. Its editorial content varied between what its limited reporting staff could glean locally after coverage of pro-Parnell meetings in Carlow and elsewhere, and surprisingly close-to-the-bone police scandals lifted from the Dublin and English papers.

It was a four-page broadsheet. Its entire front page of advertisements reflected political affiliations pretty well in that part of south-east Leinster during the period; farmers, businessmen, craftsmen and professionals who were still in the National League stood by it financially. But it was significant that nearly a year after it was launched in early 1891, its biggest display ads were house ones: it could not have survived without a subsidy.

There was no subtlety about its editorial policy. The anti-Parnell elements in the Irish Party were traitors or worse. 'Blatheration' was the term most often applied to their comments when the paper bothered to publish them, and the same bias spilled over even into the area 'Jottings': 'Well done, Parnellite Cricket Club of Mullinavat ... unlike your Blatherationist Brothers, you carry the laurels of victory from your first field ...'. Tim Healy, Parnell's most vocal and vitriolic opponent within the Irish Party, got as good as he gave, and became 'the ingrate groundling who fattened on Parnell's bread and butter.' Attacks on the anti-Parnellite clergy were obliquely aimed, sometimes appearing as letters to the editor, but obviously the product of the editorial pen:

> If it was rashness to be a Fenian, it was also a sin. So the priests say […] is it rashness now to be a Parnellite? It was and always will be a sin to be an Irish patriot. […] Our priests will pray for the Queen and Royal family […] what right have they then to preach to me the politics I must profess?

The paper wasn't above publishing letters that purported to show the political dishonesty of local personalities by throwing moral mud:

> By denouncing Parnell as a 'raskal' and joining hands with the 'clargy' you imagine you are a saint […] but […] I know the story of poor Jeannie. I remember her innocence, her happy and stainless youth. I also know who it was that blighted her life and having blasted her future sent her off across the boundless ocean to sink beneath the weight of her own shame, into misery, into degradation—but God knows her end.

There was a call for religious unity too:

> I long for the day when Catholics and Protestants will work side by side in the cause of Ireland. I hope I live to see them united like brothers. […] Surely the time has arrived when religious feuds should cease. If the Catholic priests continue to pursue their present line of action and constitute themselves the supreme authority on politics in this country, surely we cannot blame our Protestant fellow-countrymen for refusing to assist us in our attempt to get the management of our own affairs. […] Priests can boycott their barber, their tailor or their shoemaker for

being opposed to them in politics, but the Pope says (vide his Rescript) that boycotting is unChristian and sinful. The seceders, many of them more immoral than himself, betrayed Parnell because Gladstone told them to do so.

Patriotic poetry was a great standby. The more emotional, the better:

If Ireland, cursed, beggared and slandered,
Had nothing to show for her cause
Save protests, remonstrances, wailings,
Against England, her lash and her laws,
The Nations might blush for our meanness,
Or laugh at our eloquent might;
The corpses below have redeemed us,
They fought the good fight....

It is difficult to reconcile such emotionalism and outright propaganda with Matt and Ned Walker, who were quiet-spoken men, frock-coated, and gravely courteous, and who, despite the anti-clerical bias of the paper, insisted on their rights as Catholics to practise their religion in the cathedral, side by side with Parnell's opponents. The situation was full of contradictions. 'Nobody could keep us from Mass,' said Mary Anne in later years. 'But of course we always left before the sermon.'

At first, the family lived over the office and plant. In a whitewashed kitchen behind the little office area, the paper was hand-set by Matt and Ned, who were both compositors. On Friday nights, every member of the family folded the issues and counted them into orders. By eleven o'clock the job would usually be done, and the rolled-up papers, in dozens and half-dozens, piled the linoleum-covered office counter. The youngest children would already be in bed. The older ones would qualify for what Mary Anne called the 'Friday-night feed'—fresh eggs and rashers and hard-fried bread, crisped in an iron pan over the kitchen range, accompanied by soda bread and yellow salted country butter. It was a regular family custom to sit beside the roaring range, 'the heels of your bands ingrained with printer's ink' from the folding, and gorge the rich back rashers after midnight—the end of Friday, the weekly 'fast day'.

As opposition to the paper grew, volunteer folders from outside of the family grew few. But the main problem was circulation.

Years later, Mary Anne said:

> I was never Involved with politics [...] I left that to Matt. He loved Mr Parnell and, God knows, he even looked and dressed like him [...] the dark eyes, the beard and, of course, the gentlemanly manner. But nearly all Parnell's supporters copied him at the time in one way or another. Matt always wore the same sort of three-quarter that Parnell had—not quite a 'tall', a velour, and much more expensive than we could afford.
>
> He wore it in Kilkenny when he went with Parnell on one of the last campaigns. They threw lime in Parnell's face. A man came out of the crowd, he was near to Matt, and he had the lime in some sort of parcel. All the men around Parnell drew in and protected him. Matt got the lime on his hat—he put it over Parnell's face. Carlow used to be what was called a 'McCarthyite region'. It was mostly against Parnellites.

That hat reappeared during the Abbey years. One evening in 1904, Matt arrived home to the family house and found Maire and Gipsy at the kitchen table making props. He chatted away to them and asked what they were making. 'It's a tramp's costume,' replied Maire, loosening the seams of an old jacket.

Gipsy chimed in: 'We found this on top of your wardrobe. I hope you don't mind us cutting it up.'

Matt stared at the crownless top hat in his daughter's hands. It was the hat he held over Parnell's eyes. The girls were distraught.

'No, don't apologise,' he said calmly. 'That hat played a part in Irish history twelve years ago. It's playing its final act today.'

Matt had returned to Carlow late in the year before Parnell was to die. The great drama was already drawing to a pathetic close. The result of the divorce proceedings had been announced that November. It was rumoured that Parnell, disguised in a long coat and deerstalker hat with the ear-flaps down, had mingled, unknown, with the crowds awaiting the result outside the London law courts. Eight days later, the Irish Party had reaffirmed its belief in its leader and returned him. A week after that, at an emotional meeting in committee room fifteen of the House of Commons, the same leader was deposed.

Like most Parnellites, Matt had lived through the events amazed that they could have happened. There was bitterness and grief as the whole structure built by Parnell begun to crumble. Matt was out of Dublin when, incredibly, news came that Parnell had physically taken possession of the party's weekly newspaper, *United Ireland*, in Abbey Street in case it changed its policy under editor William O'Brien, the MP now opposing him. Matt rushed to Dublin to see what could be done, and the next day, while he watched Parnell address a cheering crowd in Sackville Street, O'Brien's supporters broke into the *United Ireland* office and scattered the type for an edition. Parnell led another skirmish and finally assumed control of the paper. It was an indication of the importance he came to lay, too late, in public opinion.

Later, there were conferences aimed at reconciliation, but they failed, and early in the same year Parnell sent a letter to be published in the *Vindicator*. It was addressed to O'Brien, and in it Parnell refused finally to resign the leadership 'which I have accepted at the hands of our nation and our race.'

As event followed startling event, the Walkers in Carlow faced their worst opposition. Mary Anne found it increasingly difficult to shop just where she wanted, but kept up her weekly expeditions until the opposition finally gave way. There were one or two comments in the street and remarks were made to the children on their way to and from school. Stones were thrown through windows.

Mary Anne clashed with the clergy. When Daisy and Maire failed in a religious knowledge examination, she claimed the result was biased. On another, more spectacular, occasion, Mary Ann claimed she wasn't being given room for herself and the children at Mass. To the horror of the congregation, she marched all the family up to the High Altar, where they stood, lined up inside the rails, until room was found in the body of the church. Carlow came to regard her somewhat warily.

Thereafter, she went pointedly to Mass and waited for the sermon. If it tended to be anti-Parnellite, she would walk with her entourage from the church in the middle of it.

Maire's memories of the Parnell era are more idyllic than her mother's. She remembered the first time Parnell came into her life, in Dublin: 'I must have been about seven years of age when father took me to hear him speak in O'Connell Street. I know father loved Parnell.'

Despite the political unease, Maire loved her time in Carlow. She even remembered the move from Blessington Street. In September her mother packed up 'our wee home, and all of our belongings went on a canal boat, a usual mode of travelling for furniture.' The family went down to Carlow by train and were met by Matt. Maire never forgot the shock of seeing 'how very bright was the little town of Carlow. So clean and so lovely. I didn't know what it was. Years afterwards I heard it was electric lights.' Carlow was the first town in Ireland that had electric lights.

Matt took a furnished flat on Dublin Street until their own place was ready. There was an electric streetlamp outside Maire's window on the street, so they had no need to take lamps to bed. 'It was so bright, and economical too.'

The Walkers were four and half years in Carlow. For about two of these they lived on the Athy Road, where they had 'a lovely large orchard. I was always to be found on an apple tree—my own lovely sweet apples. I would go anywhere for an apple to this day.'

She recalled meeting the O'Hanrahan family in Carlow. 'Michael, who was executed in 1916, was there. His father had a cork-cutting business in Tullow Street and his sisters went to school with me.' She was very close to his eldest sister, Eileen. After returning to Dublin, Maire would travel to Carlow each summer and spend her holidays with the O'Hanrahan family, until they too came up to Dublin and got jobs. Harry and Michael joined the volunteers and Eileen joined Cumann na mBan.

Michael joined the IRB, and was frequently to be found in the Walker's tobacco shop in High Street, which was always a hive of rebellious activity. In 1916, Harry O'Hanrahan recalled Maire's kindness to the brothers at the Jacob's garrison. Michael's execution hit her very hard. After all, he was a childhood friend.

But Maire wasn't dreaming of English firing squads as she sat in her apple tree in Carlow in 1891. It would be another twenty-five years before the curtain would raise on the greatest drama of her life.

They had known that Parnell was ailing, but the fight for vindication had gone on. In Cork, he declared in March of 1891—it was St Patrick's Day—for the complete independence of Ireland. He denounced his former colleagues and his English allies. Earlier, Tim Healy had written of him and the Party that it 'is a dreadful spectacle we present, with a lunatic trying to smash the great fabric that has been created under his authority.'

And then, impossibly, on 6 October, Parnell was dead. The last campaign was over.

Four days later, the *Vindicator*, all its columns framed in black, marked the event with words that showed it had no intention of leaving him forgotten:

> Our once fond leader, our Chief, our Uncrowned King, is dead. His early grave is open to receive him, prematurely sent to rest—murdered by the people who he loved more dearly than life itself. [...] The good men and true of Ireland will remember the slayers of Charles Stewart Parnell. They will treasure up in hatred the memory of the vile means by which he was done to death. [...] Farewell, our Chief, our dear Chief. Farewell. Farewell!

Tim Healy wrote:

> The funeral was a great affair. The crowd looked so resolute that Sir Garnet Wolseley [the Irish Commander in Chief] declared it was the only crowd he was ever afraid of.

Matt Walker's nationalism was deep-rooted. Like printing, it was practically a Walker family tradition. The Catholic branch of the Walkers was at least two generations old when he was born. It originated colourfully enough (said Mary Ann) with a virtually penniless Walker arriving in Carlow, dispossessed for his politics, with only the tools of his gentleman's hobby, bookbinding, in his bag. He set up business and plunged headlong from Ascendancy Presbyterianism into middle-class Catholicism by marrying a nun, who gave up her vows for him and lived happily ever.

Matt's father, Francis, had a comfortable bookbinding business in Carlow when he was born in 1846. Francis died an exemplary Catholic, spending most of his declining years in church or the nearby Catholic Institute, where he was honorary librarian of a famous local book collection. This was known as 'Dr Doyle's Books' because of its circulation among members of the Catholic Doctrine Society, founded by the famous and controversial churchman James Warren Doyle—'J.K.L.', an acronym for 'James Kildare and Leighlin'—whose palace was in Carlow. Dr Doyle, the Bishop of Kildare and Leighlin, was a contemporary of Daniel O'Connell.

Matt, the eldest son, learned printing, and went to Dublin to work on the then pro-Parnell *Freeman's Journal*. He was basically a quiet man, easily led in most matters, but fiercely rigid when it came to less profitable activities, like membership of the IRB, and championship of the hopeless Parnell cause in 1891. He was a man of great personal integrity with no practicality, and when he met Mary Ann Doherty in Dublin they were a well-balanced pair, for her practicality was undeniable.

Mary Ann's practical nature grew out of trade: she'd spent her youth behind a counter in, of all places, a ship's chandler's, run by a relative, and she was quite content to take Matt in hand and look after his business affairs.

If Matt was gravely courteous, and beset by all the inhibitions afflicting the country man living in Dublin, Mary Ann was precisely the opposite. She was a pretty girl, brown-eyed and brown-haired, with tight ringlets and a good dress sense. She moved quickly and grasped opportunities as they arose, and it wasn't her fault if the husband she grasped them for let them slip away. She had—and often said she needed—a good sense of humour. And she had a great tendency to romanticise, which was a help in her circumstances, too.

She was a child when her parents died, and her grandfather undertook to rear her. When he remarried it was to a widow whose husband had been lost at sea. Captain William Campbell had plied a two-masted schooner, the *Enterprise*, in trade out of Kingstown for years, but had signed on for one trip too many on a bigger schooner to the Indies, and it had gone down. The ship's chandler's, nudging the Dublin quayside, was a fascinating place to grow up; a world of dim lamp-lit interiors and tallow-soaked atmospheres with the talk and smell of the sea never far away. Leathery sailors were Mary Ann's recollection of its main clientele, and the stock was varied: equipment, clothing, barrels of meal or salted meat, tobacco pipes and chunks of black plug and twist. Another of Mary Ann's memories was of the customers cutting the pigtail tobacco 'chew' from a huge roll hanging from the ceiling. It was sold by the inch, or in special 'cuts' measured from fist to elbow. There was a bald-headed monkey on a chain in the bauble-hung parlour behind the shop, a succession of pet parrots in the family, and a glass case full of stuffed birds and lizards that recalled the late captain's distant voyages as a young man.

Mary Ann grew up in a happy atmosphere. The customers were talkative men with stories of faraway places, and she got all the affection of her elderly guardians. She learned dressmaking and millinery, and grew to idolise her second grandmother.

Inevitably, since Mary Ann was the source, the story of her new grandmother had a colourful ending. According to her, the grandmother's first husband had not, in fact, drowned. He'd been shipwrecked, but the wife never knew. The two husbands only met only after she died. She fell down the stairs and cracked her skull on one of her first husband's sea chests. 'It's true,' Mary Ann would say. 'You can see the dinge in the brass binding to this day.' And so you could.

Matt Walker stayed only a year with the *Vindicator* after Parnell died, then returning to Dublin and his old trade, leaving Mary Ann in Carlow until he could find another home. It was some years before the family was together again in Dublin, and by then the Parnell controversy was a thing of the past.

Matt's utter impracticality plagued him all his life. Consistently, he never did today what he could put off until next week, and he was an incurable optimist. He frittered money away in well-meant enterprises that he hadn't the hard-headedness to sustain, and what he didn't lose he gave away, in cash or in credit. His generosity was boundless.

The same unfortunate set of characteristics smouldered like a slow match in each of the gifted and unpractical children that he fathered. Frequently, as he and they missed chance after chance in life, it drove Mary Ann through blind fury to frustrated resignation. 'What matter?' she would say. 'In the heel of the hunt, I could have done a lot worse for myself. At least I married a perfect gentleman.'

Parnell's death brought about an incredible change in Ireland. In Dublin, once a Parnellite stronghold, the nineteenth century flickered out amid the arguments of the politicians he had left behind. The young Walkers, returning there from Carlow, were part of a generation that was already turning away from politics and seeking a different form of national expression.

Matt had been slow to recover financially from the Carlow period, but by 1898 things were looking better for him. He had a regular job on the Dublin *Daily Express*, and was one of the first Irish printers to be trained to operate the newfangled linotype machine that was just then revolutionising the printing industry. This extra skill yielded a wage over the thirty-eight shillings to two pounds a week that compositors averaged at that time, and Matt could feel that he was not badly off. He had rented cheaply a big old terraced house in High Street, near Christ Church Cathedral. Mary Ann was even able to afford the twelve pounds a year it cost to employ a general domestic, while she continued her dressmaking business in two of the airy upstairs rooms, helped by the eldest girl, Daisy.

Frank, the eldest boy, had just turned twenty-one and was working as a compositor on *The Nation*; Charlie and the two youngest children were still at school, and the slender, golden-eyed Maire (nicknamed 'Polly') was working as a retoucher in Vance's photographer's in Stephen's Green.

From the high box window of Vance's, Maire had seen the climax of the celebrations marking the centenary of the death of Theobald Wolfe Tone, the hero of the 1798 rebellion. The event was just an excuse for a large nationalist demonstration that reached its end just across the road at the Fusilier's Gate to the Green, where the foundation stone for a monument to Tone was laid. The ferocious enthusiasm of the crowd had not escaped her, and she caught her first sight of Maud Gonne and W. B. Yeats. The latter wore a large black hat and flowing cravat, and intoned a speech to the huge throng.

Later that night, the Walkers had a more personal contact with the centenary celebrations. Their house, at 56 High Street, was the place where Tone's body had been taken to await burial a hundred years before. As darkness gathered, a crowd—the tail, perhaps, of one of many torchlight processions—stopped there to recite prayers in the street. Matt and Mary Ann contributed to the occasion by placing a lighted candle in each window of the house. The Walker family knelt in their doorway as the prayers for the dead rebel were said, and the crowd responded, undulating slowly beneath its canopy of greasy torchlit flame. This time the fervour of the people and the patriotic overtones of the event moved Maire to tears.

The Dublin in which the Walkers came of age was itself in the process of physical change, but the process was less evident in the part of the city where they lived. High Street was in 'old Dublin' as Mary Ann, the Dubliner, knew it. It was the original street of the city founded by the Danes. A hundred years before the Walkers moved there it had been a desirable residential district, but in 1900, while it still managed to retain some of its former elegance, the area around High Street was slowly decaying.

The street had other associations besides the one with Wolfe Tone. Patrick Sarsfield, the patriot hero of Limerick, was said to have been born there. Not far away, at the end of adjoining Thomas Street, was St Catherine's Church and the site of the gibbet where Robert Emmet was hanged. From a house in the same street the dashing Lord Edward Fitzgerald, 'our hope and Ireland's pride', had been dragged to prison and execution 'with the keeper of a madhouse for attendance by his side.'

> *To Murphy's house in Thomas Street*
> *The bloodhounds found their way.*
> *Up sprang he like a tiger*
> *From the bed on which he lay.*
> *Up sprang he like a tiger,*
> *For their purpose well he knew;*
> *And from underneath his pillow, forth,*
> *A two-edged blade he drew.*

Strong patriotic verse like this was often heard around the Walker fireside. There was verse after verse of it; years later Maire could still recite every one of them with a burning fervour and recall her father taking the children on Sunday-morning pilgrimages after Mass in St Audoen's to see where Emmet had been hanged. The whole area around High Street—The Liberties, traditional home of the weaving trade—was a place where rebellion had fermented for generations. Dublin Castle, the symbol of British rule, lay just over the hump of street that ran past Christ Church, and St Patrick's Cathedral, where Swift was once incumbent, was at the foot of the slippery cobbled hill behind the Walker home.

In later years, Frank Walker was to recall that a feature of his life in High Street was the call of the street dealers, faintly heard across the rooftops over Back Lane if he opened his bedroom window at the back of the house. Later still, when the family had grown up, Charlie, for whom the Liberties never lost its fascination, used to visit two of the markets that grew up and epitomised the Dublin dealer. One of them made the whole of Patrick Street a market that stretched halfway across the road in the shadow of the cathedral's soot-blackened façade. Every kind of item changed hands there: second-hand clothing, meat and fish from rickety barrows or battered perambulators, furniture, footgear and flowers and an incredible array of bric-à-brac picked up around the city by the vendors.

A visiting journalist wrote in amazement:

> Between the cathedral gate and Bull Alley we could have purchased, in the open, prayer books, pig's cheeks, candlesticks, onions, crockery and second-hand clothing of all varieties, apples, wallpaper, American bacon, bouquets of dried grass, pictures of Parnell and William O'Brien, cauliflowers, ping-pong rackets, iron bedsteads and old militia uniforms.

Not far away, another Dublin institution frequented by Charlie in the days after the Walkers moved away was the open-air bird market where you could buy a canary or a bullfinch for two kinds of a song. In those days the simple process of bird-buying was bound by its own traditions. It was customary to patronise the pubs in the immediate vicinity after purchase to discuss the birds' features with the knowledgeable locals. On Sunday mornings, the sawdust floors of the bars would be lined with boxes, perforated bags and wicker cages, the air filled with birdsong as the patrons deliberated gravely over their stout or plain porter. The market was held in what was said to be the shortest street in Ireland: ten yards. It was bounded at its exit by a famous pub. Outside, on the walls behind Marsh's Library, with its medieval scholars' booths, the birds were displayed for sale in cages. 'Stubblers' sold the most. These were men who spent the week birding in cornfields on the outskirts of the city with nets. There were others who lifted only nests with young birds in them, and reared them for sale. A good lark was sure to sell. One man used to advertise his wares with a song that Charlie never forgot:

> *Caught in the sunshine,*
> *Yellows and reds…*
> *Others were reared*
> *By the Strawberry beds.*

Cages for the birds cost extra, and many people brought them home as supplied, in black or brown sugar bags with finger holes punched in them for ventilation.

Dodging school and the rumbling wheels of horse-drawn floats from Guinness's nearby brewery, the young Walkers found High Street a fascinating area in which to grow up. But to the older ones, like Frank, the area presented another picture: the bitter poverty, the hopeless situation of most of Dublin's working-class population. Like most young Dubliners of his background and generation, Frank had a strong social conscience. It fed on much of the inflammatory literature the period was producing in books and periodicals, and also on the speeches of the larger figures in the nationalist movement. He was shocked by what he saw around him in the Dublin slums, in the streets less than a stone's throw from his own home. The Act of Union had not only deprived Dublin of its air of gracious living and relegated it to the status of a mere provincial town; the fruits of the change were to be found in the homes of its poor.

Frank's friend and soon-to-be member of the new, nationalist-inspired Irish theatre movement, Padraic Colum, saw it in the same way:

> As I went through Patrick Street, the hopes and prophecies were dead. Here were decaying houses, stinking yards back of them, where families were domiciled in single rooms, where casually employed men, spiritless women, sickly children, made up households.

If Matt Walker was able to manage on his wage as a printer, his income was at least enlarged by Mary Ann's dressmaking business. The highest wage a Dublin labourer could command, if he could get work at all, was less than a pound a week. Many families tried to exist on less than ten shillings. Bitter contrasts abounded between the better-class residential areas and the slums.

In 1900, parts of Dublin were the world of the stinking, tuberculosis-riddled tenement. It was a world that was to breed political and social revolution side by side in less than sixteen years.

For the young, slightly better-off post-Parnell generation, however, Dublin was also a place of constant intellectual excitement. There was a feeling of change. Frank had joined the Gaelic League, and in Dublin these were the great days of the league and the many clubs and societies that its appearance in 1893 had inspired. Dublin was a small city, and as the revival began to gather momentum it came alive with national movements of every kind: literary, theatrical and political, and a combination of all three. For a young woman like Maire, just turned seventeen, everyone, it seemed, was discussing the arts and the new writing that was emerging.

> Everywhere, in the streets, at *ceilis* and nationalist concerts, one met enthusiasts, young people, leaders or followers of the little clubs that were emerging, it seemed, every day.
>
> The Gaelic League was non-political and non-sectarian and worked mainly for the revival of the Irish language, but there were other bodies like Cumann na nGaedheal, the immediate forerunner of Sinn Féin, whose leader was Arthur Griffith; smaller clubs that combined social and political activities; circles devoted to industrial and agricultural development, and from the beginning there had been societies for the foundation of a national theatre.

In brief, the times were right for starting things, for planning national movements, for pioneering. Said Colum:

> There was an intellectual ferment around. It was the period of George Moore's *Hail and Farewell*, of the ablest of political pamphlets since Swift's time, Arthur Griffith's *The Resurrection of Hungary*; a sudden development in Irish poetry; a new development in prose too.

The prospect was colourfully peopled. In a small office in Fownes Street, Griffith was editing *The United Irishman*, writing most of it himself and even setting it up in type. In his house in Rathgar, A.E. (George Russell) was giving intellectual nourishment to the unknown writers of the time, publishing their work, sometimes at his own expense. The Yeatses were moving individually and characteristically across the scene. While the articulate Willie was dabbling in the occult and getting the attention of literary-minded ladies and gentlemen in drawing rooms as far apart as Kensington and Fitzwilliam Square, his brother, Jack, was quietly making his name as an illustrator. Their father, J. B. Yeats, was pacing his airy studio off Stephen's Green, painting nearly everyone who was anyone and consolidating his reputation as a raconteur with entertaining and illuminating talk.

Maud Gonne, unutterably beautiful, incredibly vocal, the epitome of Irish revolution, was in Dublin again, back from her political work on the continent and in the starving west of Ireland, where she had 'stopped a famine and saved many lives'. John O'Leary, the last of the Fenians, 'with his noble and sad eyes' was still alive to inspire the new revolutionary generation. 'And they all,' said Colum, 'converged on the theatre, all bringing something to it or, perhaps more importantly, expecting something from it,'

But in 1898, which was about two years after the Walkers moved to High Street, there was no national theatre in Ireland. At least, no national theatre of the kind that Colum—soon to find himself one of its founders—talks about. Colum was working as a clerk in the Railway Clearing House, his father was the station-master at the tiny railway stop in Sandycove, and the personalities who were starting to move towards creating an Irish national theatre were still socially remote to people like him and the Walkers.

It was only possible to watch with interest, a year later, the appearance of the Irish Literary Theatre and mark its progress from a distance. Its founders were distinguished writers, landowners and sophisticates in the arts: Yeats, the established poet; Lady Augusta Gregory, the widow of a wealthy colonial official with a Big House in the west; the astringent George Moore; and Edward Martyn, the Mayo landowner and recluse whose money had been used to guarantee it. There was no immediate point of contact there with people who had to earn a living in offices and workshops while they watched the new theatre's first appearance, and eventually the movement's apparent failure.

It is hardly surprising to find Maire in later years dismissing the Yeats–Gregory–Moore–Martyn enterprise as merely the most interesting of the early national theatre groups, and attributing its disappearance after a few years solely to the fact that it was foolish enough to employ English actors and actresses to present its plays. Maire was, after all, soon to be a co-founder of an acting group that was to prove that without Irish players there could never be an Irish national theatre. But of course there were other things that contributed to the reception the Literary Theatre got when it first appeared.

The Literary Theatre was influenced partly by events in Ireland at the time and partly by the new developments in the theatre that were moving across Europe. It set out, for one thing, to combat the glitter and the artificiality of the commercial stage. At least one of its founders, Martyn, was an Ibsenite, so it didn't aim solely at establishing a poetic theatre, despite its rather flowery manifesto. This said that the theatre sought to 'bring upon the stage the deeper thoughts and emotions of Ireland', finding 'an uncorrupted and imaginative audience trained to listen by its passion for oratory'. It was emphasised that the object was to show that Ireland 'is not the home of buffoonery or easy sentiment, but the home of an ancient realism'. The founders of the theatre said they were 'confident of the support of Irish people, who are weary of misrepresentation'.

The first play staged was *The Countess Cathleen*, which had been published some years earlier by Yeats. It was produced in Dublin in May 1899, and was followed the next day by *The Heather Field* by Martyn. Both plays were performed by a company of English professionals.

Opposition began to make itself felt even before *The Countess Cathleen* reached the stage. Martyn, a devout Catholic, withdrew his support during the rehearsals after his confessor confirmed his fears that the play was heretical (it is about a woman who sells her soul for her people). Yeats had barely overcome this and regained Martyn's support when a pamphlet, 'Souls for Sale', struck at what it claimed were the plays' antisocial and anti-Irish undertones. Cardinal Logue joined in by saying that Catholics should shun the play if it was as bad as was represented. He was said not to have read it.

There were long arguments in the newspapers. Forty Catholic students signed a protest against the play, and it was staged to the accompaniment of hisses from the back of the Antient Concert Rooms in Brunswick Street. Yeats wrote about the event several years later, and referred spitefully to what he called 'the vehement opposition stirred up by a politician and a newspaper'. More than ten years intervened between the event and his comment, and it is sometimes taken now to refer to *The United Irishman* and Arthur Griffith, with whom the theatre movement was to fall out badly in its infancy. The fact is that the paper that mainly opposed the Literary Theatre in 1899 during the 'Countess row' was the Healyite *Nation*. Griffith was obviously embarrassed because of his friendship with Maud Gonne, to whom the play was dedicated, and also by Yeats's brief association with the IRB, so his paper backpedalled noticeably in its reviews.

The Irish Literary Theatre lasted for three years. It staged the rest of its plays in the more comfortable Gaiety Theatre, again with English professionals: the F. R. Benson Company.

The most significant aspect of the final performance (the main play was *Diarmuid and Gráinne* by Martyn and Moore) was the curtain-raiser. This was Douglas Hyde's one-act Gaelic play, *Casadh an tSúgaín* (The Twisting of the Rope), and it was staged with a cast of amateur players from the Gaelic League and directed by W. G. Fay. It was the first play in Gaelic presented on the stage of a regular theatre. Fay told of how he staged it without knowing any Irish:

> I got all the actors to speak their lines in English first while I gave them the business and positions. When they got these right we turned the play back into Gaelic, and in this way put it together bit by bit. [...] It was all a valuable experience for me because it proved that, given the goodwill of the actors, I could get the same acting value out of the play whether it was spoken in English or in Gaelic.

But Fay had a less happy experience with the unfortunate Bensons, who had two problems: they couldn't understand the Diarmuid and Gráinne legend, and couldn't pronounce most of the phrases and names. Said Fay: 'I came away from these rehearsals more convinced than ever that these plays, if they were to successful, must be played by Irish actors.'

The actors and actresses did not come from the Irish Literary Theatre. Most of them came from the nationalist clubs, and they were to be the first practical link in the chain of events that created an Irish national theatre.

In Mary Walker's case, the link with the theatre she was to help to establish was Maud Gonne. Like most young nationalist women in the city at the time, she looked with awe on the spectacularly rebellious beauty who then epitomised the most active side of the independence movement.

After Parnell's death there were still people in Ireland hungry for heroes and heroines. In the late 1890s, Maud Gonne was something of a symbol that combined part of the spirit of romantic

Ireland's past with downright active rebellion. The combination was ideally suited to the mood of the time. The impression she gave was created as much by the success of her social work among evicted tenantry in Mayo and Galway as by her beauty and personality, not to mention her romantic associations with Yeats, whose preoccupation with magic and ancient myths was then at its height.

The daughter of a former staff officer in the British Army in Ireland had, incredibly it seemed to nationalists, thrown herself into the cause. In London she had campaigned for the release of the 'treason felony prisoners' who had tried to blow up the House of Commons. In France she had organised a bureau to publicise the land situation in Ireland, and she was well known in America as a lecturer and fundraiser for the nationalists. She had now settled again in Dublin, a restless, vocal ally of Griffith in his campaign to organise a new political order, and she was a rallying-point for every young woman in the city who wanted an active part in the nationalist movement.

Maud Gonne was tall—nearly six foot—and dramatically beautiful, with a mass of auburn hair, superbly dressed. Yeats, completely captivated, called her 'the fiery hand of the intellectual movement':

> *For she had fiery blood*
> *When I young,*
> *And trod so sweetly proud,*
> *As 'twere upon a cloud...*

At one time she had trained as an actress, but had given it up to dedicate her income and her enthusiasm to the cause of Irish political freedom. The more outspoken Unionists in Dublin constantly recalled this, and claimed that she was nothing less than a trained agitator. Others went further and pointed out that although there was no sign of her marrying she had already had children after a romantic alliance with a young politician in France.

In 1900, however, doubts that she might be more of an exhibitionist than a patriot were diminishing, despite her somewhat unfortunate flair for the dramatic gesture. She had a tendency to make entrances on the grand scale, she was a theatrical and magnetic street orator, and her habit of riding around Dublin in an open side-car accompanied by a vicious Great Dane caused a lot of comment. But her great accomplishment was that she not only believed in what she did, but she could inspire others to help her. By 1900, nationalist Dublin had accepted her.

Soon after she started work with Griffith she began what she claimed was the first organisation to give young Irish women a chance to take part in nationalist work. Inghindhe na hÉireann (The Daughters of Ireland) started in 1900. In less than a year it helped Griffith to put a stop to British Army recruitment for the Boer War. The society fairly successfully combined political agitation and worthwhile cultural work. By mid 1900 its programme was well under way, with branches working in the provinces, while Maud Gonne operated as a link between Griffith, the new Labour movement under James Connolly, and Yeats and the literary movement.

The object was eventually to combine all into one open separatist movement. It didn't work out quite as planned because the theatre under Yeats finally opted out. What resulted was Sinn Féin.

It was natural, with the work the Gaelic League was doing to encourage interest in the traditions of the Gaelic past, the language and the old literature, that the cultural side of the Inghinidhe's work should focus on writing and the theatre. Mary Walker, who had joined it almost as soon as it started, was involved at once in the dramatic class that the Inghinidhe ran.

She was a natural choice. At nineteen she had fulfilled all the family forecasts that she would turn out to be beautiful. She was tall, incredibly slight, with red-gold hair, pale skin, and those unbelievable brown-gold eyes. In the long homespun dresses and heavy Celtic jewellery that she wore, her hair buckled at the nape of the neck, she sometimes looked like a reincarnation of one of the old Irish warrior queens, and she was often to appear in such roles in the Abbey Theatre in later years.

People seeking to apply an overall description to her said she looked 'ethereal', and this was how more than one drama critic was to describe her. An English reviewer who saw her act in 1903 described her as 'a maiden with a strange, wan, disquieting beauty'. It was a constant source of annoyance to her that she had to wear spectacles; she left them off as often as she could. She compromised eventually with rimless pince-nez held on a thin chain behind one ear. When she removed the glasses, the effect was devastating.

Maire's nationalism was as deep-rooted as her father's, and she inherited most of her mother's objectivity and sense of humour. She was, in fact, a dedicated revolutionary, and would gladly have died in the cause of Irish political freedom. Of her early days in Inghinidhe, she said:

> We used to hold classes and debates encouraging the study of Irish history, music, literature and art, and for those of us who were interested there was a small dramatic company. [...]
>
> At the time this was producing *tableaux vivants*—living pictures—at the Antient Concert Rooms. They were very popular just then, showing a scene from some period in Irish history or illustrating some legend or patriotic melody.
>
> The little group produced full-length plays only occasionally then, but its object was to encourage young Dubliners to write for the stage and to establish the nucleus of a national dramatic company which would run in conjunction with nationalist organisations in the city.

There can be little doubt that if there had been no nationalist clubs in Dublin, no outlet for young Dubliners to engage actively in nationalist work, the Irish national theatre movement would not have got properly underway a year later in 1902, if at all. Certainly it would never have achieved the enormous impact it did early on if it had not at first been sustained by such a fantastic wave of national sentiment. The ironic fact that only a few years later this very sentiment turned many nationalists against the theatre is irrelevant; it is enough that it started the movement off.

It is probably ironic as well that two of the major forces behind the establishment of the first effective Irish national theatre company, the Fay brothers, who trained the players and evolved the acting technique that distinguished the theatre, were quite unconcerned with politics. Years later, Willie Fay said:

> We had, it is true, the nominal support of Arthur Griffith, but he was a most uncomfortable ally and readier with disparagement (or worse) than praise. He could never forgive us for refusing to subordinate our art to his politics.

Fay then goes on to place the contribution of the dramatists second to that of the players:

> The Abbey Theatre was first and foremost a theatrical, not a literary movement. It was the creation not of men of letters but of actors. [...] If we had been limited by literary or political considerations we might have done some interesting work, but we should have remained parochial. We should never have created, as we did, the 'community drama'.

From this can be seen some of the basic misunderstanding that caused so much trouble in the theatre later on. It is an interesting fact that a whole range of conflicting motives inspired the people who combined to launch the Irish national theatre movement. Yeats had first set out to create a poets' theatre; Martyn, unbelievably, wanted a realist theatre that would not offend; Moore apparently wanted a sophisticated theatre of words; the Fays wanted a players' theatre, and the nationalists wanted a propaganda outlet that would pay honour to the Irish national character.

Basically, however, the theatre remains very much the product of a time, not of any person or group. It emerged at a moment of intense intellectual ferment, nourished by nationalism and helped by its plays and the Fays' great practical knowledge of the mechanics of the stage. All this sustained it for the years that it worked in small backstreet halls while its members were unpaid.

Later, when the time came to establish it on a permanent basis, in a permanent headquarters, and with all the political and intellectual freedom necessary to it as a theatre, it remained for others to take over. But by then the Walkers, and others like them, had gone.

It was early in 1901 that W. G. moved into the Walker house in High Street as a lodger, and the next link in the chain was forged. He was thirty when he launched the first national theatre company. His father was an official in the education ministry, where, as Fay put it, 'he worked for forty years, most of the time in the same room'.

This secure but unadventurous existence did not encourage Willie to follow suit, and he failed his examination for the Civil Service. It was a blow to his family when he did not take the failure seriously. They found it hard to understand how he could cheerfully turn his back on security. As Fay put it himself:

> ... allowing that it was very hard to get you into the Civil Service, it was harder to get you out, and the longer you lived, the larger the salary you got.

His interests, however, were elsewhere, like those of his elder brother, Frank. Both had developed a passion for the stage. Frank's interest had grown from regular theatregoing, whatever he could find of plays or theatrical biographies on the book barrows, and what he managed to read about developments in Europe. Willie had become a theatre-lover through the influence of a distant relative who played walk-ons in the Queen's melodramas, and was a 'corner man' in a Christy Minstrel show.

Both brothers started their working lives characteristically: Frank as a clerk in Craig Gardner's, one of the city's biggest accountancy firms, and Willie as 'advance man' for the Irish actor/manager J. W. Lacy, whose company toured the Irish 'smalls' with adaptations of Boucicault and Whitbread. Previously, the brothers had started a small amateur drama group in Dublin, the Ormond Dramatic Society, and Frank had developed a passion for fine speech after he joined a drama school run by Lacy's actress wife, Maud Randford, in Westland Row.

Later, Willie was to say of Frank:

> He was convinced that the basis of all good acting was good speaking, and good speaking depended on good voice production. [...] when he was finished with himself, if he ever was, he could make himself audible to the back of great theatres [...] and not raise his voice above a whisper. If this school had never been set up in Dublin, or if by chance he had never joined it, I think it is unlikely that he or I would have become an actor. [...] If Maud Randford had not wished to rest for a while in Dublin, there would have been no Irish players and certainly no Abbey Theatre.

By 1900, Frank was a secretary in the accountancy firm and Willie had become an electrician. Willie had also toured most of Ireland and parts of Scotland. He had been character actor, bill poster, publicity man, comedian, song-and-dance man and 'front' for a travelling auctioneer. At one point he was advance man for Lloyd's Mexican Circus, and he had worked with an all-black company, the first to tour *Uncle Tom's Cabin* in Ireland. He was no stranger to the booth-theatres that toured Ireland in abundance in the 1890s—wooden-walled fit-ups that played 'on the grass' under canvas roofs. He knew a lot about stage management and design. 'I picked up some miscellaneous knowledge,' he said.

It was soon to be used. The elements that were to go into the making of an Irish national theatre were about to combine. The link between the players and the writers—the Literary Theatre— was Frank Fay. By then he was drama critic for *The United Irishman*, had met Yeats, and was involved in correspondence with him on the technical aspects of acting and the question of what ought to be the relationship between actor and poet.

This contact with Yeats had got Willie Fay the job as producer with the Inghinidhe na hÉireann dramatic society, and Willie strengthened the Ormond Dramatic Society with the best material he could get in Inghinidhe. Mary Walker was an early recruit. Frank Walker joined the Fays' Ormond Society too, simply because he knew them well already, shared many of their views, and was a useful man to have around.

The venue for most of the Ormond Society shows was the Coffee Palace on Townsend Street. It was run by the Irish Total Abstinence movement, and had a small but fairly well-equipped stage. Frank Walker's memory of this was that it was located in a room behind the coffee bar and was only a few inches above floor level. The footlights were hooded candles.

> If you were unlucky enough to get a seat at the back, the only way you could see the whole stage was to stand up. This was fair enough as the hall had been originally been built for temperance lectures for which a general view wasn't necessary. When the Ormond Dramatic Society put on its show, the wits in the audience used to say that it was a deliberate ploy by the temperance people to locate anyone with a hint of a stagger and throw him out or convert him.

Frank Walker went on to recall that anyone could get the hall cheaply for a concert as long as it wasn't a political one.

> The only other condition was that whoever used the place would have an interval of twenty minutes so that a member of the temperance society could give a lecture. The interval was handy enough for anyone in the cast who wanted to slip out the back way for a quick drink. A lot of the audience used to do the same. Some of them got quite clever at nipping out just as the interval curtain was falling; that was the sign for the temperance people to lock the door.

One of the final plays that the Fays presented in the Coffee Palace was a 'twopenny farce' called *His Last Legs*. Its only significance is that in its cast were most of those who were to establish the Irish National Theatre Society. The moment had arrived for the amalgamation of the Ormond Dramatic Society and the Inghinidhe drama section. Already, many of the Inghinidhe girls who wanted to learn acting were taking formal voice lessons from Frank Fay for a small weekly fee. Willie was staging the Inghinidhe's patriotic plays and tirelessly lecturing its members on stagecraft.

Ireland's national theatre was about to be born.

IV

– by David Kenny

My great-grandfather's entrenched nationalism was always going to have a bearing on his children, whom he treated as equals in 'The Cause'. There was no demarcation between boys and the girls: they would all play their part if they wanted to. He was in many ways a proto-feminist given the sexist strictures of his time, although he wouldn't have known what that meant.

The greatest indication of his non-sexist outlook came on Easter Monday morning when he arrived in church with a telegram for Maire from Lily Brennan ordering her to 'come at once'. He knew he was sending his daughter to face English guns. He must have been worried, but he would not stand in the way of Maire doing her duty.

'My father idolised me,' she said. And she in turn idolised him.

Matt was a wonderful, caring father. When his wife and children moved back to Dublin from Carlow, he had their new home fully prepared for them, down to having the beds made. Not many Victorian dads were that hands-on. Maire recalled arriving to the smell of frying bacon, a lit fire, a boiling kettle and the beds ready for the tired children. Matt was upset because he couldn't find the family's good sheets and pillowcases.

He was a gentle soul, despite being a member of the IRB. I don't believe he was capable of hatred, and it is interesting to note that nowhere in Maire's writings does she express an overt hatred of 'Perfidious Albion'. Her friends O'Hanrahan, MacDonagh, the Pearses, Plunkett etc. were executed by an occupying foreign power, but she never rants or rails against the English. In fact, some of her happiest memories are of acting in England, and her visit to Anne Hathaway's cottage where she heard her 'first nightingale sing'.

I believe that Maire wanted freedom for Ireland to be Irish. She wasn't a person who loved violence. My dad told a story about her that, to my mind, sums her up.

On one occasion during her time at Jacob's, she climbed the tower to give hot chocolate to one of the snipers. He handed her his rifle in exchange for the hot mug, around which he wrapped grateful fingers. Maire raised the gun and fired a single shot into the air.

'What in the name of God are you doing, Miss Walker? You're wasting bullets,' he gasped.

Maire turned to him and said: 'I've always wanted to fire a shot in an Irish rebellion, but I've never wanted to kill anybody.'

My father worshipped Maire, and was deeply influenced by her life and views. Growing up in the 1970s and 1980s, I never got the sense of him having any sympathy for the Provos. If anything, he looked down on them. I recall him bristling at the men selling lilies outside Mass on Easter Sunday. I also remember him hurrying us through the columns of the GPO the day that Dev died, as grim-faced men and women handed out In Memoriam postcards of the Long Fellow. I was nine, and reached out to take one.

'No,' dad said firmly, linking my arm and pushing me past one of the Shinners, angrily muttering something about them not being real patriots. I was confused. We had a photo in the sitting room of dad shaking hands with Dev on the latter's retirement at the Áras. Was dad not sad that his weird-looking friend was dead?

His lack of sympathy for violent-force republicanism can only have been received from Maire, Gipsy and Bob Price. (The latter was a close friend of Michael Collins, and his equal at one point on GHQ.) Maire, while willing to lay down her life for Ireland, would never have supported the modern IRA.

Matt supported and encouraged his daughter's nationalist activities—and she was very active. Maire was a born joiner and a hard worker. She left school early, and at the age of fourteen went to Vance's photographers on Stephen's Green to learn 'finishing, framing, mounting and retouching photographs'. Typically, Mary Anne had organised this. She then went to the School of Art to study freehand drawing and designing, but her sight deteriorated and she couldn't continue. It's strange to think of Maire having the most captivating eyes on the Irish stage yet not being able to see the audience.

The family moved to High Street and Matt took her to Upper O'Connell Street to join the Gaelic League when she was seventeen. The office was over O'Byrne's bookshop, next to the Gresham Hotel. Frank had joined before her, and she was to become friends with, among others, Sceilg, William Rooney and two future presidents, Douglas Hyde and Seán T. O'Kelly. The latter was the office boy at the time. 'There was such a wonderful spirit among the people in the movement at the time, it was so friendly. I suppose our one object was the freedom of Ireland.'

She met her lifelong friend, Padraic Colum, there. 'He was a beautiful boy, and indeed is very much the same today. Every time he comes back [from the US] I think how little he has changed.'

Padraic fought in 1916, but the future soldier was not in evidence when he attended one of the monthly meetings of Inghinidhe na hÉireann.

> Mary Quinn caught Padraic with his hand in the sugar bowl. He had had nearly everything in it. It was lump sugar. She let out a good northern shout at him, and he went under the table and hid himself.

Although Matt was still a printer, he opened a tobacconist shop at the house in High Street. It was the second in the city to have its name in Irish over the door. This was a major statement, and would have drawn attention from the Castle. Not content with nailing his political colours to the shopfront, Matt sold Irish books and papers inside too.

The shop was also a 'front' for nationalist activities, with many prominent republicans meeting there. Dev was reputed to have met his wife, Sinéad, at the back of the Walkers' premises, where Irish classes were given. High Street also provided the rehearsal rooms for the dramatic society's early plays, and was the actors' HQ for the Theatre of Ireland.

According to Maire, Matt won fifty pounds in a 'sweep of some kind' and bought a small hand press and type, and started the Tower Press. He printed the *National Democrat*, edited by Frances Sheehy Skeffington, and the *Tower Press Booklets*, published by Maunsels. He was also the first publisher of Christmas cards in Ireland with Irish inscriptions. This was Mary Anne's idea.

By this time Maire had joined Inghinidhe na hÉireann, of which Maud Gonne was president. It was there that she started her acting career and was involved in her first major nationalist protest: the children's fete at Clonturk Park, Drumcondra. It was organised by Maud Gonne to clash with the visit of Queen Victoria. For a week before the event, Máire Quinn and Gonne went around the city's sweetshops, bakers and fruiterers collecting goodies for the city's children. Gonne also called on schools to invite children to the fete. 'I need hardly tell you that our own president had a great effect on the children …'.

Maire was to remember her role, doling out buns to schoolchildren at this event, with great pride in her later years, and with wistful fondness too: 'It was a very strange thing that I may have given a bun to my husband, for he was there. And why not? For afterwards he was a Volunteer and a good soldier. We met on the field of battle, which was the ultimate end of all our early work.'

He was Major General Eamonn 'Bob' Price, who organised the surrender at Jacob's for MacDonagh, and was Director of Organisation at IRA GHQ in 1921.

V

In 1905, Maire left the Abbey after a blazing row with W. B. Yeats. She effectively turned her back on a career that could have led to her Hollywood, like her contemporaries Sara Allgood and Una O'Connor. Her papers betray her regret at that missed opportunity.

Una, 'a very charming girl', had a very successful Tinseltown career, appearing in fifty-nine films including *The Bride of Frankenstein* and *The Invisible Man*, being a favourite of controversial director James Whale. Sara, likewise, had a long and financially rewarding time there.

Maire, on the other hand, spent her final years struggling for money and work in a dreary house in Laytown. She deserved more.

> I hear there is plenty of money, but it is very hard work. You would need to be very young to really enjoy it. I would have liked it when I was young, but it [Hollywood] wasn't born then, any more than the picture theatres. So there you are.

The split has been written about at length many times before. In essence, W. B. Yeats wanted direct control, with Lady Gregory and Synge, over the theatre's direction. He was tired of all the endless votes and general democracy that the society's players liked so much. Annie Horniman provided money for the payment of wages, and the group went into uproar.

Maire and others, including Frank Walker and Padraic Colum, wanted the theatre to remain amateur, a propaganda tool for the nationalist movement. Colum in particular was annoyed that there were no sixpenny seats for the great unwashed (as Yeats might have put it) to enjoy the Abbey's plays. Ostensibly, this was patriotism versus professionalism, but as with everything there were grey areas too. Whom would be paid, and how much? A new level of competition, outside of the artistic, emerged.

Yeats, Gregory and Synge became the Abbey's three directors. Many of the actors were incensed at losing their independence to an arrogant Anglo-Irish poet, an overbearing Queen Victoria lookalike, and a young, Protestant playwright who had a bullseye target stitched to the seat of his pants. Some were angered by the idea of a politically neutral theatre, and others at the idea that some, but not all, would be paid. Allied to all this resentment there must have been an element of 'self-kicking' too, as the move was inevitable from the start. Yeats himself wrote that he had always seen it on the cards.

Frank Walker was seething at the takeover, and also unhappy with the wage he had been offered. Joe Holloway describes him becoming 'sulky' while taking direction from Lady Gregory on one occasion after the takeover. While he and Maire initially agreed to sign contracts, their days were numbered. They left, with Frank's influence over his younger sister being a considerable factor in her departure.

Regardless of Frank, she would have left anyway. Given her republican outlook, she would not have been content with merely being the employee of a successful company. Maire wanted a national theatre, and, to her, this was synonymous with the original group she had helped to found. The Abbey was less about the drama for her and more about the action to come.

Some have said, unfairly, that she just wasn't happy with Yeats's offer of remuneration, the elevation of Sara Allgood to leading actress, and the added 'inducement' of being offered the job of wardrobe mistress—apparently, it was beneath her. This has been overstated by at least one historian. Maire's mother was a dressmaker and the movement's part-time wardrobe mistress. The position was definitely not beneath her.

One can understand her distress at the prospect of playing second fiddle to Allgood, and probably not wanting to take on this extra task, but Maire was not a snob. She was an egalitarian, and everyone in the theatre was on level pegging with her, at least in her eyes. It was a co-operative.

She was not a prima donna, and this is borne out by the warm reception she was afforded on her return in 1910 by Sean Barlow and his stagehands: always the best barometer of an actor's popularity.

The split was traumatic for Maire, not least because of Yeats's treatment of her. His rage was said to be uncontrollable when she stood up to him. He even threatened to sue her for breach of contract.

On top of this, the Yeats family and the Walkers were good friends. John Yeats was infatuated with Maire. She also worked in the embroidery department of the Yeats sisters' Dun Emer, and there are photographs of John snr and Jack B. Yeats in a Walker family album. John Yeats sketched Matthew Walker at the Contemporary Club, a place of debate about literature, politics and society. Other members included Douglas Hyde, Michael Davitt and John O'Leary.

Maire fled to Gurteen Dhas, the home of John, Lily and Lolly Yeats. This is where my father's story that John B. had proposed to her got legs. Maire would have told Ted of the proposal, so I believe it to be true. John B. was four decades older than devout Catholic Maire, by the way, so romance was never going to be on the cards there.

According to John B. Yeats's biographer, William Michael Murphy, Maire was reduced to a nervous wreck by W. B.'s bullying behaviour, which says a lot about his personality. John B. spoke to Lady Gregory on Maire's behalf in an attempt to sway W. B.

> I am very sorry Moira [sic] has committed suicide. Whether she will ever again come to life I know not. All her charm as an actress comes from her quality of pride and self will, and it is exactly this quality which is now in revolt....

John B. Yeats believed that Maire needed to be brought back into the Abbey as soon as possible, because the theatre was likely to lose her permanently and it would be Yeats' and Gregory's loss.

John B. kept up the pressure on Lady Gregory, through a mixture of flattery (of her) and battery (of W. B. Yeats). His son had been particularly mean to Maire, and had caused her to turn 'extraordinarily white and languid', adding: 'What do Willie or the two Fays or Synge know about poor young girls? It is not intellect and gifts of words and arguments that are wanted.'

Maire was persuaded to stay at Gurteen Dhas until the controversy had blown over. While there, John painted what he called a 'friendship' portrait of her, as well as several sketches, one of which came to rest in Michael Yeats's hallway. Eventually, Lady Gregory spoke to Maire and her spirits rose. She must have been in a very bad way, as John B. wrote: 'she is a new girl. The distressing dumbness is gone, and she is full of quick response and at times even talks …'.

John B. was in love with her, so he can be forgiven for some favouritism. While he spoke highly of Sara Allgood's abilities as an actress, compared to Maire she was second rate and 'would never touch the heart [of the Irish people]. She will not cast spells of listening wonder as Maire can.'

He was wasting his ink. Maire was a victim of politics. She was caught between the ambitions of Sara and Molly Allgood—the latter was engaged to Synge—and the seceders led by her brother, Frank, and Padraic Colum. Her ties to the heart of the Abbey were broken.

As arrangements had been made by Horniman for a short and well-publicised English tour, Maire remained with the company until the end of the year and went with them to England.

She must have known that clashing with Yeats meant throwing away a promising professional acting career. She was considered the greatest tragedienne on the Irish stage, and she was still in her early twenties.

Her decision to leave influenced others, including James Starkey (Seumas O'Sullivan). According to Joseph Holloway, the pair were 'love's young dream'. This discovery was a shock to me—Maire had a boyfriend during the early Abbey days. To me she is the ethereal beauty in Yeats' and Russell's paintings. Otherworldly, virginal … she is my grand-aunt after all. But there is no inclusion of any details about her private life in this book.

The rancour her departure left didn't dissipate with the years. She later wrote that 'Lady G.' was 'bitter with me after I left the Theatre—and I can't blame her for that.' She can't have been that bitter, as she sent Maire a Christmas card every year. 'She was a queer old thing,' but Maire was 'very fond of her.'

If Lady Gregory was bitter over the split, then Sara Allgood was still sparking like a faulty arc light. She was particularly nasty. Maire wrote that she wasn't a welcome guest at the Abbey when she returned in 1910 to perform in *The Shiuler's Child*.

> Everything was changed […] no Fays, no Synge. […] I cannot tell you how much of a difference that made to me. I never met with such rudeness as I met there, with the exception of Lennox Robinson, Sydney Morgan and J. A. O'Rourke—and of course the stagehands.

Sara was cast as Nannie O'Hea to play opposite her, but after the first rehearsal she refused to play the part.

> Arthur Sinclair, Kerrigan and O'Donovan, whom I didn't know before, were very rude to me—it nearly broke my heart when Sara Allgood and the three men got up and walked out of the green room when I came in. It was very hard to act with them whenever I had to.

On the other hand, Robinson, whom she met for the first time, 'was always a gracious gentleman […] a real friend.'

The play went very well, and Maire got a great reception when she came on. 'Dear old Dublin welcomed me back. Many friends came up behind to say how they liked the play.' One old 'friend' was mixed in his praise:

> When I was taking off my make-up I heard someone stumble up the stairs. […] there was a knock on my

door and W. B. Yeats appeared [...] he said: 'You were as beautiful as ever, Miss Walker. A very fine performance indeed, but I don't like the play'. Yeats turned on his heel and went out. I thought he came because he couldn't ignore me. But it meant nothing to me.

There is no doubt that Maire respected Yeats, but she didn't like him. She remembered her first time seeing him outside the Inghinidhe HQ in 1901. In her eyes he presented a strange figure. She finds it hard to resist a pop at him in her NLI papers. He was walking with 'very short steps' while he waited for Maud Gonne.

I didn't know who he was, walking up and down [...,] a very tall, thin figure. His coat was loose about like a cape flowing in the wind, and he wore a broad sort of hat. He greeted Gonne with a gracious bow and she floated off with him.

She contrasted this poseur to his brother. 'Jack B. was so unlike his brother in every way. He immediately sat down and became one of us. [...] He had us in stitches of laughter.'

Ten years later, she was still noting W. B.'s vanity. On the first morning of their voyage to the US for the Abbey tour, Maire recalls W. B. posing on deck. He came up in a:

white or cream flannel [suit, ...] our poet had one made for himself [...] and who would think of him being so vain to wear this garment, and a black tie, floating in the wind.

Lennox Robinson then arrived on deck wearing the same suit, 'but not looking the same' (presumably less vain). Yeats disappeared back to his state room and re-emerged later wearing a black suit. 'I don't remember seeing him wear the cream again.'

Yeats's influence on others also irritated her. Pádraig Pearse, whom she respected deeply, came in for a lash over his apeing of W. B.'s mannerisms. In this book she speaks about their mutual-admiration society. In her papers, she is more forthright:

> P. H. Pearse was very much attracted to Yeats. [...] I thought at times he tried to imitate him. On one occasion there was a performance of [Pearse's] plays at the Abbey.... Well, at the show Pearse gave a speech about acting. [...] He based it on the Abbey acting and he tried, I thought, to imitate Yeats in gesture and voice. He walked up and down on the stage when he was speaking, and I was fairly well disgusted with him the way he spoke about W. B. How well he had trained the Abbey players....

Yeats could be very cruel (as Maire knew only too well). The ever-popular Willie Fay was also a victim of his nastiness. Maire recalled that Lady Gregory and Yeats were forever interfering in productions. This made Fay's work as manager, actor and producer almost impossible.

> He was a good actor and a very good producer, but a bad manager. [... The growing Abbey] needed a different type of man to manage it. [...] Fay couldn't do it and couldn't see that. Yeats, who is very cruel when he likes, told W. G. just that.

Yeats, typically, did not refer to her in his Nobel Prize speech, but referred to the early actors as 'clerks and shop girls'. This must have hurt Maire deeply. To be forgotten about is one thing, but to be called a mere shop girl is another. Maire was gifted, artistic and literate. Although they didn't have money, her family was middle class. Her father had a printing business and a tobacconist shop (run by her sister, Daisy). Her mother was a dressmaker. They were well-respected people. When Maire was preparing, hurriedly, for the second US tour, Lady O'Connell, no less, offered to lend her clothes from her own wardrobe.

Yeats also praised the more 'loyal' Sara Allgood in his speech. This would have hurt Maire immensely—and by extension, my father, Ted. I can't claim to be impartial here either; I am biased against Yeats too. I can't help it.

Maire's 'terrible row' with Yeats (to use Michael Yeats's description) dogged her for the rest of her life. In fairness to him, though, it is highly unlikely that the Abbey would have survived to this day if she and the seceders had had their way.

Her departure led her on to other things, such as the foundation of the Theatre of Ireland, which is covered in this book. Her post-Abbey life between 1913 and 1916 was dramatic in its own way.

There were so many things afoot […] it was very hard to give up all our time to drama as I was in C na mB and Joe Plunkett and Tom MacDonagh were in the Volunteers. […] I felt I was going back to where I began in 1900, and the activities in C na mB were very serious, so drama was put aside for the present.

VI

Maire gives a detailed and colourful account of her time in Jacob's in this book. What she doesn't mention is that she was the last woman to leave, and was in a state of nervous exhaustion. Min Ryan (Richard Mulcahy's wife) recalled bringing her to Ranelagh and putting her to bed.

Maire doesn't speak of the personal trauma of losing her friends Tom MacDonagh, Willie Pearse, Plunkett, and her childhood pal Michael O'Hanrahan. The immediate period after the Rising was horrendous for her. On top of these losses, she had to care for her little sister, Gipsy. The latter's fiancé, James Crawford Neil, was shot by a looter on his way home to Fairview from Glasthule, where he had spent the evening with the Walkers. Crawford Neil was an up-and-coming poet who worked in the National Library. He was Protestant, but converted to Catholicism when he fell in love with Gipsy. He had also given up drinking, as he was known to be a bad alcoholic. Gip walked with him to Blackrock, and he had gone on into town, avoiding Sackville Street.

On Liffey Street, near the Gaelic Press offices, he encountered some children who had looted a sporting goods shop. One of them had either a pistol or a rifle. Crawford Neil, who wrote poetry for children, pleaded with the group to go home, warning that they would be shot as looters or combatants if found with the firearm. In the confusion, the gun was discharged and he was shot through the spine.

Gip spent days looking for him, and eventually found him in Jervis Street Hospital. He knew he was dying, but kept up a brave front. The pair asked the hospital chaplain to marry them. He refused, saying, 'I won't marry a woman who will be a widow in a few hours.'

James died in her arms a short while later. She kept his letters and his poems and often read them in her old age. I have them here. My father attempted to write a musical around the story of their doomed relationship. Her sadness affected him for the remainder of his life.

Gip found love again with Eddie Kenny, a vivacious Louth man who ran a chain of cinemas with his partner, Joe Stanley. He was an amateur jockey, overflowing with energy and humour. They married in 1925, and Ted was born in 1927. Sadly, Eddie died young too, possibly from TB, in 1935. Gip never recovered, and dad spent his life looking after her, just as Rónán Ceannt took care of Áine.

When the Abbey plaque to its 1916 rebel actors was unveiled in 1966, Gip's name was absent, although she had been active, carrying despatches for Cathal Brugha. My father, who was RTÉ's theatre critic, had to embarrass the directors into inviting her to the ceremony. He never forgot that slight. There is a photo of her with Seán Lemass at the event. This was the last picture of any of the Walkers at the Abbey. Gip died in 1967, not long after I was born.

I've written a brief passage about Crawford Neil into Maire's 1916 account, as I believe he should be remembered in these pages. Maire published his only volume of poetry, *Happy Island*, in May 1916. I am threading his and Gip's story through the greater family biography on which I am now working. I also mention, briefly, the following story in the revised text.

While Maire was tending to the men in Jacob's, her father was making a little bit of history across the Liffey. After alerting her to the Rising, he walked from Glasthule into the GPO. He was seventy, and had corns on his feet.

Matt blustered his way through the British lines and presented himself to Pearse, saying, 'I'm here to do my bit for Ireland.' Great-grandad and Pearse were comrades in the IRB, and he was well respected among the men present, being a veteran nationalist. Pearse thanked him and said his offer had been noted, but he was too old to fight. Matt, being Matt, refused to leave until he was given something to do. Pearse thought for a moment and then tasked him with finding a printer's to produce propaganda for the week. The *Irish War News* was born.

Matt returned to the Gaelic Press, and with his son-in-law, Joe Stanley, son Charlie, Thomas Ryan and James O'Sullivan, they took over O'Keeffe's on Halston Street. There had been talk of invading the *Irish Independent*, but Connolly thought this would overstretch the garrison. The same was said of the nearby Gaelic Press.

Throughout the week, Joe Stanley showed extraordinary bravery, returning to the GPO for extra copy. Matt did too. In one witness statement he is described arriving at the Stanleys' dairy on Parnell Street with his hair and beard badly burned and in a state of exhaustion. He had single-handedly put out a fire at the Gaelic Press, presumably while getting supplies. Perhaps an incendiary shell had missed the GPO and landed in Liffey Street.

Matt and Frank Walker printed the 1917 version of the Proclamation as part of the anniversary commemorations. It is now rarer than the original. Unfortunately, I do not have a copy.

Matt was also given the job of delivering Pearse's farewell letter to his mother. He did this three weeks after the Rising. It can't have been easy for him. This loveable old gentleman went blind in 1928, and died a few months later. His wife, Mary Anne, passed away in 1936, after spending the last ten years of her life confined to bed after breaking her hip. That handicap didn't stop her ruling her little family empire with all the vigour she had shown in the Carlow years. Her funeral was attended by six cabinet ministers and the President's ADC. Her coffin was draped with the tricolour and followed by a cortège of street dealers from the Liberties. They wept openly.

Annie (stage name Eileen Doherty) died in 1959. Her Abbey acting career ended in the 1920s. She never set foot on stage again.

Apart from the death of her friends, Maire had one very positive encounter in Jacob's. Her future husband, Eamonn 'Bob' Price (they married in 1929), who was a captain in the second Dublin Battalion, organised the surrender of the men for MacDonagh. In his private letters to Maire, Bob speaks of how he fell in love with her when he saw her 'falling in with the men' outside the factory.

Bob was from a poor background, but worked hard at school and moved on into the pre-1916 Civil Service. His family were strong nationalists, and he inevitably found his way into the Gaelic League and the Volunteers. He saw Maire for the first time at Maud Gonne's Clonturk Park fete. He would have also known her from the stage, the League and other groups. She was friendly with his sister too: Leslie Price (who married Tom Barry) was Director of Organisation for Cumann na mBan.

Not much correspondence about their early relationship remains, but it is possible to presume that they were an item from early 1917 on, when Bob was released from Frongoch. He returned to Dublin tasked with setting up a new GHQ and reorganising the Volunteers.

Michael Collins may have brought the couple together. Maire became treasurer of his Irish National Aid Association, which supported the dependants of imprisoned and dead Volunteers. She may have kindled her romance with Bob through this organisation.

My father had a wealth of anecdotes about Collins's bravery, which were handed down by Bob and Maire. And Gipsy too— she said that 'a woman couldn't sit in the same room as Mick without him slipping his hand up her skirt.'

Bob and Collins were close, but there might have been some friendly rivalry there as well. In 1917, Bob beat the Big Fella decisively during the election for the 'centre' of the Leinster 'Fintan Lalor' circle of the IRB. Collins was seen as 'new', and perhaps overly ambitious, while Bob was an old, trusted, safe hand. He was popular among the men as well, having a good sense of humour, integrity and bravery. He also like a jar, as the puritanical Ernie O'Malley points out in his book, *On Another Man's Wound*. But then, Collins's crew were generally heavy drinkers.

Bob was Director of Organisation IRA GHQ in early 1921, and spent most of his time out of the office on the road, meeting Volunteers around the country (like O'Malley). He dressed in civvies and posed as a travelling salesman, but also carried a Webley. Bob is worthy of his own biography, and was working on it up to his death. Maire submitted the only portion he had written down to the Bureau of Military History.

I mention the fact that he was a heavy drinker because, according to an elderly relative, it caused friction in their marriage in later life. According to her, Bob cut quite a forlorn, but immaculately dressed, figure when in his cups. He appeared to be a man struggling to contain a drink problem and retain his dignity, while carrying many terrible memories.

It is possible that he suffered from post-traumatic stress, like many other Volunteers, after his service during the Tan and Civil Wars. A few years ago I discovered that he was on the Military Tribunal that whitewashed the Ballyseedy Massacre, the worst atrocity perpetrated by Free State troops on unarmed republican prisoners (they were tied to a mine and blown up). I often wonder if that weighed guiltily on his mind.

Bob retired from the army as a Major General, and helped raise my father in Laytown (Maire and he lived in Marion Villas). He seems, from what I recall from my dad, to have been a distant figure, and died, most likely as a result of his alcoholism, in 1951.

Maire's service after 1916 was unspectacular. Women were confined to more of an auxiliary role than in the period leading up the Rising. She was chiefly involved in what she described as 'ordinary Cumann na mBan duties': fund-raising, distributing money to prisoners' families, canvassing for Sinn Féin, and parading at public meetings and funerals, including those of Thomas Ashe and Richard Coleman. She also attended to the sick during the flu epidemic of 1918.

That same year she moved to Drogheda, where Joe Stanley and my grandfather, Eddie Kenny, were setting up the country's first chain of cinemas. She then moved to the duo's Cavan picture house and set up a branch of Cumann na mBan in the town. She assisted local republicans, but 'there was not much to be done', she said in her pension statement. Although she was 'on call', her involvement in the national movement was coming to an end.

Maire continued to tour with plays to raise funds for Pearse's St Enda's, including a trip to Liverpool in 1920 with 'Maire Nic

Shiubhaligh's Irish Players'. The remainder of her life was spent in Laytown helping Gipsy raise my father after Eddie died.

She joined the Irish Countrywoman's Association and staged plays around the country, in which my father sometimes appeared, and gave elocution lessons. She frequently performed on radio, but this work eventually dried up. Maire seemed destined to fade away, but never gave up.

Her last stage appearance was in 1952 as Kathleen Ni Houlihan with an obscure company in a backstreet hall off Mountjoy Square. She wasn't paid for her time. Her last paid job was as Laytown's first librarian. Maire always dealt in 'firsts'.

She was plagued by ill health in her final years, and died in Drogheda in November 1958. Her funeral was attended by the president's ADC, her old friend Lennox Robinson and members of the original Abbey company, including veteran stagehand Sean Barlow. One of the floral tributes read: 'From the Directors of the Abbey Theatre in memory of a great actress.'

Maire's cause of death was a stroke. I don't know if she was a smoker to the end of her life, but she was a committed puffer during her middle years at any rate (according to her papers in the NLI).

> The Abbey was where I learned to smoke. [...] I became a desperate smoker. J. M. Synge used to make his own cigarettes. He would come around in the wings and make them for us. He was such a charming man.
>
> He showed me how to make them, and when I was leaving he came to me and said, 'Maire, if you stay on with us, I will give you a machine to make them and a whole lot of tobacco so you will never be without a cigarette.'

It seems oddly appropriate that a habit she picked up in the Abbey may have contributed to her death.

This book was 'born' in 1948—the year that Maire made her stage 'comeback', appearing with Gip and Ted in *The Gaol Gate* at the Olympia Theatre in a programme commemorating the 150th anniversary of Wolfe Tone's death. The audience greeted her return with rapturous applause, and her friends suggested that dad should take down her reminiscences. He started on the spot writing his first notes for *The Splendid Years* on the back of an envelope.

It took several years to finish. Dad told *The Irish Times* that it was 'the start of a long, long interview.' He took notes from his aunt anywhere and everywhere, as incidents came back to her. Most of this book was transcribed by the fireside in Laytown.

Dad's manuscript, somehow, managed to get burned along the way. It must have been disheartening for him, but he persevered, starting again from scratch. The end result was this book. It opened a few doors for him. He went on to have a very successful career as a newspaperman, working for *The Times* and the *Independent*. (His 'scoops' included interviews with Ernest Hemingway, Tyrone Power and Laurel and Hardy.) He was then headhunted into RTÉ at the very start of TV in Ireland, becoming one of its newsroom pioneers.

He retired as Foreign Editor in the mid-eighties due to ill health, but never stopped writing, and somewhere there is an unpublished horror thriller called *The Children of Dorchas* I am still waiting to uncover.

In his unpublished notes about this book, dad says, 'I was never quite happy about *The Splendid Years* as its scope was necessarily limited.' I know from what he told me that this wasn't the only reason he took it out of print almost immediately after its release. He was deeply unhappy with the job Duffy's had done.

The corrections I made to this book are from handwritten notes in one of his two copies. They don't trouble the original narrative, and were to my mind as a thirty-year editorial hack, generally cosmetic. In some places they are hard to decipher. Where there was doubt, I left the original text 'stet' (to use sub-editorial terminology). I also disagreed with some of his deletions. I would have argued the toss with him about these if he was still alive. I have also resisted the temptation to festoon the following pages with endless annotations of my own. They tend to slow down the pace of a book, and it is not my place to muck around with Ted's 'flow'. I think I have filled in most of the necessary blanks with this introduction. I hope I have done him justice.

One of my reasons for bringing out this revised and lengthened edition is because Maire's voice has been hidden for sixty years. Historians are aware of her, as there are copies of *The Splendid Years* in various libraries, but the general reader is not. Maire's original dedication was 'To all other amateur dramatic societies'. *The Splendid Years* was never intended to be a scholarly work for academia. It was for 'ordinary' people. I want her to be heard again. I'm very proud of her and her family. And of my dad, of course.

I say the above is *one* of my reasons. The chief reason is that I wanted to do this for my dad. It's his book, and it is a shame that he never had the self-confidence to follow through on his other literary projects. He was a brilliant writer who had the gift of making history accessible. He ensured that his aunt lived on. It's through his words that we can take inspiration from Maire's selfless dedication to country and community.

Her exploits are typical of many of the women from the revolutionary period. It has long been a source of annoyance for me that 'the sisterhood' have been airbrushed from our history books. This is, thankfully, being rectified. I hope *The Splendid Years* plays its part in this regard too.

Finally, I have decided not to print pictures of Maire in old age. She and dad didn't include any in the original version of this book. Her 'strange, wan, disquieting beauty' (to quote a contemporary Times critic) faded with the years. Perhaps the actress who made her debut as an old woman (Kathleen Ni Houlihan) didn't want to be seen as a pensioner.

Daisy Walker's daughter, Kathleen (Gregan) Carey, my own beloved 'auntie Kathleen', told me a poignant yarn about Maire and Gipsy's final days. It might help to explain my decision.

One day, in late 1957, a journalist from *The Irish Times* walked up the laneway to Tedville, the green corrugated-metal house where Gip lived with Ted. He asked my grandmother if 'Maire Nic Shiubhlaigh, the famous Abbey actress' was at home.

Gip replied that she was on holidays in Dublin and wouldn't be back for a number of days. The hack thanked her and turned, crestfallen, to head back to the railway station. As he walked off, he raised his hat to a portly, white-haired old lady, who was struggling up the laneway laden down with shopping bags.

'Who was that, Gip?' asked Maire, putting down her shopping.

'Oh, no one. He was just looking for directions,' replied Gipsy.

My grandmother had seen Maire approaching. She lied to the journalist as she didn't want her big sister to be remembered, and photographed, in the press as an ailing old woman. She wanted people to remember her as the hazel-eyed, twenty-one-year-old beauty of John B. Yeats's portraits. I am respecting that 'ownership' of Maire's memory.

Let her remain forever young, wan, disquieting and beautiful. Let her continue to live through *The Splendid Years*.

Foreword
by Padraic Colum

TO SAY that it is a story written with liveliness and modesty is to pay an insufficient tribute to *The Splendid Years*. Character is in the writing in spite of the fact that a second name goes with Maire Nic Shiubhlaigh's in the heading: a real person is projected, and this saves the story from becoming a mere chronicle. Her collaborator has done his work so well that it would be inept not to remark upon Edward Kenny's part in the writing of the book: it is not as if he had just listened to and transcribed what was said in sessions; it is as if this young journalist had set himself not only to reproduce the words but the voice we heard in *Deirdre, The King's Threshold, In the Shadow of the Glen* and in *The Shadowy Waters.* His is indeed a fine piece of work.

Maire Nic Shiubhlaigh has been a participant in some of the great moments in recent Irish history; here is communicated the sense of expectancy that these moments held for the generation that came of age in the times of Yeats, Arthur Griffith, Pádraic Pearse…. A young girl takes lessons from a youngish man who earns his living in an accountant's office, and we are at the beginning of a movement that is to give Ireland a theatre that is to rank with the world's celebrated theatres. 'The beginning of a ship is a board; of a kiln, a stone; of a king's reign, salutation.' The combination that seemed to begin so casually produced actors and actresses like Willie and Frank Fay and Dudley Digges, actresses like Maire Nic Shiubhlaigh herself, and Sara Allgood; plays like the memorable ones of which she gives such clear account. But it did so because there was an intellectual ferment around. It was the period of the first Irish plays, but it was also the period of George Moore's *Hail and Farewell!*, of the ablest of Irish political pamphlets since Swift's time, Arthur Griffith's *The Resurrection of Hungary*, of a sudden development in Irish poetry; a new development in prose, too, one might say, when one remembers that a young man once came into the hall in Camden Street where a rehearsal was going on who, known only to a few people for a few lyrics at the time, was to write *Portrait of the Artist as a Young Man* and *Ulysses*.

As one reflects on the period the prospect widens and becomes more peopled: Arthur Griffith was editing *The United Irishman*, David Moran *The Leader*, Pádraic Pearse *An Claidheamh Soluis*, A. E. *The Irish Homestead*. There were exhibitions of Jack Yeats, exhibitions by A. E. that gave arresting colours and arresting figures to the Irish landscape; in his studio in Stephen's Green J. B. Yeats was painting the men and women of the time and talking endlessly and illuminatingly; Maud Gonne with her beauty and single-mindedness was present as only she could be present; John O'Leary, the last of the Fianna, with his noble head and sad eyes was there to inspire another generation. And they all, representative people, people of importance, converged on the theatre, all bringing something to it, or, perhaps more importantly, expecting something from it.

Looking back to those years I see a young woman with brown eyes and a beautifully modelled face whom J. B. Yeats delighted to sketch and paint, whom Frank Fay delighted to instruct, happy for a day when he had her voice ring to the walls, and whose voice indeed was as fresh and clear as the voice of a bird in the early morning when she appeared as Lavarcham in A. E.'s *Deirdre*. Where she lived in High Street became a place of voices, of winged words. There Willie Fay insisted on having room and board; there Frank Fay would come to delight himself with passages from *The Shadowy Waters*. And there her hospitable father and mother surrounded all these flights with the simplicity of a Dublin home where it was possible for the younger girls to move, casually it seemed, into the theatre. Maire's brother, Frank, who just took any part for which he was needed, again and again proved himself an exciting actor.

And now I am reminded of an entertaining incident. His most exciting appearance was in *On Baile's Strand* where as CúChullain's son he played opposite Frank Fay's CúChullain. Now Frank Fay was far from heroic in his build, but he could project himself as a heroic figure as he did not have to draw the audience's attention to his bodily equipment. But he had to take hold of the arm of the young man who was his son, and ejaculate: 'That arm had a good father and a good mother, but it is not like this,' and strip his own to show an arm as meagre as any townsman's. It was wonderful that he could do it and leave only a momentary sense of incongruity.

The Splendid Years gets down memorably to the theatre as theatre; many have written about it as if literary expression were all that there was to the Irish theatre, words and the delivery of words, as if the theatre were devoid of entrances and exits, boards and footlights. ('Four boards and a passion,' Frank Fay used to say longingly when one met him going back to his accountant's office.) A theatre comprises many inventions, and here we are being told of some of them. The occasion is the production of *On Baile's Strand:*

> Fay adopted simplicity and the artistic blending of colour as his keynote in the staging. Great emphasis was laid on lighting. Amber-coloured hangings draped the interior of a great hall. A huge door, closed, showed intricate Celtic interlacings on panel and lintel. When it was opened a glimpse was revealed of a luminous blue sky over a bay. Two plain thrones stood in the centre; brilliant hand-painted medallions on the walls completed the fittings.

It had been remarked by a few of the discerning that the extraordinary accomplishment of the Fays was in the fact that Willie could diminish and Frank could enlarge himself on the stage. How well that extraordinary metamorphosis is put before us:

> Willie Fay, the comedian, the businesslike stage manager of a few moments before, was no more. He was

transformed into a tiny ragged sprite, cringing before the glittering king of his brother. The other figures paled into the background. Frank Fay spoke, fondling his lines, and they flowed across the footlights, hovering a moment over the hushed auditorium, his little figure gaining power through the beauty of his words, first as the proud king, hero of a thousand battles, then as the horrified, grief-stricken father verging on madness.

The National Theatre Society, evolving into the Abbey Theatre, has a history that has often been recounted. But there was also the Theatre of Ireland and the Irish Theatre, which had their own distinctive plays, their own actors and their own producers; in both organisations Maire Nic Shiubhlaigh was a guiding spirit. In connection with the Theatre of Ireland let me recall a remarkable actor who belonged to it. He was Joseph Goggin. I have reason to remember a production of *The Fiddler's House* when he played opposite Maire Nic Shiubhlaigh. He had a distinguished appearance and real poetic power. So obviously did he look the artist that Oliver Shepherd took his as the model for Mangan's face; his features are perpetuated in the bronze in Stephen's Green. But the Theatre of Ireland could only give performances now and again in different places, while the Abbey, even though it was in the doldrums at the time, had continuity and a fixed place. Then there was the Irish Theatre, whose patron was Edward Martyn. It is a pity Martyn's plays were not more often produced: they had constructive power, a power that the rest of our dramatists are badly lacking. Willie Pearse, Thomas MacDonagh and Joseph Plunkett, before they took on their greater roles, were connected with this theatre. But, like the Theatre of Ireland, their financial resources were too meagre to allow their development.

Meagreness of financial resource, indeed one might say an almost total lack of it, set up a dead end before the theatre movement in those days. Had it not been for the fact that an English patron gave Yeats a theatre, the National Theatre Society might never have been stabilised into a National Theatre. The spirit of the young people who were willing to keep up two jobs, their own and the theatre, was magnificent. But in what other city in Europe would they have been left to do their work, unaided, after their genius, enterprise and single-mindedness had been shown? Readers of today will be startled by the statement that when Maire Nic Shiubhlaigh went back to the Abbey it was the first time she got a salary out of the theatre. It was the same with the dramatists in the early days—they got nothing, absolutely nothing. If one had been paid ten pounds, or even five pounds, he would have gone dancing down College Green. If he had even been given an inaugural supper in the house of some of the richer Dubliners who made conversation out of his plays, he would have been pleasantly surprised. 'The Splendid Years', the authors name the time. They were splendid because of the spirit of a few people. They were austere days for the young men and women who made them splendid. They gave to and they got nothing from the Dublin of those days.

Preface

by Edward Kenny

IN THE following pages, Maire Nic Shiubhlaigh tells her story of the young years of the Irish national theatre movement, from its beginning, for her, in an amateur dramatic society of about sixteen actors and actresses, of which she was one, until the Easter of 1916. It is a story of hard work for little material reward, of a constant striving for recognition and of triumph over many difficulties—in short, the story of the pursuit of an ideal. Because of the nature of our collaboration in preparing it, I have been asked to tell something here of how the story came to be published and to explain its scope as a history of the theatre.

The Splendid Years had its beginning in a short lecture about her association with the original Irish National Theatre Society, which Maire Nic Shiubhlaigh gave to undergraduates at University College Galway in 1947. Her talk evoked so much interest that she was asked to repeat it elsewhere, this time including her recollections of the early years of the Abbey Theatre in Dublin, and a little later she spoke at a third gathering of her experiences as a member of an Irish Volunteer garrison in Dublin during Easter Week, 1916. The notes of these three talks, considerably augmented of course, and documented as fully as possible, comprise this book.

As far as recording the narrative is concerned, I have been in a fortunate position insofar as, being a close relative of the teller, this is a story with which I have grown up. Snatches of it emerging in conversation have been told around our family fireside over a long period of years. In preparing what follows for the publisher, we have adopted much the same system. Those additions that have been made to Maire Nic Shiubhlaigh's original lectures have been made without haste, in conversations that have taken place over almost two years. The newspaper cuttings, lists of plays, etc. that comprise the Appendices, I have added merely as a guide to the student. In this regard, particular attention is directed to the period from 1906 until 1912, covering the career of the Theatre of Ireland, the story of which has probably never been told before.

A follower of the Irish theatre during the years covered in the following pages once said, in effect, that he would happily endure any of the physical discomforts imposed by small, ill-equipped and draughty halls merely for the pleasure of hearing Maire Nic Shiubhlaigh and Frank Fay recite verse. It was a sentiment endorsed by other discerning playgoers of the period who recognised the accomplishment of that small band of original Irish players who were indeed, as was later written, 'in love with the voice'.

Maire Nic Shiubhlaigh is a typical graduate of that school of acting— and beautiful speech—founded by the brothers Frank and W. G. Fay. Many writers have described her not only as a tragedienne of power and intensity, but as the possessor of one of the most beautiful speaking voices ever produced by the young Irish theatre. Most of the major roles in the early Irish plays fell to her as the National Theatre Society's first leading lady. Some of the first Irish dramatists wrote specially for her; when he wrote some of his first verse-plays, Yeats probably had her in mind as one of the actresses who would help to interpret them on the stage. She was the original Nora Burke of Synge's *In the Shadow of the Glen*, the original Dectora of *The Shadowy Waters*, and a striking *Kathleen Ni Houlihan*, while her performance as Moll Woods in the original production of Seumas O'Kelly's *The Shuiler's Child* (staged modestly in Dublin by the penniless Theatre of Ireland) evoked widespread critical acclaim in Ireland and abroad.

Then, too, the Walker family had remarkably close associations with the Irish theatre during its first years: Frank Walker was also a player-founder of the Irish National Theatre Society, while at a later date two of the younger sisters joined the company and pursued careers of their own on the Irish stage as

'Eileen O'Doherty' and 'Betty King' respectively. It is interesting to note as well that on the Abbey Theatre's opening night two members of the family were on the stage; two more were in the auditorium selling programmes in the time-honoured tradition of the amateur dramatic society; and another—my grandmother— was behind the scenes, stitching the costumes.

The Splendid Years, however, is not the story of the Walker family—rather is it the story of the infant years of the Irish theatre, as seen by one of the theatre's founders. Students of the movement who have devoured the mountain of books written on the subject may notice an occasional lack of reference in this story to certain events in the theatre's history. These gaps are intentional. This is Maire Nic Shiubhlaigh's story of the theatre, and concerns itself only with those events with which she was familiar at the time. The essential history is there all the same.

Maire Nic Shiubhlaigh grew up during one of the most colourful periods in Irish history. She was fortunate enough to participate in many of the events that made that period colourful. As she tells us, in retrospect the Dublin of the young century was 'full of earnest young people, all of them anxious to do something useful for Ireland,' whether it was the launching of a national theatre or the planning of insurrection. It is a matter of history that this period produced *both* an Irish national theatre and an insurrection; what may not be so immediately apparent is the connection between the two. For Maire Nic Shiubhlaigh, and many of her contemporaries of those years, the theatre began in the politico-cultural clubs that existed in Dublin at the turn of the century. Like a number of her fellow players she abandoned a career in the theatre only to pursue the original ideal during the Easter insurrection. And here the link between the theatre and the Rising becomes apparent: the young enthusiasts of those years, the homogeneous elements making up the nationalist clubs of the period and providing the impetus necessary, not only for the foundation of a theatre but for the building of a nation. In both cases it remained for others to build upon these foundations.

For the Irish theatre was not, of course, the creation of any one person or small group of people. It was the product of a period—a period of great intellectual activity and of a generation dedicated to the national ideal. It emerged on the wave of enthusiasm created by the young people who 'wanted to do something useful for Ireland,' and for many of whom the wheel had turned full circle when the first shot was fired in 1916.

These were important years in Irish history. This is how Maire Nic Shiubhlaigh remembers them.

To all other amateur dramatic societies.

Part One

The Irish National Theatre Society

Chapter One

1900–1901
The Curtain Stirs

LOOKING BACK now it seems a strange thing to say that, for many of us who were closely involved in it, the beginning of the Irish theatre came as something of a surprise. Before 1902, when the Irish National Theatre Society was established, few of us who made up the original company of Irish players had much general experience of the stage. Most of us were young folk—the eldest amongst us would have been no more than thirty—and none of us, apart from W. G. Fay, who was responsible for our appearance together, had ever acted professionally. We knew little of the drama apart from what we had read or been told of dramatic movements on the Continent, or what we saw for ourselves in theatres in Dublin.

There was little to indicate that our first appearance as a company of amateur players, producing two Irish plays in a small Dublin concert hall, would begin a movement that would change in many ways the course of theatrical history. We were all quite unknown; young Dubliners, drawn into the company partly because of an interest in acting, partly because of an interest in Irish nationalism. Most of us came out of nationalist clubs in Dublin, or were connected in some fashion with the nationalist movement. Almost everyone in the Irish theatre was during its first years.

Remembering this simple beginning, the excitement of what was my first important appearance on a stage, I find that my memory of the occasion is still quite clear when other more recent events have passed from my mind. But this is not strange. There are outstanding events in everyone's life. Small memories of the occasion stand out quite clearly, little irrelevant recollections of people and of the small mishaps that always occur behind the scenes when any little group of inexperienced players anywhere prepares for a first performance. Quite easily I can remember my surprise at the sight of A. E. dressed in strange Celtic robes for the small part he was taking in his own play, *Deirdre,* standing calmly behind the little stage, displaying none of the agitation one would expect of a man awaiting the production of his first play, and looking rather odd in Druid's costume with the steel-rimmed spectacles he was wearing, while he held a script for someone uncertain of lines. And Willie Fay being very important as producer and actor, making sure that everything was all right while Frank, his brother, was just as nervous then as he always was in later years before a new play began.

And I can remember the response of the audience later in the evening when Maud Gonne played the woman in *Kathleen Ni Houlihan,* and the applause, which lasted long after the curtain had finally fallen. It was all very wonderful. It may be of course that the passage of years and the excitement of the time can magnify the memory of such an event out of all proportion, yet I think not. It would be stranger if memories of this occasion were not so clear. The production of these two plays was to mean much for all of us who helped with them. It was the prelude to many things.

For most of us it had begun quite simply a few years earlier, in what was at that time one of the smaller nationalist clubs working in Dublin: Inghinidhe na hÉireann (The Daughters of Ireland). Inghinidhe na hÉireann was a politico-cultural society of young women founded by Maud Gonne as an auxiliary of the old Celtic Literary Society, of which Arthur Griffith and William Rooney were then members. It was probably the only organisation of its kind working in Dublin at the time that offered young women an opportunity to take part in national work. It had a wide following amongst young girls all over the city. Like most other little Irish clubs of the time, its activities were varied. Politically, it was something of a thorn in the side of the administration; culturally, it did much good work. We used to hold classes and debates, encouraging the study of Irish history, music, literature and art, and for those of us who were interested in acting there was a small dramatic company.

At the time this was producing *tableaux vivants* at the Antient Concert Rooms, a small theatre in Brunswick Street— 'living pictures', very popular just then, showing a scene from some period in Irish history or illustrating some legend or patriotic melody: William Rooney's *Dear Dark Head*, or perhaps something out of Moore's *Rich and Rare* in which would appear a lady, richly bejewelled and garbed in silks, wooed by a glittering Sir Knight to the accompaniment of appropriate choral music. The director was Alice Milligan, who also wrote some of the plays later produced by the company, *The Harp that Once* and *The Deliverance of Red Hugh*, and some members of the Celtic Literary Society contributed pieces of their own in the years that followed: Padraic Colum gave *The Children of Lir* and *The Saxon Shillin'*, two of his first works for the theatre. The little group produced full-length plays only occasionally then, but its object was to encourage young Dubliners to write for the stage and to establish the nucleus of a national dramatic company that would run in conjunction with nationalist organisations in the city.

This was 1900. In Dublin these were the great days of the Gaelic League, of innumerable little clubs and societies, of diverse movements, aimed at the establishment of a new national order. The revival had just begun to gather momentum. Dublin bristled with little national movements of every conceivable kind: cultural, artistic, literary, theatrical or political. I suppose a generation arriving amidst the bickerings of Parliamentarians, of Parnellites and anti-Parnellites, had turned from politics and begun at last to seek national expression elsewhere. Everyone was discussing literature and the arts, the new literature that was emerging. Everywhere, in the streets, at *ceilidhs* and national concerts, anywhere that crowds gathered one met enthusiasts, young people drawn from every side of the city's life, leaders or followers of all the little clubs and societies that were appearing every day. The parent group was the Gaelic League, which was non-political and non-sectarian and strove principally for the revival of the language, but there were other bodies like Cumann na nGaedheal, the immediate forerunner of Sinn Féin, whose leader was Arthur Griffith, as well as smaller clubs that combined social with political activities, circles devoted to industrial and agricultural development, and from the beginning there had been societies for the foundation of an Irish theatre.

In these first years the most important of the latter groups was the Irish Literary Theatre, founded by a few of the older writers, W. B. Yeats, Lady Gregory and Edward Martyn, for the production of Irish plays in Dublin by Irish writers. The Literary Theatre was influenced partly by conditions in Ireland at the time and partly by the new dramatic movement that was sweeping across Europe in revolt against the commercialism and artificiality of the professional theatre.

Just before 1900, Yeats and Martyn had begun to write new and original plays, producing them in Dublin at the Antient Concert Rooms and the Gaiety Theatre, but they had made the mistake of employing English players for the work. After a short and stormy career, their enterprise had died. They found that English voices, no matter how well trained, could never lend themselves effectively to the expression of Irish idioms. Their productions in three years included Yeats's *The Countess Cathleen*; Edward Martyn's *The Heather Field* and *Maeve*; George Moore's *The Bending of the Bough* and Alice Milligan's *The Last Feast of the Fianna*. Dublin received these at first with loud protests—some of the plays were sufficiently in advance of their time to arouse bitter controversies—and then, what was worse, with a lack of interest. Admitting defeat after the failure of *Diarmuid and Gráinne*, the final production, Yeats said: 'There was always something incongruous between Irish words and an English accent.' The Irish Literary Theatre had died in early 1901. Its failure had meant the cessation until capable Irish players were available of any really important movement towards the establishment of a national theatre in Ireland. Yeats, strangely enough, had made little attempt to look for Irish players; he waited until they discovered themselves. The two men responsible for us 'finding ourselves' were Willie and Frank Fay.

Willie first came to prominence when he was appointed producer and stage manager with Inghinidhe na hÉireann the year the Literary Theatre died. This was an honorary position to which he gave much of his time. He was the son of a Dublin civil servant, an electrician by trade, and decidedly an actor by inclination. In later years when he became better known as an Irish player, a humorous tradition grew up in Dublin that he knew more about his hobby than he did about his work. Whether there was truth in that or not may still be a matter for debate, but he certainly displayed a far greater interest in what went on behind the footlights than he did towards what might be taking place inside them. When we who formed the nucleus of the Irish National Theatre Society met him he was a young man with a rough-and-ready but surprisingly wide and practical knowledge of the theatre.

Besides touring Ireland with every conceivable kind of makeshift fit-up, playing *The Shaughraun*, *East Lynne* and all the other time-worn favourites in barns and country halls, he had found time in about 1898 to establish a small amateur theatrical company in Dublin called the Ormond Dramatic Society. With his brother, Frank—whose interest in the stage was as profound but not so spectacular—he used this to experiment with different types of popular drama in the city's small halls and concert rooms, playing Boucicault and Whitbread to enthusiastic, although not very critical, audiences.

He was a small man of indeterminate age, slightly built, with a battered felt hat, a long mackintosh and an old briar pipe that he never seemed to take out of his mouth. Steel-rimmed spectacles perched at a dangerous angle on his thin nose. He used to cycle down to rehearsals each evening, stopping the machine carefully outside the Inghinidhe rooms, then carrying it into the hallway with him. At that time he used to tell us that he was 'in the throes of one of his infrequent spells of inactivity,' which meant that he was resting in a job as an electrician before travelling off across the country again with some new fit-up. Apparently, by way of an antidote to this inactivity, he was willing to divide his time between his work in the city, the Ormond Dramatic Society and Inghinidhe na hÉireann Theatrical Company. He was that sort of wanderer who cannot stay away from the stage for long, and looked as though he would never settle permanently anywhere. We used to call him a 'professional amateur'. He became the greatest comedian the Abbey ever had, and was the theatre's first and perhaps best producer.

In 1901 his work as producer with Inghinidhe na hÉireann was confined to those occasions upon which the company produced full-length plays. At that time our efforts in this direction were received with interest in nationalist circles in the city, and were usually well attended, but, probably because the plays were indifferent affairs, we did not have much of a following amongst regular theatregoers. The Dublin public seldom thought of going out of its way to a small hall when professional entertainments were available in the bigger and better-equipped theatres in the centre of the city. There was plenty to attract it there.

Dublin was then, as always, a sort of testing ground for visiting companies. The playgoer had the choice of anything from the *Hamlet* or *Othello* of Martin Harvey to the broadest farce or melodrama. Shakespearian stock companies paid frequent visits, and there were snatches of Goldsmith and Sheridan now and then, while the Bensons, H. B. Irving, Forbes-Robertson and Ellen Terry had appeared on the boards of the Gaiety and the old Theatre Royal from time to time. Those who liked variety or meaty melodrama could go to Dan Lowrey's or the old Queen's. From farther afield came the *Comédie Française,* with refreshingly different fare to that offered by the British visitors. The French players always excited considerable comment, and had the reputation of being pioneers of a particular form of playing. They were later mentioned as models for native Irish players.

Fay came regularly for rehearsals to the Inghinidhe na hÉireann rooms, and occasionally as a guest to the society's monthly debates. Sometimes he brought along his brother, Frank, a slightly built man like himself who worked with a firm of accountants in the city. Frank used to sit rather uneasily in the background at these gatherings, surrounded by earnest young women who chattered incessantly at him while Willie held forth tirelessly and with the most unexpected eloquence on theatrical matters. Probably he did not like us very much, but the deference with which Willie treated him on all occasions set him high in our estimation, and he always restrained himself sufficiently to answer our questions courteously while he kept one eye fixed on the clock.

Though he was older by only a year or two than his brother, he looked nearly twice Willie's age. His square-cut face, serious expression and deep, carefully controlled voice added years to his appearance beside the other, whose mobile, Puck-like features gave him a schoolboyish look. Willie referred to him endlessly on all subjects; if asked for an opinion while not in Frank's company, he invariably deferred judgement until he had consulted with 'the brother', as he called him. Surprisingly, although nothing was done without his sanction, 'the brother' seldom had the last word in any matter. Whether it was because his views on all subjects were identical to Willie's or not, it was always the younger man's suggestions that were implemented. The latter's judgement on most matters concerning theatrical work was unerring, and in any case he always had plenty of authoritative arguments with which to back up his theories. He would never have undertaken anything, however, without Frank's sanction.

It was less than a year later that Frank Fay shared the position of leading Irish player with his brother. He was not, as the other had been, anything in the nature of a 'professional' actor, for he spurned the questionable joys of fit-up caravan travelling. He widened his knowledge of theatrical work by concentrating on the less colourful activities of the Ormond Dramatic Society, whose interests he looked after during his brother's widespread travels in search of technical theatrical experience. He was an actor of merit, but strangely enough it was not in this respect that he shone most. His talents lay in a slightly different direction, for he was a dramatic instructor of genius. Later, when he took over the training of the first Irish theatre company, he achieved the factor essential for the production of Irish plays: proper voice control.

I doubt if any productions of Yeats's early verse-plays could have been as effective as they were without him. He was directly responsible for bringing out the peculiar inflections of the Irish voice that are so important in plays of this sort. In preparing plays he laid the utmost emphasis on the importance of words, and made beautiful speech, whether it was the delivery of dialect or the lyrical speaking of verse, his goal. Thus he produced a company of Irish actors unique in the history of the theatre who were, as one writer later recorded, 'in love with the voice.' A popular error still identifies W. B. Yeats with the training of the Irish players and the establishment of the acting tradition that has kept the Abbey Theatre alive through the last fifty years. If the poet were alive now he would be the first to disagree with such a theory: to Frank Fay must go the credit of training the actors.

Without Willie Fay there might never have been an Irish theatre company; without Frank Fay there might never have been a competent one.

At about this time Frank started a small elocution class in the Coffee Palace Hall, Townsend Street, for people interested in the stage. I was one of his first pupils.

He was a painstaking teacher. Besides many long and not very comfortable sessions, which we passed learning the fundamentals of correct speech, we were taken to most productions of note on the Dublin stage. Fay believed in emphasising his teachings by comparison, and from the front row of the sixpenny gallery we watched the work of every great figure of the time while he purposefully examined each performance. He was particularly enthusiastic about the work of the French players, especially Coquelin. The latter, he claimed, was the only actor who had the courage to cast off the 'genteel' conventions that burdened the work of the English players.

The British productions of the time were indeed in marked contrast to the continental ones. It used to be said, especially in the case of the smaller companies, that before an Englishman went on a stage he took a course in military foot-drill. The movements of all the minor actors appeared to be worked out to the minutest detail beforehand to fit in with the idiosyncrasies of the 'star', hence a sort of robotic effect; a lack of spontaneity. The continental artists on the other hand cast all these conventions aside, and apart from the principal movements essential to the picture they presented, they moved as they considered the characters they portrayed should, quietly or noisily—mostly noisily—and with a delightful freedom. Few of us knew French, but we could always follow the stories of these productions with ease.

Meanwhile, during our term of study with his brother, Willie Fay had come into contact with the Literary Theatre, and he had been asked to produce, as a curtain-raiser for Moore and Yeats's *Diarmuid and Gráinne*, a short Gaelic piece, *Casadh an tSúgáin* (The Twisting of the Rope) by Douglas Hyde. He had accepted, not only for the experience of working in Irish but for the distinction of being associated with the play, which was the first of its kind ever presented on a regular stage. It was during the work that he began to think that if there were people in Ireland who could act in plays in Gaelic, there must be some who could do so in English. He began to visualise the formation of a group of Irish actors to do plays of an Irish character.

This idea—a national theatre movement—was not altogether original. Before Fay thought of it, Norwegian Ole Bull had already broken virgin soil by turning a little group of raw amateurs into a highly efficient dramatic company and erected a Norwegian National Theatre. European dramatic circles still rang with this achievement. It was echoed partly in Paris, where in a frugally equipped backstreet hall, André Antoine, a man with little or no theatrical experience, had created the *Théâtre Libre*. It was from the example set by these two pioneers that Fay got his inspiration. Both projects had started from practically nothing. The Norwegian company had begun with a prepaid advertisement in a daily paper that modestly suggested that if anyone was interested in the foundation of a national theatre they would be enrolled as members, and Antoine's progress had been hampered by financial difficulties from the outset.

Fay was sure that such an enterprise could be established in Ireland. Further, he learned from the failure of the Irish Literary Theatre that a national dramatic project in Ireland that was purely literary was impracticable. In other words, if there were no one in Ireland who could act, there would never be an Irish national theatre. It is doubtful if he was predominantly influenced by any sentiments such as a nationalistic or patriotic type of expression through the drama; he was concerned principally with the establishment of a new standard of acting that would be characteristically Irish. In that, he was successful.

It was after his work on *Casadh an tSúgáin* and the dissolution of the Literary Theatre that he broached the subject of a native Irish theatre company with the handful of us who attended Frank's classes. Rather sceptically—for we were all working folk—we asked where the money was to come from. 'From us and a group of sympathisers that I'll soon find' was the reply.

Sympathisers, however, were hard to come by, and Fay could find only five pounds. It might have daunted a lesser man. Unconcerned, he began work with his brother on the training of The Ormond Dramatic Society and the Inghinidhe na hÉireann personnel. In the meantime he searched for a suitable play.

One day in the middle of a rehearsal he was handed the script of a new work by George W. Russell, or A. E., the name under which he wrote. It was a two-act piece called *Deirdre* based on the legend of the death of the Children of Usnach. Fay was interested. The subject was, for him, an entirely new departure. But he considered the play too short. 'It should have another act,' he said.

A. E., who at that time was contributing to *The All-Ireland Review*, said that he had written the play partly for a Christmas issue of the magazine and partly 'because everybody nowadays seems to be writing plays.' He had never intended it to be produced, and said so. Fay argued that the play was one to which, in production, he could give full value. We never knew what agitated conferences were held at the distinguished writer's quiet Rathgar home, or to what lengths the little man went to persuade his victim to write the extra act and permit its presentation. Few of us entered into it until a wet winter night a fortnight later when we attended a meeting at the Coffee Palace and learned that the play was to go on after all. Fay's financial resources had dwindled and Inghinidhe na hÉireann had agreed to subsidise the production. That night, muffled in topcoats in a draughty corner of an empty stage, a handful of us formed a new society by merging the Ormond group with the Inghinidhe dramatic class. Fay allotted parts, and the first two acts of *Deirdre* were put into rehearsal. The third act, we hoped, would be ready in a week.

We were a very small company. Included were the two Fays, Máire T. Quinn, Helen Laird, Dudley Digges, P. J. Kelly, Padraic Colum, Fred Ryan, James Cousins, Charles Caulfield, Brian Callender, Frank Walker (my brother) and me. Not many of the names are familiar nowadays. Few of us became professional. Most of us joined the society simply because it was part of the new nationalist movement.

We made our first appearance two months later. Word soon got out that the society, which now had the name of 'W. G. Fay's Irish National Dramatic Company', intended to present a play by an Irish author on an Irish subject with a cast of Irish actors. In itself, of course, that was not enough to attract more than passing notice, but the fact that the play was written by A. E. was a different matter. The author was widely known as a poet, journalist, artist and mystic, and with *Deirdre* he had entered a completely different field.

'There's only one thing I'm worried about,' Fay said. 'The programme will be a bit short. We'll have to fill up with concert items.'

As it happened, however, that wasn't necessary. W. B. Yeats came down to rehearsal the next night with a script of a new play under his arm. 'I've been talking with Miss Gonne,' he said, 'and we thought you might put this on with *Deirdre*. It runs for about twenty minutes.'

The script was read. It suited our needs admirably. The subject—a historical one—was excellent; the piece blended comedy, pathos and just the right shade of national feeling. Fay was pleased. It was arranged to produce it with the longer play.

Yeats called it *Kathleen Ni Houlihan.*

Chapter Two
1901–1902
Enter Kathleen, Stage Left

THE FAYS were very much aware that with the productions they were breaking entirely new ground, and they gave themselves wholeheartedly to the work of rehearsal. Willie, who included a knowledge of scene design amongst his many other accomplishments, painted new sets in which he experimented with what he called a new type of 'suggestive colourings', and Frank looked after the production. They could talk of nothing else but the plays, and the standards that would have to be set in their presentation.

A. E., whose attitude towards the whole thing had turned from reluctance to something bordering on enthusiasm, also displayed a keen interest in the rehearsals, and even had a part in his own play—that of Cathmha, a Druid. Máire T. Quinn was cast as Deirdre opposite Dudley Digges, and I was given the part of Lavarcham, an old woman, Deirdre's nurse. Other parts were taken by Frank Fay, Padraic Colum, Fred Ryan, P. J. Kelly and James Cousins.

Maud Gonne created the title role of Kathleen Ni Houlihan. Her interpretation was a triumph of restrained, sensitive acting, but although she remained a member of our committee for several years, she never again took part in plays. She felt that her work was not in the theatre. Willie Fay, Dudley Digges, Charles Caulfield, Máire Quinn and I made up the rest of the cast in the Yeats play.

We rehearsed when and where we could. The performance was scheduled for the hall of St Teresa's Temperance Society in

Clarendon Street, but it was not until a week before we opened that we had the use of the stage. Sometimes we went out to A. E.'s house at Rathgar to try out *Deirdre*. On other occasions we descended on the homes of sympathetic friends and took possession of libraries and drawing rooms—anywhere that did not too obviously upset the occupants. Alternatively, of course, if Fay was what he called 'flush', or between us we could muster the necessary cash, we took the Coffee Palace, where we fitted as much as we could into a few valuable hours. In the meantime, Fay and A. E. painted scenery.

We had many visitors to the rehearsals. Yeats would come in, discuss technicalities with the Fays and sit back in the shadows, watching. Yeats always seemed to be in the shadows. Occasionally his voice would make itself heard during lulls in the hammering as he made suggestions. He looked strangely out of place with his flowing cravat, loose clothes and unruly poet's hair beside us in our work-a-day attire.

One could never claim to have known Yeats well. Unlike A. E., whose manner was benevolent, his attitude was haughty. A. E. muffled in his great tweed coat, or, peering pleasantly through a tangle of spectacles and beard, was always ready to talk with us and listen to our theories. Yeats on the other hand appeared to give only half his attention. In conversation you got the impression that he looked through and beyond you towards another world.

Naturally, being a brilliant and rather mysterious person, apparently detached from the material things of life, he was the idol of most of the young people who filled the Dublin universities. His every move was followed closely during his visits from London, where he lived at the time. He was a striking figure: tall, and commanding attention. He had a dark complexion with a high forehead, jet-black hair and deep eyes. His full-lipped mouth gave him a rather sulky look at times. It is hardly accurate to say that he was wayward, but he was exceptionally strong-willed. During the years that followed, when he acquired the leadership of the Abbey, he carried it through some of its most critical years, fought all its battles and denounced its enemies and critics with a vigour almost terrifying in its finality. Those who moved on the outskirts of the theatrical movement used to say: 'Yeats thrives in a row.' I have frequently seen him shaken by fits of the most uncontrollable rage.

Of course, being the foremost Irish writer of the time, surrounded by this aura of mystery, and already famous enough to be satirised by the wits in England, where many people admired him but few, surprisingly, understood him, he qualified as a sort of jibing-post in some circles in Dublin, and many funny, but not altogether just, stories were told about him. It was understandable of course: he was on the one hand completely divorced from material considerations—an impression that his association with occult societies, and the strange, unrealistic note that ran through some of his poetry, helped to foster—on the other he was a fighter of the fiercest calibre who could descend completely from the plane he usually occupied and crush all who opposed him by the sheer force of his personality.

Later years were to show evidence of this trait—his attitude on the occasion of the first production of J. M. Synge's ill-fated *Playboy of the Western World* was one—but he had already proved himself a fighter during the furore in Dublin some years earlier over his *Countess Cathleen* when the audience rose in protest because his central character sold her soul to the devil. Yeats had completely surmounted all this opposition with an acid pen and a scathing word. Dublin, in fact, was still rather uncertain about him. He was a puzzle to some; he was admired and copied by others. Young literary-minded people looked at him with a sort of awe and were struck almost dumb when he spoke to them. If he saw the effect he was creating, he seldom showed it. The witticisms that were woven around his actions, if he noticed them, he disregarded or glanced at with a sort of lofty detachment. Yeats was a poseur, but he was never the insipid poet. He commanded the respect of men and the adoration of many women.

St Teresa's Hall, Clarendon Street, Dublin, where *Deirdre* and *Kathleen Ni Houlihan* were produced on 2, 3 and 4 April 1902, was approached from the Dublin South City markets, off Exchequer Street. It was a small place, with room for about three hundred, and had a tiny stage that did not give much room for movement or extravagant gesture. The boxed-in scene, manufactured by Willie Fay, took up most of the space from wall to wall. Off-stage during the action, we lined up in the wings in the order of our appearance, backs to the wall, noses almost touching the side-pieces of the scene, and sidled crab-like into position for our entrances. Awaiting our cues, we held our breath. It was quite likely that a vigorous movement would have brought our chests into contact with the canvas walls and caused them to fall inwards. As it was, the whole scene wobbled dangerously when we moved.

There were no dressing rooms. We had to dress upstairs and get backstage through the auditorium before the audience began to arrive. This meant that if there were any latecomers amongst the cast they would have to show themselves to the audience before the curtain went up. Maud Gonne arrived late the first night and caused a minor sensation by sweeping through the auditorium in the ghostly robes of the Old Woman in *Kathleen Ni Houlihan* ten minutes before we were due to begin. Frank Fay pursed his lips and stamped away in annoyance from his peephole in the proscenium when he saw the occurrence. 'Unprofessional!' he called.

Willie Fay, whom nothing seemed to bother, made us up. His brother, dressed as Concobhar, the King in A. E.'s play, moved from one to the other of us, feverishly running us over our parts. He was always on edge before a first production and had the unhappy knack of communicating his nervousness to others.

Long before the curtain rose, the hall was filled with a mixture of Ormond Dramatic Society clientele and the literary and artistic cliques of the period. Gleaming shirt-fronts mingled with the less resplendent garb of the Dublin worker. Before the footlights lit up the banner of Inghinidhe na hÉireann—a golden sunburst on a blue ground—hanging near the stage, the aisles were crowded with standing-room-only patrons. It was an auspicious opening.

Deirdre was presented first. It is a sombre play based on the legend of the destruction of the Red Branch, and the death of the three sons of Usnach through the love of one of them, Naisi, for Deirdre, the girl whom Concobhar the King had chosen as his bride. It is probably the best-known and most often dramatised of all the tales of ancient Ireland. During the first ten years of the Irish theatre movement, no fewer than five writers took it for their theme. J. M. Synge, the last to do so during my time with the theatre, never saw his version produced. He had only just finished it when he died. Of the remaining four writers, two wrote English versions; one, Father Thomas O'Kelly, dramatised it in picturesque Gaelic; and the fourth, T. W. Rolleston, wrote it as a book for cantata.

The events as they are recounted in the old texts took place at about the time of Christ. Concobhar was the High King of Ireland, Deirdre his intended bride, and Naisi one of the rulers of the sub-kingdoms. Concobhar, fearing that the beauty of the young girl would attract other men, hid her in a lonely valley under the care of an old woman, Lavarcham. A Druid prophecy that she is the girl fated to bring about the destruction of the Red Branch is set in motion when she meets the three sons of Usnach hunting. Naisi immediately falls under her spell and persuades her to flee the country to Alba, where Concobhar's wrath cannot reach. They live there for seven years until Concobhar sends word offering his friendship. They return to Ireland, the three warriors are murdered, and their death brings war on Ulster in which the Red Branch is divided and the prophecy fulfilled.

A. E.'s treatment differed slightly from that of the other writers who used the legend. His Concobhar—elsewhere depicted as a bitter, treacherous old man—was not a jealous king, but a lawgiver who tempered his anger with Solomon-like justice. Oddly, the characterisation was considered by some people to be a mistake. The bitterness of the old Concobhar had served to accentuate the pathos surrounding the death of Naisi and his brothers, demonstrating more fully the reason for their destruction.

But whatever its faults—and if there were any I did not notice them—the production of these two plays is one of my brightest memories. How many who were there that night will forget the Kathleen Ni Houlihan of Maud Gonne, her rich golden hair, her pale, sensitive face and burning eyes as she spoke the closing lines of the Old Woman turning out through the cottage door:

They shall be remembered forever,
They shall be alive forever,
They shall be speaking forever,
The people shall hear them forever...!

Watching her, one could readily understand the reputation she enjoyed as the most beautiful woman in Ireland, the inspiration of the whole revolutionary movement. She was the most exquisitely fashioned creature I have ever seen. Her beauty was *startling*. Yeats wrote *Kathleen Ni Houlihan* especially for her, and there were few in the audience who did not see why. In her, the youth of the country saw all that was magnificent in Ireland. She was the very personification of the figure she portrayed on the stage.

Deirdre was presented under a gauze upon which Fay played a green arc, giving the stage a ghostly, mist-like appearance. Costumes, made from designs by A. E., blended perfectly into the sombre background. The characters had the appearance of figures rising out of a mist.

Critics were, as critics always are, divided in their opinions. Although most writers welcomed our arrival unreservedly, others adopted a condescending attitude. These notices were full of smug pats on the back and suggestions that it would have been impossible to carry out. Probably because we sprang from a modest source, and were Irish, some sections of the Dublin press were never, during our early days, very enthusiastic about our work. For many years they displayed a sort of grudging interest in what we did. It was odd that, later, our reception in England should be more generous. The reviewers there were usually more constructive too.

Kathleen Ni Houlihan, however, with its intensely patriotic theme, captured the attention of all. Even the smuggest and most patronising critic could find no fault in this sincerely written little piece. The story of the 1798 Kilalla family, whose eldest son on the eve of his marriage follows the mystical figure of Ireland, which comes to him in the form of an old woman and leads him away as 'a young girl with the walk of a queen,' was a happy choice for a first appearance. Yeats was congratulated over and over again. Of Maud Gonne's performance it was said:

Her interpretation of the part was marked by a high degree of histrionic power, and her beautiful voice was heard to advantage in the many snatches of folksongs with which her speeches were interspersed.

'We feel sure,' said one reviewer, 'that *Kathleen Ni Houlihan* will be a success wherever it is acted.' That prophecy proved correct. The play will remain one of the classic short pieces of the Irish theatre.

In the audience that night was one who was to play a major part in our future—a short figure in rusty black with a long Victorian veil—Lady Gregory. She came backstage after the show to see us. As she shook hands she smiled and said: 'You were very good!' (She had a lisp and a peculiar foreign-sounding accent.) 'I hope to see more of you.'

We later saw her talking earnestly with the Fays and A. E., pointing at parts of the stage and apparently suggesting improvements and renovations. Although we did not know it we were witnessing the conception of the Irish National Theatre Society and the real beginning of the movement that was to bring us into the Abbey Theatre.

Chapter Three

1902–1903
'The Sowing of the Seed'

THE SUCCESS of our first appearance created a new spirit within our little company. The interest of the public and the many congratulations lavished upon us by the leading literary figures of the day made certain the feeling that there was a future for a company of Irish players, no matter how small such a company might be or how modest its efforts.

The question that now faced us was on what basis we should establish ourselves before continuing with the work. Our next play, whatever it might be, would have to be ready quickly. Now that we were before the public in a favourable way it was imperative that we remain there and cap our first effort with something more ambitious. But before we began work it was necessary that a more permanent society than that formed by Fay be established.

We met again to discuss our position, and found that despite the attendances at our first two plays we had very little money left when bills had been paid. It may be added here that though the production was under its auspices, Inghinidhe na hÉireann had refused to take any of the profits.

We had no illusions about what the future might hold. We realised that our way would be full of difficulties. The only way to make progress was to work as a unit. It was no use simply appointing a committee in the manner of the casual dramatic society and foisting the responsibilities of the company onto it without any further help from the members. We would all have to work together; that was the only way we could hope to succeed. There was another side to the question, too, but one that was easily got over. Each of us had work of our own to do during the day, and the only time we could find to devote to rehearsals was in the evening. Lack of cash made the establishment of the venture on a professional basis impossible, but that, in any case, would not have mattered. At this stage the prospect of appearing as professionals did not attract us. Until we were in a position to do otherwise *through our own efforts*, we would remain amateurs. That was to be the special character of the society.

In the end we found that two principal facts had emerged from our talks. The first was that the society was to be a purely co-operative one with a committee that would defer to the desires of the society as a whole, each member, whether actor or committee-man, was to have an interest in the affairs of the group, the choice of plays, etc. The second was that all the members were to be amateurs. The latter arrangement was twofold, since it also did away with the petty bickering and desire for individual advancement that mar so many theatrical enterprises of the professional sort.

A. E., who, with Sir Horace Plunkett, was leading the agricultural co-operative movement in Ireland, promised to arrange for the registration of the society, and a committee was appointed as follows: president, W. B. Yeats; vice presidents, Maud Gonne, Douglas Hyde and George Russell; stage manager, W. G. Fay; secretary, Fred Ryan.

A fortnight later, the Irish National Theatre Society was formally established:

> to continue—if possible on a more permanent basis—
> the work begun by the Irish Literary Theatre, to create
> an Irish national theatre by producing plays in English
> and Irish, written by Irish writers, or on Irish subjects, or
> such dramatic works of foreign authors as would tend to
> educate and interest the public in the higher and more
> vital forms of dramatic art....

It was the sowing of the seed that blossomed into the whole Irish theatre movement.

We settled down to await the arrival of new plays. Fred Ryan, our new secretary, had one in the last stages of completion, and Yeats had promised us a short comedy. In the meantime we held meetings at each other's houses—gatherings at which much tea was consumed while Willie Fay taught us something of stagecraft and Frank taught us something of elocution. On half-holidays and Sundays when the weather permitted we made our way out of Dublin, usually towards Glen Dhu or Kilmashogue, some of us on foot, others astride clamorous bicycles—the most modern mode of conveyance in those days. In the shadow of the Dublin hills we lit furze fires and lunched, afterwards climbing the craggy heights and testing our voices on the summer air. Sometimes A. E. accompanied us, cheerfully levering his huge bulk across boulders. On these occasions he usually wandered off to some secluded glade with Willie Fay and set up easel and canvas, sketching and smoking.

It was about this time—June 1902—that we acquired what we intended to be a modest theatre at Lower Camden Street—the back shed of an egg and butter store, ingeniously and inconveniently hidden from its neighbours behind piles of provisions and other miscellaneous wares. It was hard to find, small, draughty and uncomfortable, but beggars could not be choosers, and although our independent spirit just kept us out of the former category, we were in no position to make demands. Bad and all as the place was, the rent—about ten shillings a week—was quite outside our means, and it was with some trepidation, and several invocations to the gods in favour of theatrical pioneers, that we took it over.

I may say here that Camden Street is one of the busiest shopping quarters in Dublin. It straggles across the centre of the city and pursues a course through a maze of smaller streets towards Rathmines. Along its narrow way, shops big and small jostle each other and marketers throng narrow pavements. At that time no one in his proper senses would have expected to find a theatre there, and even if he had it would have required an expert guide to discover ours. Its entrance—an open hall-door—peered shyly at passers-by between a butcher's and a family grocer's.

It was a wet and windy day when I went down to see it. With considerable difficulty and several false starts I managed to find it, stumbling down an inky passageway full of interesting smells reminiscent of sawdust and onions, and came out into a fair-sized room where Willie Fay, covered in dust and wearing a dilapidated boiler suit, hammered away at what looked like the beginnings of a stage.

Willie, as I said before, could get work out of anyone. It was only a matter of minutes before I was shaking the dust out of a pile of frowzy old curtains and holding wood for him to saw. As the others arrived they were rapidly enlisted to help with the other jobs he had been thinking out while he worked. That first night in Camden Street was a memorable one. There was many a crookedly driven nail in the framework of our stage, and many a swollen thumb in the company. When we began to get tired, Fay leaned back with a hammer in his hand and said: 'It's not such a bad little place, is it? … Well, not *very* bad, anyhow…?'

Not very bad…. It was about fifty feet long by thirty wide. One of the walls was lime-washed, one was papered, and the others still bore traces of a deep-green paint in the places where damp had not reached. If there was an intact pane of glass in the windows, it wasn't visible. The iron roof complained noisily in the breeze; there were no seats; the ceiling leaned towards us and looked as though it leaked. The only comfort was the sight of a rusty stove, pushed into a corner with the end of its chimney-pipe protruding from its rear. We hoped it was still workable.

In dismay we glanced at Fay. 'A little bit of hard work will do wonders,' he said, and scratched his head.

The next night we brought a carpenter friend down to 'do the hard bits', rolled up our sleeves and got to work. Frank, with four or five others, adjusted the roof, pushed putty into the more noticeable cracks and replaced the broken windowpanes with boards. We painted the walls green and bordered the plywood proscenium of the stage with cream. Fay brought some planks and converted them into benches for the audience to sit on. The stage was ridiculously small—little bigger than a rostrum—with tiny cubicles on either side in which to dress and make up.

In a fortnight we had done all in our power to make the place presentable, but it could by no stretch of the imagination be termed beautiful. Joseph Holloway, one of our more prominent associates, writing later of it, said:

> It breathed the air of unsophisticated Bohemianism, and, somehow or other, gave the impression that if high art blossomed here, it did not mature in very luxuriant surroundings....

He was one of our admirers, but he could not, in truth, have said more in favour of the place. There was a truly primitive air about it.

But whatever its shortcomings, this little hall became the first Irish theatre. Although, as we later discovered, it was completely unsuitable for public performances, it became our first headquarters; not only a rehearsal room but a meeting place where we discussed our ambitions with each other and the many outsiders who became interested in our work. Here, more than anywhere else, were the foundations of the theatre laid. It was here that we gathered around us that collection of politicians, artists, poets and dramatists who formed the core of the movement. In many ways our meetings bore little resemblance to those of a theatrical company. Rehearsals, to the casual onlooker, seemed to form only a small part of our activities. It was only with the approach of new plays that time was given over wholly to preparations for an appearance and a space cleared amidst a chaos of props, scenery, work-tables and draperies where we could more easily enact a scene. In the intervals between productions Frank Fay held his elocution classes in one corner, Willie painted his scenery in the next, and around the stove, in a wide circle of benches, the remaining members of the assembly sat and deliberated gravely and youthfully on topics of the day. It was here, too, that we received our first touring offer and discussed the opening of the Abbey.

We gathered many new members. Sara Allgood joined us; the wonderful, gifted Sara who became such a vital part of the theatre in later years. She too had been a member of Inghinidhe na hÉireann, and already enjoyed a reputation in the city, both as a member of the Inghinidhe dramatic class and as a singer of Irish folk songs. She needed little training. She had a magnificent contralto voice that, even before it was fully developed, had that quality that later made it the most famous on the Irish stage. Rich and full, that voice carried her across the world. It was pure gold—a 'gift from God' someone said later—and she could use it as she willed. But it was not only her voice—which many considered rivalled that of the young Bernhardt—that made Sara Allgood the most famous of the Irish players. She was an actress too, much more of the theatre than any of us in those early days. Her métier was tragedy, but she was equally at home in peasant comedy, and, as was proved later, when she played with William Poel's company, in Shakespeare.

Once, too, after she left the Abbey, she startled Dublin by appearing in musical comedy, playing a part in a production of *The Chocolate Soldier*. Her versatility was amazing. Dublin will never forget her Juno in *Juno and the Paycock*, but other memories of her survive too—as Mrs Delane in Lady Gregory's *Hyacinth Halvey*; Mrs Grogan in William Boyle's *The Building Fund*; or Widow Quinn in *The Playboy of the Western World*.

She was a great actress and an unforgettable character. She used to come down to Camden Street full of a vivid gaiety and run through her parts with amazing ease. In 1940, when she went to Hollywood, the Abbey lost one of its greatest personalities. She was not seen enough in films. It seems she preferred to give more of her time to the training of young players than she did to playing itself. And yet she was one of the few stage-players who could adapt themselves successfully to films; she could make her personality felt on a screen, no matter how big or how small a part she was playing. And that is a severe test for any actress who has had the sympathy of a live audience for most of her career.

People were anxious to meet the little company. Not many nights passed without some new face materialising from the murkiness of our entrance hall. James Joyce, a young clerk then, and his constant companion, Oliver Gogarty—an intriguing combination, for where one was shy and retiring the other was talkative in the extreme—paid us occasional visits and argued learnedly, and with the earnestness of youth, over the finer points of stage management; and once George Moore came amongst us with an air of sophisticated boredom, shook hands flabbily all round, and captured Frank Fay for a technical discussion on the French stage.

The distinguished author of *Esther Waters* was so far above our heads that few of us could speak to him coherently. He had a pleasant but condescending manner, and his conversation, sprinkled with familiar references to the famous, was enough to rebuff the advances of those who, even if they did make theatrical history at night, earned their bread and butter during the day. Probably he felt that a visit to Camden Street was indicated because of his earlier association with the Literary Theatre; he seldom came to see us again while we were there, though he often visited the Abbey in later years.

A. E., muffled in his blanket-like coat, hunched on a bench near the stove, was probably our most popular member. With his spade-shaped beard and soft unruly hair he looked more like a benevolent uncle than a distinguished thinker and one of the greatest minds of his generation, poet, artist, essayist, and one of the forces behind the great cultural upheaval that was taking place. He wore narrow, steel-rimmed spectacles that magnified thoughtful eyes set deep under a high forehead. The eyes arrested attention. They were brilliant and shrewd, and they reflected their owner's emotions constantly, lightening or darkening with the changes in his voice. He had a faintly northern accent.

I cherish my acquaintance with A. E. It is a privilege merely to have known this man who quietly did so much, culturally and economically, for the Ireland of his time. In his unobtrusive way he gathered about him all the young writers of the period, nourished their ambitions with friendly advice, even launching the more promising of his protégés. His anthology of Irish verse,

New Songs, published in 1904, contains the first writings of some of our most distinguished poets.

In those days the *conversazione* was very much a feature of Dublin social life. Most of the small societies throughout the city devoted much of their time to debate, and their activities were echoed on a somewhat larger scale by many of the more prominent figures of the period who 'held court,' as it were, in their own homes. Of these functions, A. E.'s Sunday evening reunions were perhaps the most popular. He had a little cottage-style house at Coulson Avenue, Rathgar, to which he invited all the literary and artistic workers, known and unknown, of the day. His advice on most matters concerning literature and art was much sought, and as a result these gatherings were colourful affairs, combining somehow the functions of a learned debate and a pleasant social evening. One discussed the work of new writers and analysed the work of established ones. Distinguished men of letters mingled with literary-minded clerks and shop assistants near the little fireplace, and first manuscripts often changed hands for publication.

For most of us during these years, A.E. was the real leader of our movement. To the casual onlooker he might have appeared just another, and not very prepossessing, member of the little society, a bulky figure, sitting well out of the chatter and the noise, puffing a pensive pipe. But his readiness to help on all occasions, his intense nationalism, the work he was always doing to further the interests of Ireland, both artistically and economically, made him, for me, the central prop of our whole movement. He argued, but he seldom fought—when he did it was with a crushing finality that knocked all the fight out of anyone who crossed swords with him—but he did more, perhaps, for the Ireland of his time than any other man. He worked quietly, without any attempt to gain individual distinction. He would always have been the first to run from publicity of any sort.

I have sat with him, listening to his advice, watching the quiet way in which he directed his followers into the channels for which they were most suited. He drew extensively from his deep fund of knowledge, and was always ready to place it at the disposal of anyone he thought sincere. In 1905, when A. E. left the National Theatre Society, I think it was then, for me, that the society died.

Lady Gregory, now an established member of the committee, paid Camden Street occasional visits. These usually took place with the approach of new plays, when she forsook the quiet of Coole House, her home at Gort, County Galway, and took rooms in a Dublin hotel, entertaining lavishly during her stay. As the work of new dramatists wishing to avail of the society passed from Fay's hands through a reading committee to her before we saw it, she always insisted on reading over selected pieces to us in her hotel drawing room. Her odd, lisping voice had a peculiar effect on speeches, especially those of the poetic sort, and later the strange, lilting lines of Synge suffered much through her pronunciation.

I think she rather fancied herself as an actress. Years later, when circumstances delayed my arrival at the Abbey for an appearance as Kathleen Ni Houlihan, she horrified Yeats and the company by calmly announcing that she would play the part herself. Her interpretation was hardly a flattering one, and not only because of her extraordinary sing-song delivery of the beautiful lines. Her appearance, at times oddly reminiscent of an elderly Queen Victoria, can hardly have been in keeping with the character Yeats had in mind when he wrote the play. But her arrival in such fashion as an Abbey Theatre actress received, to her delight and Yeats's dismay, widespread publicity, and she often spoke of the occasion afterwards, referring proudly, and a bit pathetically, to her appearance in the play as the realisation of a lifelong ambition.

But she was a pleasant, if at times rather condescending, person, who treated us all as children in need of special advice. She was a member of a well-known Galway family, the Persses, and the widow of a former British Colonial official, Sir William Gregory, and was drawn, almost by chance, into the dramatic movement. She has written somewhere of meeting Yeats in London in 1898 and being struck by his theories of playwriting and his hope one day to found a theatre for the production of experimental plays. It was after this that she joined in launching the Literary Theatre.

When this failed she turned, like Yeats, to the most promising of its successors, and came to us in 1902 a small and not very striking woman in middle age, full of a great enthusiasm for our work and a conviction that the Irish National Theatre Society should succeed where the Literary Theatre had failed.

In these and later years she often had her own way as far as the affairs of the society were concerned, for although she was not altogether overbearing, she was tenacious, which is much the same thing. I have many memories of her during these years: presiding maternally at one of those suppers she loved to hold in the theatre on first nights; or, in different circumstances, drawing up her short, rather bulky figure, squaring her shoulders and smiling grimly in a thin-lipped manner in face of opposition. Or again in later years, bustling with her strange, strutting walk through the Abbey, meeting distinguished visitors in the vestibule before the curtain rose on new plays, smiling her fixed social smile, or talking rapidly in her odd, flat-toned way. Her interest in the theatre was profound, and with the years it quickened.

When in 1910 she assumed part control of the Abbey, the theatre became a life interest—as she wrote herself, one of her 'enthusiasms'. She was the Abbey's self-appointed champion, and it is doubtless that but for her perseverance the theatre might have closed its doors during the lean years after its establishment as an independent concern, its control vested in a directorate. With Yeats, she fought all its battles and surmounted all its difficulties.

She was a most hospitable hostess. During these early years her arrival in Dublin for a new play was usually accompanied by an invitation to the Nassau Hotel, where she would entertain a few of us elegantly with tea and French cakes in her suite while she discussed new shows. Occasionally she would have confectionery sent down to Camden Street, coming in herself later in the evening and, like an understanding aunt, sitting beside the stove while we brewed tea and ate.

It was in Camden Street during a rehearsal of her play *Twenty-five* that she instituted what was later to become one of the most popular features of Abbey Theatre first nights—the

'Gort barmbrack suppers'. The Gort barmbrack was a cartwheel of a fruit cake, filled with the richest ingredients and made especially by her own bakers at Gort for the casts of her new plays.

It was a huge affair, several pounds in weight, and usually took two to carry it. It must have been two feet in circumference and fully eight inches in depth. Wrapped around with silver paper, and adorned with candied peel and glacé cherries, it held a place of honour on a table near the stove. I will always connect barmbrack with rehearsals and the smell of grease-paint. Abbey openings years later would never have been considered complete if there was not one—and it had to be a genuine Gort one—on the table in the green room, a serrated knife beside it for anyone who wanted a piece. Many times have I gulped the last crumb of a slice down before stepping onto the Abbey stage, and many times has my reluctance to part with any of it, even after my cue had come and gone, made me temporarily inarticulate before the footlights.

As a theatre, the Camden Street rooms were a dismal failure. In December 1902 we produced Fred Ryan's *The Laying of the Foundations*; a one-act comedy by Yeats called *The Pot of Broth*; P. T. McGinley's *Eilis agus an Bean Deirce* (Eilis and the Beggarwoman); and *The Racing Lug* by James Cousins.

Our little hall was uncomfortable, not only for us but for our audiences, which nightly became smaller. There was a breeze that used to manifest itself during the action and blow the stage draperies back in our faces, while it strangled what little enthusiasm the audience could muster. The loyal few who came to see us—half of them were non-acting associates of the society anyway—used to huddle together on the benches for warmth. Between the acts they moved about in topcoats to get their circulation working again. To make matters worse, it rained without pause for the three nights that we played. Press notices were not encouraging. Critics began to introduce sly little digs into their regular reviews of our progress at what they called 'The dying Irish Dramatic Muse'. Wrote one:

Surely it would be possible to house the much-advertised Irish dramatic muse? … She has many friends and there must be many more waiting to be wooed. It may be, of course, that the mission of the society is not to the dramatic Gentiles, that it preaches only to the elect, the chosen people.… If one may judge by last night's audience the elect are few and strangely coy.…

It seemed to us that our work would suffer in such a cramped space; it was certain that we could make no progress without audiences. It was decided to abandon all hope of establishing Camden Street as a theatre. *Connla,* or *The Sleep of the King*, a historical fantasy by James Cousins, and *The Townland of Tamney*, a one-act comedy by Seumas MacManus, were our last productions there. We took the Molesworth Hall for future appearances and kept the Camden Street rooms on as a headquarters, rehearsal room and workshop for the manufacture of scenery.

Our 1903 season opened on 14 March when we gave Yeats's fine 'morality', *The Hour-glass*, its first production at the Molesworth Hall, with Lady Gregory's one-act *Twenty-five*. Yeats's play, which after its production was compared with *Everyman*, was a new departure for us. Fay's setting, too, caused widespread comment. In search of a remote poetical effect in keeping with the character of the play, he threw away realism altogether. The scenery, such as it was, was calculated to centre the onlookers' attention on the dialogue. Against a background of dark-green tapestries, the only properties used were a rough desk bearing a heavy book, open to show an illuminated text; a tasselled bell-pull; and a wrought-iron bracket holding the hour-glass. Costumes merged into the background, and only those of two of the ten characters had tints of warmth in them. The dark colour scheme heightened the effect of the piece and the brilliance of the actors as nothing else could have done. It was an outstanding example of that classic simplicity of decor that is so often sought on a stage but seldom achieved. It was undoubtedly one of the most satisfactory settings for which Fay was responsible during his time with the theatre, and was probably never surpassed, although several attempts were made to improve on it through the years.

In about 1911, Yeats, who was constantly seeking original settings for his plays, had the piece produced at the Abbey in a Gordon Craig setting—a complicated affair of manoeuvrable screens and passageways, the characters masked and brightly dressed. The Craig screen-scenery was a new departure for the Abbey, and doubtless Yeats saw that by employing it he could make use of every available inch of the theatre's limited acting space: the screens could be moved in a matter of moments to achieve various effects, gave an impression of great space, and allowed for extra lights through the absence of overhead pulleys and ropes, but many considered it out of place at the Abbey, where box scenes were always employed. Used for *The Hour-glass*, the screens were hardly an improvement on Fay's scene of 1903, which struck a more sombre note.

This was the original *Hour-glass* cast:

The Wise Man	Dudley Digges
Bridget (his wife)	Máire T. Quinn
His Children	Eithne and Padragan Nic Shiubhlaigh
His Pupils	P. J. Kelly, Seumas O'Sullivan,
	Padraic Colum, P. Mac Shiubhlaigh
The Angel	Maire Nic Shiubhlaigh
The Fool	Frank Fay

Lady Gregory's *Twenty-five*, the first of her one-act plays that the society produced, was a sentimental and rather weakly constructed peasant piece about a young man who saved his former sweetheart from eviction by playing cards with her husband and allowing him to win fifty pounds in the process. We staged it with fair success for a number of years, but since it never seemed to give complete satisfaction to its author it was rewritten in 1907 for production at the Abbey under the title of *The Jackdaw*. Stripped of its former tragedy, and transferred from its original setting in 'Kilbecanty' to a huckster's shop in 'Cloon' with a lively Kiltartan dialogue, it has since become one of Lady Gregory's most popular short comedies.

Chapter Four

1903
Beyond the Pale with Synge

OUR FIRST invitation to appear outside the city came just before the Easter of 1903. It was from Father John O'Donovan, parish priest of Loughrea, and later administrator of the cathedral there, who asked us to appear in the town for his church fundraiser. He was a great friend of the nationalist cause and was gathering funds for the building of the cathedral—one of the first in the country built solely by Irish hands with Irish products. We were glad to help him, not only because of the worthiness of the project, but for the experience of playing to a provincial audience.

The visit gave us a pleasant weekend as guests of the jovial Father O'Donovan and his curates, all of whom treated us with a respect that was in marked contrast to the treatment we had been receiving in Dublin. Whereas in the city we were still being regarded by some as harmless eccentrics who gave uninteresting plays in draughty unsuitable halls—it took some time to live down the effect of those two appearances at Camden Street— in Loughrea we immediately attained the status of distinguished visitors, and spent a luxurious two days as guests of the clergy in the town's leading hotel.

We gave *Deirdre* and *The Pot of Broth*—a programme we hoped would suit all tastes—at the town hall. We had been at some pains to choose a suitable bill.

Willie Fay, recalling memories of his own days on the road, informed us that provincial audiences were uncertain quantities, even in the larger towns. Either Fay was wrong, however, or we had chosen well: we had a large and appreciative audience, and many had to be turned away. The good priests, leaving nothing to chance, as is the way of the rural Irish clergy, had been thorough in their preparations. Our appearance had been announced from the altar for a week before we arrived, and as an extra precaution a special fleet of bell-ringers—Loughrea was one of the few towns in Ireland to retain the ancient crier—had been engaged to work the surrounding area.

The result was impressive. The hall was filled to capacity long before the curtain was due to rise; we could have played an extra night to an audience composed completely of the disappointed ones who had travelled from outlying districts to see us. The event ended with a reception at the parochial house to which all the clergy and 'strong' farmers for miles around had been invited. We returned to Dublin amidst loud congratulations. Altogether, the visit was a pleasant one.

Apart from its significance as the first time we played to audiences outside Dublin, this engagement could not have come at a more opportune moment in our careers. It was a prelude to a more ambitious trip a few weeks later, which, although few of us realised it at the time, was to have a profound effect on our future. Our first invitation to play outside Ireland came late in April, about a week after we got back from the country. Stephen Gwynn, then secretary of the Irish Literary Society of London, was visiting Dublin, and came down to a meeting at Camden Street. He told us he had been in Ireland a few months earlier and seen some of our plays. He showed enormous interest in the work of the society, and was particularly struck by the theories of the two Fays. The formation of such a company, he said, was an event long awaited, and he thought that if we felt ready for it he could arrange for us to visit England. The Literary Society would probably be able to bring ten or twelve players over. Would we like to appear in London? We could gain much valuable experience by playing to more sophisticated audiences than the ones we knew in Dublin.

Now, I cannot overemphasise the importance of this. Upon this visit, although few of us realised it in 1903, depended the whole future of the Irish National Theatre Society. It marked the first major turning point in our careers. Quite apart from the fact that it introduced us to a public before whom, if we had had to depend on our own resources, we could not have appeared for many years, if at all, it had a remarkable sequel. If Mr Gwynn had not been in Dublin then, if he had not seen our work when he did, our movement might have pursued a completely different course in the years which followed.

Naturally we agreed to his suggestion; such an idea had been beyond our wildest hopes. Mr Gwynn went back to England. A few days later a formal invitation to appear in London the following month arrived from the Literary Society, which was to provide full travelling expenses and a theatre. We were stunned by our good fortune. Fay wired back our acceptance. Because most of us were working during the day, he stipulated that the visit should be a weekend one in order to allow us to travel on a Friday or Saturday and be back in Dublin again by Monday before our offices and workshops reopened. We were engaged for a Saturday-evening performance with a short matinee the same day. On 1 May we left Ireland—most of us for the first time—arriving in London late the following morning. After a few hours' sleep and a quick rehearsal we went before our first English audience at three o'clock the same afternoon.

For the matinee, we chose *The Hour-glass, Twenty-five* and *Kathleen Ni Houlihan*. In the evening we gave *The Pot of Broth*, repeated *Kathleen* and finished with *The Laying of the Foundations*.

The Queen's Gate Hall, South Kensington, where we played, was not an established theatre. In memory it was something like the Molesworth Hall in Dublin. Backstage accommodation was scanty and the stage itself was small, but any inconveniences were more than balanced by the hospitality of our hosts, and the enthusiasm of the audiences was as surprising as it was gratifying.

Although it was not the first time that Irish plays had been seen in the city, it was the first time they had been given there by Irish-born players. It was, as many writers pointed out, an event of great importance. The audiences, mixed ones, and a little puzzled at first, soon saw what we were driving at and helped us through what was for many of us a trying ordeal. There were plenty of congratulations afterwards.

Critics were particularly pleasant. They remarked especially upon the 'style deliberately adopted', the ability to fade into the background when not speaking and the absence of unnecessary stage business. Above everything, the aims of the movement intrigued them. It was the *Times* critic, A. B. Walkley, who said of the society:

> It is a part of a national movement, it is designed to express the spirit of the race, the virtue of it in the medium of the acted drama. That is an excellent design. If the peculiarities of Irish thought and feeling can be brought home to us through the drama, we shall all be the better for the knowledge, and the art of drama, too, cannot but gain by a change of air, a fresh current of ideas....

And William Archer, writing in *The World*, was no less pleasant when he said:

> I remained to admire and applaud with the utmost sincerity. The company, indeed, were amateurs, with many of the characteristic faults of their class, but in almost all of them there was a clear vein of talent, and the work they presented was all of it interesting, and some of it exquisitely and movingly beautiful....

All the other daily and weekly periodicals devoted columns of space to reviews, all of them full of praise. It was a remarkable achievement for a company that had been founded less than twelve months earlier.

We returned to Dublin flushed from our victory and not a little awed by the high praise that had been showered upon us: our visit had brought us into personal contact with many of the most eminent figures in the London theatre world. We had, it seemed, arrived. Who was to blame us if we thought it was but a step to even greater triumphs? But any hopes we had of being acclaimed in Dublin were soon dashed. Our next appearance could not compare in any way with the popular success of the London one.

In October, just five months after our return, we introduced a new play by an author whose work was later to make the name of the Irish theatre famous all over the world, and had the unusual experience of turning a powerful nationalist club in Dublin against us. The play, a first attempt, was entitled *In the Shadow of the Glen*. The author was an obscure journalist named J. M. Synge.

It was early in June of 1903 when Lady Gregory called us to her rooms at the Nassau Hotel and read Synge's play over to us. The piece was a one-act comedy based on an Irish folk tale the author had heard from an old Aran Island *seanchaí*— the story of the aged husband feigning death to test his youthful wife's fidelity, denouncing her, but forgiving her lover. The plot, strictly speaking, was not original, but the treatment was. It was completely different to anything we had known before; the play itself was a masterpiece of dramatic construction. It was, in fact, the first of the Irish 'realist' dramas, and the quiet young man who sat unobtrusively in the background while Lady Gregory read aloud his words was to take his place amongst the greatest dramatists the Irish theatre produced.

John M. Synge—who came to us with his play directly from the Aran Islands, where the material for most of his later works was gathered—was born near Dublin in 1871, graduated from Trinity College, and shortly afterwards left Ireland for the Continent, living alternately in Germany and France, where he made a rather precarious livelihood as a violinist and contributor to literary magazines. Yeats had discovered him in Paris about 1897 and, recognising the quality of his writings, had brought him back to Ireland, where he introduced him to Aran, prophesying that in the beautiful lyrical prose of the western peasant he would find an original vehicle for dramatic composition.

He was right. Synge went to Aran for a month, and stayed there on and off for a matter of years. He drew his inspiration from the hearths of the tiny whitewashed cabins and the rocks of the western seaboard, gathering tales and expressions from old and young. In a short life—he died at the early age of thirty-eight—he wove them into sombre dramatic tapestries embroidered with the rhythmic language of the true Irish peasant. His prose, highly musical and enriched with flashes of the most beautiful poetry, he devised simply by transcribing directly from the Gaelic of the islands. It is most difficult for an actor to master, and most effective if delivered correctly.

He was a gentle fellow, shy, with that deep sense of humour that is sometimes found in the quietest people. His bulky figure and heavy black moustache gave him a rather austere appearance—an impression quickly dispelled when he spoke. His voice was mellow, low; he seldom raised it. But for his quiet personality he might have passed unnoticed at any gathering.

During rehearsals of his play he would sit quietly in the background, endlessly rolling cigarettes. This was a typical gesture, born more of habit than of any desire for tobacco—he gave away more cigarettes than he smoked. At the first opportunity he would lever his huge frame out of a chair and come up onto the stage, a half-rolled cigarette in each hand. Then he would look enquiringly around and thrust the little paper cylinders forwards towards whoever was going to smoke them. In later years he became the terror of fire-conscious Abbey stage managers. He used to sit timidly in the wings during plays, rolling cigarettes and handing them to the players as they made their exits.

He could speak wisely and constructively of his own work. He would later write in a preface to his *Playboy of the Western World*:

> All art is a collaboration, and there is little doubt that in the happy ages of literature, striking and beautiful phrases were as ready to the storyteller's or the playwright's hand as the rich cloaks and dresses of his time…. In Ireland, those of us who know the people have the same privilege … on the stage one must have reality and one must have joy, and that is why the intellectual drama has failed and

people have grown sick of the false joy of the musical comedy that has been given them in place of the rich joy found only in what is superb and wild in reality. In a good play every speech should be as fully flavoured as a nut or an apple, and such speeches cannot be written by anyone who works among people who have shut their lips on poetry....

Synge was a genius, one of the great literary figures of his time, but brilliance often ripens under the most difficult conditions. *In the Shadow of the Glen* was sufficiently in advance of its time to arouse in Dublin audiences a completely unfounded indignation. Its production raised a storm of protest in some sections of the press that was stupid and ridiculous, disconcerting its unfortunate author, and amazing most of us, who had never looked upon the play as anything but an exceptionally well-written comedy.

Indeed, from my point of view as an actress, there was nothing wrong with *In the Shadow of the Glen* at all. Though it looked, and was, a difficult play to interpret, each of the four characters offered scope to whoever would be chosen to play them. But there was a division of opinion against it in the society. Dudley Digges, our juvenile lead, believed that it was an unsuitable piece for us to play, and he was joined in this by some other members who said that they would be compelled to withdraw from the society if it was put on. As it had already been decided to produce the play, there was nothing to be done but let them go. Dudley resigned with three or four others, taking with him Máire Quinn, who later became his wife. He was, of course, missed. Digges, an old and well-liked member, was the best young actor the society had, and without him our organisation was incomplete. It was many years before the vacancy created by his withdrawal was filled.

Happily, however, for him, his resignation did little to affect his career. Soon after he left us he had an offer to appear in Irish plays at the St Louis American Exhibition of 1903. Here, playing opposite Máire Quinn, he rapidly ascended to leading parts on Broadway, where he worked for many years. Afterwards he went into films—he was probably the first of the 'Irish players' to do so—living between Hollywood and New York until his death.

With Máire Quinn gone, I was cast as Nora Burke, the young wife in the new play. I found the part a difficult one to master as it was completely unlike anything I had done before. At first I found Synge's lines almost impossible to learn and deliver. Like the wandering ballad-singer I had to 'humour' them into a strange tune, changing the metre several times each minute. It was neither verse nor prose. The speeches had a musical lilt that was absolutely different to anything I had heard before. Every passage brought some new difficulty, and we would all stumble through the speeches until the tempo in which they were written was finally discovered. I found I had to break the sentences, which were uncommonly long, into sections, chanting them, slowly at first, then quickly as I became more familiar with the words.

Neither Fay nor Synge offered me much help during rehearsals. I found it difficult to understand this until Fay explained that I had been chosen specially for the part because of my comparative inexperience as an actress:

> When you *read* a book or a play you supply your own characters. The author just makes suggestions which you, the reader, enlarge upon. If you were a more experienced actress you might read into this part something which, perhaps, was never intended. Be the *mouthpiece* of Nora Burke rather than Nora Burke. You will be corrected only if you are inaudible or if your movements are wrong.

To our surprise, the attitude of those who had left the society was echoed on a larger scale by some sections of the public and the press even while Synge's play was still in rehearsal. The piece was 'un-Irish' wrote some reviewers, an 'insult' in fact to the peasant women of Ireland whom Nora Burke was taken to typify. There was an immense furore about it. A number of writers, claiming that Synge was slyly attacking the institution known as the 'made marriage' and attributing it solely to Ireland, raised all sorts of objections. Others wrote: 'Nora Burke is a lie.' Of the play they said: 'It is no more Irish than the Decameron. It is a staging of the old-world libel on womankind—the Widow of Ephesus.'

Now, I do not propose to analyse the extraordinary attitude adopted towards the play. Indeed, the attacks were launched so suddenly that few of us were even able to gather what they were all about. Perhaps it was that the Irish play-going public of that time was so used to the 'genteel' comedy of the established theatre— the entertaining, but not very realistic, stuff that was time and again put before it—that it couldn't swallow a credible satire. In those days if an actress played an unpleasant part, then it followed that she was an unpleasant person. Similarly, if a dramatist wrote a nasty play he was a nasty fellow. Then, of course, there was the fact that Ireland was on the threshold of a renaissance. Everybody, writer, politician, artist, was at pains to eulogise over the beauty of the Irish character. The advent of a comparatively unknown writer who painted an unpleasant if realistic picture of the peasantry at such a time was, to say the least, unwelcome. The Dubliners who raised the loudest objections could not accept *In the Shadow of the Glen* as a play. They refused to be entertained.

But though these objections disconcerted us at the time, they did not halt our progress or lower us in the esteem of every section of our public. Time vindicated Synge as a dramatist of genius. That unanimous admiration did not come to him until after his death was an ironic turn of the wheel of fortune that typified his not-too-happy career as a man of the theatre. Plenty of reviewers accepted *In the Shadow of the Glen* amicably on its first production. The most unfortunate feature of the affair was that a great many of those who raised the loudest objections were members or leaders of some of the nationalist clubs. Arthur Griffith, who had hitherto been one of our staunchest friends, wrote vehemently against the play in *The United Irishman*. His denunciation of the play was, in my opinion, the saddest aspect of the whole unnecessary controversy. It was many years before Griffith, who was a man of the most violent likes and dislikes, looked with favour again upon the National Theatre Society.

Not all of the comments in the newspapers were condemnatory. Quite a few people looked upon the whole thing as a joke. It was one of these who wrote in the letter columns of the old *Daily Express* (and introduced a welcome note of light relief into the controversy):

> It is not only Ireland that is insulted. There are notorious plays that insult other nations.... It is impossible to deny that the people of Egypt, now downtrodden under a foreign yoke, are insulted by the play of *Antony and Cleopatra*. We all know that the heroine of that play is necessarily a typical woman.... *Macbeth* is an insult to the humanity of Scotland—think of the murder of Macduff's children!
>
> ... *Romeo and Juliet*, a play which describes the children of Catholic Italy as disobeying and deceiving their parents, is as little deserving of tolerance. Why insult every learned and laborious German by representing him as selling his soul to the Devil in the play of *Faust*? But I have given enough instances. I now invite those who are sensitive for the honour of all countries to meet me tonight on O'Connell Bridge at 10.30. They will know me by my Gaelic League button and the pike which I shall carry in my right hand.... We will then adjourn to a spot where the police will not disturb us until eleven.

Which, if it did nothing else, at least showed us that there were those in Dublin with a sense of humour who were capable of accepting a play merely as a play and not as an indictment of all Irish national aspirations.

Poor Synge, bewildered by the attacks, retired completely into his shell. He was puzzled and hurt that his play should be received in such fashion. After a hurried curtain call on the first night, he withdrew quietly from the scene.

In the Shadow of the Glen was first produced at the Molesworth Hall on 8 October 1903, with a new Yeats play, *The King's Threshold*, and a revival of *Kathleen Ni Houlihan*. Oddly, in view of the press attacks, there was little trouble from the audience—a little hissing from the back that was quickly quelled. Yeats made a very definite speech against the attacks on the first night.

The end of 1903 was now in sight, and since it was necessary to end the season on a more pleasant note than disapproval, not to say denunciation, we looked in haste for a new play that would be less unpalatable to the public taste than Synge's. One of our members, a young man who had been with us since the foundation of the society, had a piece in preparation for some time. Fay asked him to rush the writing of the closing scenes, and we put the first part of it into rehearsal early in November. The play, a three-act tragedy, was called *Broken Soil*. The author was Padraic Colum.

Colum, who worked then as a clerk with the Great Southern Railway, had entered the Irish National Theatre Society through his association with Inghinidhe na hÉireann. He was a close friend of Arthur Griffith and, like the Fays, had been a constant attender at the Inghinidhe debates, even taking part in a number of *tableaux* under Willie Fay's direction. It was during the period 1901–1902 that he wrote his first play, *The Children of Lir*, following up its production by the Inghinidhe company with another, *The Saxon Shillin'*—a short piece, sprinkled with political propaganda, and of little theatrical value since it was hastily put together for production at the Annual Drama Festival of Cumann na nGaedheal.

Broken Soil was his first important work, and although it is not his best play—he later rewrote it with more effect under the title of *The Fiddler's House*— it was a poignant and well-constructed little character study set in the midlands. Like his later plays, *The Land* and *Thomas Muskerry*, it depended for its effect on a conflict of emotions rather than action. Con Hourican, a wandering fiddler, and his daughter, Maire, find themselves torn between the desire to travel the roads and the wish to remain within the comfortable seclusion of their small farm. The climax comes when they, forsaking comfort and friends, return to their wanderings.

We had long been familiar with the story, since the author, who was a slow worker, had been writing the play in the intervals of his clerical job. He used to come down to Camden Street with bits of it that he had written out during the day, and read them to us over the little stove. We were able to watch it grow and discuss it as he went along. It was a simple story, simply written, with a facility surprising for a person of Colum's age—he would have been no more than twenty at the time—and it showed a profoundly sympathetic insight into the Irish peasant character. More importantly it caught the public fancy after Synge's play, and was the means of turning most of those who had denounced us back again in our favour. Reviews were long and pleasant, and in striking contrast to those of *In the Shadow of the Glen* two months earlier. The piece became one of the most popular in our repertoire. We played it several times during these years, on both sides of the channel, and its popularity never seemed to diminish in any way. London indeed, when we visited it again in 1904, was particularly enthusiastic about it, and several of the better-known journals singled the play out. It was the *Daily Telegraph* critic who wrote:

> The piece possesses that quality only too rarely met with either on the stage or in the pages of romance, the quality of the unusual, while in the development of his theme, Mr Colum reveals a reticence and a strenuous simplicity admirably fitted to produce in the spectators' minds a profound impression of the truth and fidelity of the picture presented.

Broken Soil brought our 1903 season to a most successful conclusion.

Meanwhile, our first London visit was bearing fruit in a way we had not envisaged. We heard of a wealthy Englishwoman with an interest in the theatre who had seen our performances at the Queen's Gate Hall and become interested. 'She is anxious to do something for us,' said Yeats.

Hearing that we intended to produce a new Yeats play with *In the Shadow of the Glen*, she came to Dublin and offered to dress the production for us. Her name was Miss A. E. F. Horniman. It was Miss Horniman who built the Abbey Theatre, and gave us the use of it.

Chapter Five

1903–1904
Annie Horniman

MISS HORNIMAN was a tall, quiet Englishwoman, a member of a wealthy Manchester commercial family, and well known as a patron of drama in England, where she had already done much for the experimental theatre. Through Yeats, whom she knew in London, she had visited the Queen's Gate Hall on the occasion of our appearance there, and had been sufficiently attracted by our work to make it known that she wanted to assist us.

She came to Dublin about the summer of 1903, took rooms in a large hotel, imported bales of the most expensive dress materials, engaged a team of English theatrical costumiers, and began fitting us out for the production of a new Yeats play, *The King's Threshold.*

Few of us ever got to know her intimately, although she was an extremely likeable person who made a point of meeting us all and never tired of advising us wisely on stage matters. During her stay in Dublin she often came down to rehearsals at Camden Street with Yeats, showing at all times the greatest interest in our methods and sitting near the stove talking in her quiet, witty way. It may be said here that her interest in us never had anything to do with the national aims of the society. Miss Horniman, who merely hastened the destination of our company by building the Abbey the following year, was interested only in the development of drama. It is questionable, too, if during these first years of her association with us, she fully realised the basis on which the National Theatre Society had originally been established. If she had, she might have thought twice before financing it. Her interest in us was not as an Irish national co-operative movement, but as a society with a fresh approach to the drama, which, therefore, deserved encouragement.

Since she had already financed a number of such groups in England, she regarded our group as yet another small company in which by her aid she would receive a governing interest. In view of subsequent events it was a pity that her position was not sufficiently clarified at the outset. When she began to exert her influence in the affairs of the theatre, she indirectly brought about the death of the original National Theatre Society.

But in 1903, none of us could see into the future. As far as most of us were concerned, Miss Horniman's offer was heaven-sent. Before her arrival in Dublin, our careers had not been very profitable financially—even if they had proved to us that there was a future for what we were doing. The National Theatre Society might at last have been exciting interest, but it was certainly not making money. The arrival of a complete outsider, who was prepared to assist us materially by dressing even one of our productions, was something it would have been foolish to ignore.

We blessed our new-found friend, who, as it turned out, spared neither time nor money on the society. Miss Horniman was generosity itself: she gave wholeheartedly and with an almost embarrassing readiness. Certainly it would be untrue to say that the Irish theatre does not owe her a debt of gratitude. Her assistance, which only began with the dressing of Yeats's play, placed the Irish National Theatre Society on its feet. There is little doubt that if she had not helped us when she did, it would have been many years before we could have emerged from the small halls in which we were playing at that time.

From the start, she was as good as her word. Miss Horniman dressed *The King's Threshold* expensively and elaborately. The play, a dramatisation of the legendary silence of Seanchan, was staged very effectively by Fay, who made use of draperies in a manner reminiscent of *The Hour-glass*. The scene on the steps of the king's palace was devoid of all unnecessary decoration and provided an austere effect of greens and greys that contrasted well with the dresses of the characters, most of which were richly jewelled. Very sincerely we thanked Miss Horniman, and she returned to England. She soon became a pleasant memory. Our surprise can be understood when, a few months later, Fay called us around him and announced that she wanted to help us again. 'Miss Horniman wants to build a theatre in Dublin,' he said, 'and give us the use of it.'

Most of us were overjoyed, although, at a debate held later on the matter, there were certain murmurings against Miss Horniman's proposal. Some members, who were perhaps more discerning than the rest of us, foresaw a danger of the national ideals of the movement being shelved if an outsider was allowed in. But older heads on the committee counselled acceptance of the offer. The society replied, agreeing to perform in any theatre Miss Horniman might provide for the purpose in Dublin. She answered by return asking Fay to find a suitable building or site. 'I can only afford to make a very little theatre, and it must be quite simple,' she said later.

Nevertheless, we believed that she was prepared to provide up to one thousand pounds for the project—a sum that would have been ample for the conversion of a small hall near the centre of the city at that time. In actual fact, the figure for the acquisition and alteration of the building that became the old Abbey Theatre was, I think, something in the region of thirteen or fourteen hundred pounds, but Miss Horniman provided the extra money without complaint.

We set about finding a suitable site. The object, of course, was to get one as close to the centre of the city as possible. As it happened, our luck was in. Owing to a recent corporation by-law that stipulated that all theatres in the city should undergo extensive alterations in order to install safety devices in the case of fire, a number of the smaller Dublin halls were closing down. One of these—attached to the Mechanics' Institute in Abbey Street and within easy reach of the tramway terminus—closed its doors a few weeks before we began our search. It happened to be on the site of one of the oldest theatres in Dublin. The remains of the original building had been razed, and a small theatre built, where popular plays had been performed up to about the middle of the last century. This had degenerated through the years into a cheap music hall, which had been closed by the authorities.

The building was later taken over by the Mechanics' Institute, which had rented it about ten years later to a well-known theatrical company. The directors of the latter, after fighting a losing battle against a law that demanded an enormous fee for the patenting of serious theatres, had bowed to the inevitable and mixed its dramatic entertainments with music-hall turns. 'The Mechanics', as it was widely known in Dublin, was a popular if rather noisy place, typical of a number of small music halls in the city. When the new corporation fire law was enforced, it had found it impossible to carry on, and closed down altogether. Being already fashioned as a theatre, the place suited our needs admirably.

The advice of a well-known Dublin architect, Joseph Holloway, was sought, and after some small legal difficulties had been overcome the lease was acquired, together with that of an adjoining building in Marlborough Street—formerly the old Dublin city morgue. It was estimated that the task of making both buildings one and decorating the interior would take about eight or nine months. Work was begun early in 1904. It was hoped that the opening night would be in December of the same year.

Meanwhile, we continued with the programme that we had laid out for the first part of 1904. In January we produced an experimental play by Yeats called *The Shadowy Waters*; the following month we gave the first production of Synge's *Riders to the Sea*.

Yeats's play, which he termed a 'dramatic poem', was written for the theatre, but depended more for its effect upon the delivery of its verse than upon any dramatic situation. A walk 'among the seven woods of Coole' had suggested a dream of beings happier than men, moving about in the shadows. To these beings Yeats had tried to give a local habitation and a name, and *The Shadowy Waters* was the result. It is set on a galley crossing a sea hidden in mist, and when the curtain rises, Forgael, a sea-king, lies sleeping while his sailors plot his death. Another ship is seen in the fog, a battle ensues, and the second vessel is captured. Aboard is Dectora, daughter of a slain emperor. Forgael subdues her and his own rebellious sailors by means of a magic harp. The sailors flee to the other ship, and Forgael and the woman drift on alone 'awaiting death, or what comes after, or some mysterious transformation of the flesh that is every lover's dream.'

As a literary effort the piece was fine, but the author took some pains to envelop the piece in all-pervading mysticism, which did not allow for easy interpretation on a stage, and the audience, as a result, were in some doubt as to where the dramatic elements came in. One reviewer wrote:

> There is a great deal of weird and intangible dialogue in the piece, which, as at present acted, leaves the audience in a thick mist as to what the motive may be.

Another termed it: 'weird, puzzling, and depressingly gloomy.' It is hardly likely that the piece as it was then was ever really intended as a serious dramatic work. The verse was particularly fine, and we had the play in rehearsal for some time as an exercise in elocution, but it found its way onto the stage in 1904 rather by accident. Yeats, writing of it in 1906, said that he began it when he was a boy, but that by the time it was first produced the plot had been so often rearranged, and had become so overgrown with symbolical ideas, that the poem was obscure and vague. He later rewrote it with more effect, and it was produced in its new form at the Abbey on 8 December 1906.

In contrast to this production, Synge's *Riders to the Sea* was an immediate success. This time there were no murmurs from those who had so forcibly objected to the author's first work, and critics were almost unanimous in their praise. The piece, of course, has since been acclaimed as one of the most perfect short dramas in the English language. An unusual combination of mysticism and realism, its stark, almost bitter tragedy, lifts it far above anything else of the kind the Irish theatre produced. When he wrote it,

Synge wove his most sombre tapestry. It was his masterpiece.

The story of the old woman whose sons have slowly been claimed by the sea was not altogether original, but the circumstances were of little importance. Synge's prose, his unique sense of dramatic values, made an original plot unnecessary. It was pure tragedy. There was no sentiment; no unnecessary situations, no conflicting side-issues. From the moment the curtain rose, the audience was drawn inexorably towards the climax.

This was the original cast:

Maurya	Honor Lavelle (Helen Laird)
Bartley	W. G. Fay
Cathleen	Sara Allgood
Nora	Emma Vernon (Miss Vera Esposito)
Men and Women	Maire Nic Shiubhlaigh, P. J. Kelly, Seumas O'Sullivan, George Roberts, Maire Ni Gharbhaigh, Doreen Gunning

One of the most effective passages in the play is that which introduces the *caoin* of the Aran Islands—the bitter, songlike lament of the women as they follow a coffin to a place of burial. Its inclusion is vital for the successful presentation of the piece, and the producer who dispenses with it will never achieve the effect the author intended. Many present producers ignore its value, and in almost every case the play loses much of its tragedy and the poignancy of the climax is blunted. As Synge meant it to, it provides a strange, eerie background to the final speech of Maurya, the old woman.

The custom of keening itself, at one time fairly general in Ireland, is now peculiarly western. Doubtless it is a relic of some ancient civilisation, handed down with variations through the centuries. In Aran of latter years it became the practice for relatives of a dead man, or one who had been lost at sea, to hire a special party of women to sing the *caoin* before, during and after a wake, and the wealth of a family was measured by the number of singers it could afford. The lament itself has a strange, savage quality about it when sung by an expert. Its effectiveness probably lies in its repetition. Over and over the women repeat the lines, softly at first, rising gradually on a sustained note to the eerie splendour of the climax. Rocking backwards and forwards to the beat of the music, they seem to lose themselves in the beauty of the lilt.

As an interesting sidelight on the original production of *Riders to the Sea*, it may be worth adding here that the *caoin* that was sung by us in 1904 was a transcription of a genuine Aran lament. It was not composed specially for the production; it was given to two of us in rather peculiar circumstances by an old peasant woman living in Dublin. We learned it just as she sang it herself, recalling, perhaps, some island tragedy similar to the one around which Synge wrote his play.

We never learned her name, but she shared a home with her married daughter in a decaying tenement off Gardiner Street. The room, in which an entire family lived, formed a most unusual background for a woman of her upbringing. It had evidently been used as a drawing room by the house's original tenants, and had a massive marble fireplace that almost filled one whole wall. The floorboards were rotting away, and the room was filled with the usual flimsy furniture, an iron bedstead in one corner. The contrast between all this and the woman herself was startling: she was still dressed in the clothes of the islands, the shawl and red petticoat, which her daughter said she refused to give up in favour of other garb.

There was an air of poverty about the room, but it was scrupulously clean. The building, of course, was one of the many Georgian mansions in that part of the city which had gradually fallen into disrepair, eventually being taken over for use as tenements. The old woman had no English. We spoke to her in Gaelic for a time. Then she sang the *caoin*, standing, looking across the bed towards the window, her eyes closed, her arms outstretched, her head thrown back, swaying backwards and forwards with the rise and fall of the music. We had come expecting a chant or some kind of conventional lamentation, nothing like this. It was strangely moving to see this old figure standing at the window of a crumbling tenement, looking over a city street, singing:

Tá sé imighthe uaim!
Go deo! Go deo! Go deo!

They were thin, piping notes. The sounds from the street outside contrasted strangely, the noise of passing vehicles. But listening, one forgot the unusual circumstances. The *caoin* seemed to possess her. Synge might have written his play around her alone, an old woman counting the loss of her sons with a bitter satisfaction.

We staged *Riders to the Sea* in the Molesworth Hall towards the end of 1904. Herbert Hughes, the Irish composer, and a friend of the society, transcribed the *caoin* as it was sung on the stage, and later presented me with a copy. It is doubtful if it has ever been published. Here it is, as it was sung on the first night:

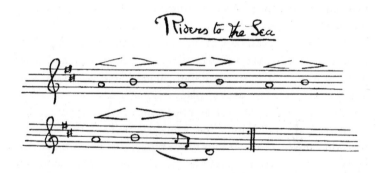

Synge's play was the Irish National Theatre Society's last production at the Molesworth Hall. Later in 1904, on 26 March, we visited London again, and got an even better reception than before. A few months later we were playing at the Abbey Theatre.

Chapter Six

1904–1905
The Abbey Opens

IN COMPARISON with the other theatres in Dublin at that time, the original Abbey Theatre was very small; in fact, it must have been the smallest downtown hall in the city. But for us, emerging from the out-of-the-way Molesworth Hall, with memories of our earlier appearances in Camden Street still vivid, it was wonderful to be able to play in a real theatre at last. We had a 'green room'—a sort of common room where we could meet and wait between the acts of plays—a stage, which, even if not very big, was reasonably well equipped, and we had a more or less draught-proof auditorium that would not offend those people who were used to the comforts of the bigger theatres. We could at least be sure that there would never again be murmurs about hard chairs and cold breezes.

The theatre opened for the first time on Tuesday, 27 December 1904. It is easy to describe.

The building itself took up most of a corner with the pit entrance looking into Abbey Street within sight of Nelson's Pillar, the door to the main vestibule stalls and balcony opening onto Marlborough Street. Passing through the double glass doors here, one entered a tiny lobby, to the left of which was the green room, later moved into the lobby to give extra space and allow for a coffee bar.

Around the vestibule, which held the booking office and cloakrooms, hung portraits of Lady Gregory, Miss Horniman, Willie Fay and me. The lobby was a cramped space in those days, little more than ten or twelve feet in width, and hardly much longer. The theatre seated something like five hundred, not much more, but it was an attractive little place. Its atmosphere always led to a feeling of intimacy between player and audience member. Standing on the Abbey stage, the feeling, absent in so many other theatres, of being one with the audience was always present. Actually it had been the intention to have a projecting platform in the manner of the Elizabethan Theatre, but it was found that this would occupy too much space. The actual stage, although small, proved big enough for us. None of our sets was elaborate.

The decoration of the house had been carried out in nearly every case by Irish workers, although some of the articles, such as the electroliers, came from the Continent. Two stained-glass windows, fashioned in the image of a tree in leaf, on either side of the Marlborough Street entrance, were the work of Sara Purser. A picture of Sara Allgood, which later hung in the vestibule, is also her work. J. B. Yeats, the poet's father, painted pictures of Miss Horniman, Lady Gregory, Frank and Wille Fay and me, also for display in the lobby.

As was only to be expected on such an occasion, we had a full house. It was the most fashionable theatrical event of the year. Distinguished-looking visitors kept drifting into the tiny vestibule, scrutinising the fittings, discussing the history of the society and standing in little knots on the stairs. Yeats was impressive in evening dress, and kept coming behind the scenes every few minutes to see how things were getting along.

Backstage, Willie Fay, dressed for his part in one of the new plays, with a wild wig slipping sideways over his face, swung from a baton high in the flys, arranging the lighting. Beneath him passed an endless procession of figures carrying ladders, tools, canvas screens and draperies. Idlers at the back of the drawn hessian curtain eyed the swelling audience.

Standing as far out of the way as possible, those of us who were unoccupied ate a scrap meal of bread and cocoa. It was all we had to eat for hours. Every member of the society had been in the theatre since early afternoon.

In between bites we watched the auditorium through a crack in the curtain. The pit and gallery were full. The stalls were slower in filling, but the crowd was increasing all the time. A number of people sitting in the front seemed oblivious of the pre-curtain chatter as they listened to the violin music of Arthur Darley, our one musician.

Darley was a great addition to the little company. A violinist of note, he was a well-known collector of traditional Irish airs. Yeats had taken him along to play between the acts when we were in the Molesworth Hall. He used to stand in the corner of the stage, just outside the curtain, fondling his violin self-consciously and playing plaintive little pieces much appreciated by audiences. Few reviews would have been complete without a mention of him. It turned out later that he had known Synge in Paris before the writer came to us. Both had played in the same orchestra.

The sound of a familiar voice drew our attention backstage again. In a dark corner, sitting on an upturned property basket, sat Synge himself, rolling the inevitable cigarette.

'God bless you,' he said. 'I hope you're as happy as I am. I'm so honoured that my little play should be chosen for the first week.'

In the Shadow of the Glen was billed for the second night. For our opening we played a triple-bill: Yeats's new one-act *On Baile's Strand*; a revival of *Kathleen Ni Houlihan*; and the first production of *Spreading the News*, Lady Gregory's clever little cameo of an Irish fair-day incident. During the following week, Synge's play was shuffled with Lady Gregory's in support of *On Baile's Strand.*

Many considered that Yeats's new play was his best. In it, as one writer put it, he emerged from the shadows with less of the mystic and more of the human element in the composition than in some of his earlier verse-plays. The piece, a dramatic setting of the legend telling of the slaying of his own son by the unwitting CúChullain, belonged to an older order of drama than some of his other lyrical works. With the introduction of Barach, the fool, Yeats approached the Shakespearian model, but never sacrificed his own originality of treatment, wrote the reviewers.

Fay adopted simplicity and the artistic blending of colour as his keynote in the staging. Great emphasis was laid on lighting. Amber-coloured hangings draped the interior of a great hall. A huge door, closed, showed intricate Celtic interlacings on panel and lintel. When it was opened, a glimpse was revealed of a luminous blue sky over a bay. Two plain thrones stood in the centre; brilliant hand-painted medallions on the walls completed the fittings. A golden arc played across the front, helping the colourful costumes of kings, councillors and the resplendent CúChullain of Frank Fay to blend into a pale background.

That night I played Kathleen Ni Houlihan for the first time. This made the occasion doubly memorable for me. I suppose every player has a favourite part. This was mine. From the very first appearance of the company in 1902, I had hoped that I would some day appear as the Old Woman in Yeats's play. People have said that through the years my playing of the part has been creditable, but I would like it known that every time I have played Kathleen I have modelled my performance on the one given originally by Maud Gonne. Although I have seen many famous actresses play Kathleen since, I know of no performance that surpassed hers on the little stage in St Teresa's Hall.

The evening progressed, and the subtle humour of Lady Gregory's new play, the first of her famous 'Cloon' comedies, captured the heart of all in the auditorium. The overbearing 'Removable Magistrate' and his dull-witted policeman, Jo Muldoon, seeking out the perpetrator of a crime that was never committed; the melancholy Bartley Fallon, handcuffed to the infuriated Jack Smith, whom he is supposed to have killed; his mournful fear that if they are put together in a cell, 'murder will be done that time surely'—a perfect piece of dignified comedy by Willie Fay.

And then the scene had changed. The curtain had risen on the new Yeats play. I was standing in the wings, a forgotten prompt script in my hand. Willie Fay, the comedian, the businesslike stage manager of a few moments earlier was no more. He was transformed into a tiny ragged sprite, cringing before the glittering king of his brother. The other figures paled into the background. Frank Fay spoke, fondling his lines, and they flowed out across the footlights, hovering a moment over the hushed auditorium, his little figure gaining power through the beauty of his words, first as the proud king, hero of a thousand battles, then as the horrified, grief-stricken father verging on madness, his anguish intensified by the quiet irony of the fool. That moment—a brief one in a memorable evening—will remain long in my memory. The Fays had never acted so well together.

That evening ended too soon. Silently we gathered on the darkened stage, the muffled roar of the applause coming through the fallen curtain. Yeats passed through the green-room door, crossed the set, then stepped in front of the audience. Faintly his words came back:

> We shall take as our mottoes those words written over the three gates of the City of Love of Edmund Spenser— over the first gate was 'Be bold!'; over the second, 'Be bold, be bold! And evermore be bold!'; and over the third, 'Yet be not too bold'....

More applause, the tiny building vibrating with the echoes. Then quiet, and the murmur of voices as the audience began to file out.

Backstage, I remember, Frank Fay spoke first. He said: 'This is only the beginning ...'.

Fay was right. Although we had settled at last in permanent and suitable surroundings, we had still far from arrived. The hard work, the gradual improvement of our standards, until the Abbey became more than a mere theatre, the hub of a great national dramatic movement, still lay ahead if we were to justify our existence and the hopes that were placed in us. Our arrival in the Abbey did not mean just the continuation of our earlier work. As Fay had said, it meant the beginning proper. But we had great hopes for the future.

Perhaps we were over-optimistic. If fortune smiled on us at all this first year, it did so a trifle crookedly. Less than six months after our opening, there was dissension within the group. Before the year was fully ended, the original Irish National Theatre Society was dead, and most of its members had left the Abbey.

The Splendid Walkers: Clockwise from back left: Matthew, Charlie, Maire, Frank, Mary Anne, Gipsy, Annie and Daisy.

Power Couple: Matt and Mary Anne, photographed in the mid 1890s.

Wan and Beautiful: A rare colourized photograph of Maire, circa 1904.

Picture Perfect: Maire's portrait by John B. Yeats, which hangs in the Abbey to this day. Picture courtesy of the Abbey Theatre.

Mirror, Mirror: Maire in an example of some early 'state-of-the-art' trick photography. Picture courtesy of the Abbey Theatre.

Maire in a promotional shot. Picture courtesy of the Abbey Theatre.

Production for the first time on any Stage of On Baile's Strand and Spreading the News, on Tuesday, 27th December, 1904, and every evening till Tuesday, 3rd January, 1905.

ON BAILE'S STRAND, A PLAY IN ONE ACT, BY W. B. YEATS.

CUCHULLAIN, the King of Muirthemne	F. J. Fay
CONCOBAR, the High King of Ullad	George Roberts
DAIRE, a King	Arthur Sinclair
FINTAIN, a blind man	Seumas O'Sullivan
BARACH, a fool	W. G. Fay
A YOUNG MAN	P. MacSiubhlaigh
YOUNG KINGS and OLD KINGS	Maire Ni Gharbhaigh, Emma Vernon, Sara Algood, Doreen Gunning, R. Nash, N. Power, U. Wright, E. Keegan.

SCENE—A Great Hall by the Sea close to Dundalgan.

Costumes designed by Miss Horniman.

SPREADING THE NEWS, A COMEDY IN ONE ACT, BY LADY GREGORY.

BARTLEY FALLON	W. G. Fay
Mrs. FALLON	Sara Algood
Mrs. TULLY	Emma Vernon
Mrs. TARPEY	Maire Ni Gharbhaigh
SHAWN EARLY	J. H. Dunne
TIM CASEY	George Roberts
JAMES RYAN	Arthur Sinclair
JACK SMITH	P. MacSuibhlaigh
A POLICEMAN	R. S. Nash
A REMOVABLE MAGISTRATE	F. J. Fay

SCENE—The Outskirts of a Fair.

On Tuesday, Thursday, and Saturday, 27th, 29th, and 31st December, On Baile's Strand will be followed by :—

KATHLEEN NI HOULIHAN, A PLAY IN ONE ACT, BY W. B. YEATS

KATHLEEN NI HOULIHAN	Marie Nic Shiublaigh
PETER GILLANE	W. G. Fay
BRIDGET GILLANE, his Wife	Sara Algood
MICHAEL GILLANE ⎱ his Sons	P. MacSiubhlaigh
PATRICK GILLANE ⎰	U. Wright
DELIA CAHEL	Maire Ni Gharbhaigh

SCENE—A Cottage near to Killala, in 1798.

On Wednesday and Friday, 28th and 30th December, and on Monday and Tuesday, 2nd and 3rd January. On Baile's Strand will be followed by :—

IN THE SHADOW OF THE GLEN, A PLAY IN ONE ACT, BY J. M. SYNGE.

DAN BURKE, Farmer and Herd	George Roberts
NORA BURKE, his Wife	Maire Nic Shiublaigh
MICHAEL DARA, a Young Herd	P. MacSuibhlaigh
A TRAMP	W. G. Fay

SCENE—The last Cottage at the head of a long glen in County Wicklow.

The next production will be a new play in three acts, by J. M. Synge.

Leading Lady: The programme for the Abbey's opening performances, featuring Maire and her brother Frank (P. Mac Shiubhlaigh) in various roles. Picture courtesy of the Abbey Theatre.

Elocutionist

Maire nic Shiubhlaigh
(late Abbey Theatre)

209 Griffith Avenue
Whitehall – Dublin

Individual and Class Tuition in

Elocution . . . .
Stage Technique .
Acting . . . . .
Microphonic Detail
Auditions arranged

Terms on application.

Maire's business card, post Abbey Theatre.

Gipsy Bride: Maire (right) is matron of honour at Gip and Eddie's wedding.

Gip and Ted in 1930.

Take Note: Ted as a young newspaperman. He joined RTÉ's TV newsroom in 1960/61.

Farewell, Chief: Ted and de Valera meet at the Áras. The president was a regular visitor to the Walker family home on High Street.

Alone She Stands: Gipsy (right) pictured at the unveiling of the Abbey plaque in 1966. Also pictured are Helena Molony (seated) and Seán Lemass. Picture courtesy of the Abbey Theatre.

Chapter Seven

1905
Farewell to Camden Street

OUR OPENING was successful, both artistically and financially, and though our attendances thinned somewhat towards the middle of the week, they recovered sufficiently towards the end to compensate. Reviewers, too, were particularly pleasant, forecasting a favourable future for the group, and our reception by cross-Channel writers was no less gratifying than it had ever been. By mid January we were in rehearsal for our next play, which was a first production. It was a three-act piece by Synge, his first attempt at a play of more than one act, called *The Well of the Saints*.

As a literary achievement, this play is one of the best that Synge wrote. Its three acts are devoted almost completely to the development of a central character, Martin Doul, a blind beggar, fighting against a miracle that has restored his sight, but destroyed the illusion of life that his blindness has created.

The story deals with an incident in the lives of Doul and his wife, both blind, who believe the stories they have been told of their own physical beauty. When a travelling friar passing through their village restores their sight with blessed water from a saint's well, the illusion is destroyed and they see themselves as they really are—old and ugly. Their sight fails a second time, and when the friar offers to cure them again, this time permanently, Doul repulses him roughly. The play ends with the beggar, still refusing to submit, being driven from the district by the infuriated villagers.

The Well of the Saints, beautifully written and perfectly constructed though it was, could never have been popular with the audiences to which we were playing. Its principal appeal lay in the beauty of its writing, the literary skill of its author, not in any great dramatic situation. The picture it presented of Doul and his wife was anything but a flattering one. Being written by Synge, some of our audiences read into it a satirical attack on the Irish peasant's attitude to the church, and it received long notices in the Dublin press. Synge's point of view was again defined—as it was every time a play of his was produced—as 'that of a man not in sympathetic touch with the people from whom he purports to draw his characters'. One man added:

> The suggestion, moreover, was of a tendency that will carry Mr Synge's dramatic development far away from the ideals that have hitherto ruled that small body of literature in the English tongue which expresses the ideals and characteristics that are recognizable as Irish and appreciated as national.

After an excellent house on the first night, our audiences fell rapidly away. The last performance was played to a scattered houseful. It was an unfortunate start to our new career.

Shortly after the production of this play, we gave up using the Camden Street rooms and transferred our equipment and scenery to the Abbey, where we had the use of the stage for rehearsing. It was difficult to leave Camden Street. Our removal marked the passage of one of the most pleasant periods in the society's career. The little fifty-foot hall, for all its drawbacks, had been the scene of so many important events during the society's first years that leaving its draughty interior was like forsaking an old friend. Even the abandonment of the murky passage entrance with its piles of provisions brought a lump to the throat. We were moving on.

The Abbey's green room now became the centre of our activities. Here we met and debated in the lengthening evenings, brewed tea or cut slices of Gort cake. And although the room was even smaller than the Camden Street one, it began slowly to assume the appearance of our old quarters as the weeks passed and old friends visited us. A. E. still smoked his pipe in a quiet corner while the room echoed with the buzz of conversation; Willie Fay still met visitors, and climbed aboard his beloved hobby-horse of stage management; and Frank still held elocution classes. As before, there was a constant coming and going of supporters and associates of the society who were willing to help out in any way they could.

During the first years of our career in Camden Street and the Molesworth Hall, all ticket checking, ushering and programme selling during performances was done by those of us who might not be acting, or by these non-acting 'associates'. There had never been any shortage of volunteers. Willie Fay, for example, had friends who helped him with the changing of scenery and lighting and so on. The position of wardrobe mistress was held by my mother, Mary Anne, who was a bespoke dressmaker by day. She was assisted by J. A. O'Rourke, who was a tailor and one of our most talented players.

In the early Abbey days, lack of funds forbade the purchase on any extensive scale of a permanent wardrobe collection, and our ingenuity knew no bounds. Many of our most effective properties and dress accessories were created by us—and my mother—from cardboard, papier mâché, tin (in the case of shields and spears in period pieces), and odd bits of paste jewellery picked up occasionally in the city. In these times, too, before the theatre acquired the well-known gong (hanging behind the stage, it was beaten before the start of a play), the rise of the curtain was heralded in a less musical but nonetheless effective manner by three solemn knocks delivered to the floor behind the proscenium by whoever happened to be idle. Dignity at all costs, as we used to say.

After our arrival at the Abbey it quickly became necessary to acquire part-time theatre staff, and they were drawn from amongst the non-acting associate members of the society. Usherettes, ticket-checkers, booking-clerks and technicians were appointed, and a number of these provided the nucleus of the full-time theatre staff employed after the company became professional. Many of them remained with the theatre in this capacity all their lives.

One of the most notable personalities was the late Nellie Bushell, usherette in the stalls until her death, who, during the years of the Black and Tan war, often turned the torn-ticket box into a miniature arsenal, concealing the arms of fugitives who sought a few hours' refuge in the theatre. Originally a poplin weaver, she had always been actively associated with the political clubs, being a member in later years of Madame Markievicz's Fianna na hÉireann, the original Irish scout force, headquartered after its foundation in 1909 at our old premises in Camden Street.

Backstage, too, under the direction of Willie Fay, there were plenty of helpers who looked after the technical side of productions, and there was the beginning of a permanent staff of technicians in Seaghan Barlow and Udolphus Wright, the stage carpenter and house electrician respectively, both of whom gave up much of their spare time in the first days of the movement to work as players and scene-shifters, and both of whom were appointed to these jobs on a full-time basis in later years.

Like dramatic societies everywhere, we had a faithful, if small, 'following'. There were a number of people outside the dramatic movement who had seen our first performance in 1902 and had followed our career closely afterwards. Many of these friends turned up for every new play we gave; in fact, some of them came to see the company each time it appeared whether the play was a new one or not. Some took a seat in the auditorium for as often as three or four nights in succession—as long as a play ran.

I think, of all the people who occupied a place in our first-night life at this time, the most interesting was Joe Holloway, the Dublin stage-diarist and the man who had supervised the conversion of the old Mechanics' Building for Miss Horniman. Indeed, Holloway was probably one of the most colourful of the many figures who moved on the fringe of the dramatic movement after 1903 or 1904.

He was a Dubliner of the old period, born not very far from the Camden Street rooms. He was an architect, but a private income had probably enabled him to give up his profession early.

None of us ever heard of him practising on an extensive scale; he had the reputation of being essentially a man of the theatre. It was quite true. Although it is doubtful if he had ever been moved to act, or even to write a play, he probably knew more about the history of the Dublin stage in his lifetime than any man then living in the city. He was probably the first Abbey Theatre historian; his diaries contain first-hand accounts of almost all the dramatic or musical entertainments in the city from the days of his youth until his death.

He was a stocky little man in middle age, with a long black overcoat, a bowler hat, a bushy moustache and hair that stuck out at all angles. He used to wander into our rehearsals almost every evening in search of news for his diaries. Every night he wrote down a full account of all theatrical activity in Dublin during the day. At the end of each year the penny copybooks and jotters that he used were bound in leather and stacked on his library shelves for future reference.

Visitors to his home at Northumberland Road would be amazed at the bulkiness of the volumes; some of them contained almost a thousand closely written sheets. Each year they encroached further upon his available space. Towards the end of his life they lay piled in rows on the floor of his room, some of them overflowing onto chairs and desks.

He often said that his interest in the stage had begun when, as a boy, he saved his pennies for the Queen's or the Mechanics' or Dan Lowrey's and how he spent most of his out-of-school hours in the lobbies of the concert halls, hoping to get an opportunity of entering. Thereafter he was a regular playgoer. When we met him he could recall at a moment's notice a first night of ten or fifteen years back and, by a casual delve into his diaries, produce exhaustive accounts of incidents long forgotten in the history of the Dublin stage. He knew every play, every actor and every playwright who came to the city in his lifetime.

Holloway seldom missed a play we gave. In the Abbey, his seat in the front row of the stalls was always reserved and always filled on a first night unless he happened to be ill or away from Dublin. And in these early days of the theatre, when half-empty houses were the rule rather than the exception, he was our greatest support. We could always depend on his slow enthusiastic applause from the front. If a line misfired or was greeted with silence, the silence was usually followed by the rhythmic beat of his heavy palms. Quite unconcernedly, as though there were no one else in the theatre, he would record his approval. Afterwards he would come around to the green room and, if it was a first night, drink pots of strong black tea while he discussed points in the play we were giving.

I may mention here that anything Joe Holloway had to say about our work was always worth listening to. Although he was not a very sound drama critic, he *was* an experienced playgoer. His opinions were typical of the great mass of theatregoers in the city at that time, and he was worth his weight in gold as a sort of barometer by which to gauge the public's reaction to our work. For this reason alone, and quite apart from the fact he was our friend, he was a valuable addition to the theatre. Holloway was the finger that we, as players, kept on the pulse of Dublin.

Lady Gregory retrieved some of our losses on 25 March 1905 when we gave the first performance of her play, *Kincora*, a full-length costume piece dealing with an important period in Irish history: the events leading up to the defeat of the Danes in Ireland at Clontarf. *Kincora* was a powerful and popular play. The two principal characters, Brian Boru (the king who 'wars but for peace'—a popular figure, played by Frank Fay) and his high-spirited war-loving queen, Gormleith, were finely drawn and a joy to act.

Reviewers acclaimed the work, for it was a new kind of thing for the Abbey, being legendary, but without the poetry or symbolism of Yeats, which did not always succeed outside literary circles. It ran for a week, playing to full houses.

On 25 April we produced a three-act comedy, *The Building Fund*, the first play of William Boyle, whose works were to take a big place in the Abbey's repertoire for several years. *The Building Fund* threw symbolism and experiment aside and was written with one purpose only in mind: entertainment. It was an immediate popular success. Set in County Louth with a small cast of five, it painted a magnificent and highly amusing picture of a miserly farmer, Sean Grogan, and his equally grasping mother. It was the first of several clever pieces that were to come from Boyle's pen for a number of years. In Boyle, the Abbey soon discovered that it had the popular writer of straightforward comedies that appeal to every type of audience. He was a valuable addition to the company, for it is always useful for a theatre to have a reserve of popular plays that it can put on at short notice.

A succession of rollicking comedies poured from his pen thereafter. One, *The Eloquent Dempsey*, enjoyed remarkable success in 1906.

The first half of this first Abbey Theatre year came to a close with Padraic Colum's *The Land*, a sensitively constructed three-act piece written to celebrate the emancipation of the small farmer by the Irish Land Act of 1903. It received even greater praise than *Broken Soil*. One reviewer wrote:

> Mr Colum has indeed accomplished a strong and illuminating piece of dramatic work, which is all the more to be praised because it expresses a definite and personal point of view. *The Land* is the work of an artist, but of an artist who loves the smell of ploughed earth and the falling rain, and balances this love exquisitely with the love of spiritual things…. There is tragedy here, the bitter tragedy of the conflict of ideals, and Mr Colum has used his materials with knowledge and sympathy, with great technical skill, and with that hint of poetic exuberance which is the breath of true art. His characters—the despotic land-loving father; the town-smitten girl, Ellen; her despairing liberty-craving lover; her makeshift father who has been in gaol for the cause; and the rest—are all distinctly and imaginatively drawn.

The first production of Colum's *Land* has other memories for me. It was the last play produced by the old Irish National Theatre Society. A little later the society, which we had founded in 1902, was dissolved, and its place taken by a limited company controlled by a directorate.

Not all memories of the change are pleasant. The events that followed this reorganisation of our enterprise resulted in the withdrawal from the National Theatre Society of most of its original members. I was amongst those who left.

Chapter Eight

1905–1906
Walking Out of the Abbey

BEFORE I GO into the events which led up to the secession of players from the Abbey this year, it may be as well to say that for some time prior to its arrival in the theatre a vague sense of dissatisfaction had begun to grow up within the National Theatre Society.

In 1903, a little before Miss Horniman came into our lives, a number of minor disagreements amongst members of the committee had given rise to the feeling that all was not quite as it should be within the group. A few of the members had begun to feel that the co-operative policy of the organisation was not being observed, and some of the more nationalist-minded players felt that the society was no longer as national in character as it had been originally. I mention both these points because they have a direct bearing on what followed during our first year in the Abbey. As far as I am aware, the full story has never been told before.

In 1905 the dissolution of the old National Theatre Society and the establishment in its place of a limited company was, of course, inevitable. With the arrival of the society in the Abbey it was considered necessary to establish the organisation on a definite businesslike footing without delay. It was agreed that the only course open to us was to float a company with each of the player-members of the original society holding shares. The capital accruing from the sale of the remaining shares would enable us to carry on as amateurs for as long as it took to establish ourselves as a regular theatrical company producing plays with the same frequency as other theatres in the city.

Under this arrangement it was estimated that if we worked hard enough on the preparation of plays, we would, with luck, be self-supporting within a year. It would, of course, mean twelve months of strenuous work for the players—the more frequent production of plays would give us little time away from rehearsals—but it was work that we were all prepared to do. Hard work and enthusiasm had always been the measure of the members' sincerity. And the organisation had first been founded upon the basis of achievement solely through our own efforts.

The new scheme was put into operation about the middle of 1905, when the Irish National Theatre Society, Limited, made its appearance. This, a limited liability company, had a directorate composed of W. B. Yeats, Lady Gregory and J. M. Synge. Each of the players became shareholders of the company with one share each, and the rest of the shares were distributed.

With our enterprise thus established, everything appeared to be well within the theatre. But this was only partially true. The establishment of the business company, although it had been carried out with the consent of most of the members, had altered the spirit within the group. Some of the friendliness, the comradeship, vanished soon after the new arrangement came into force. When the directorate began to make decisions on certain matters without notifying the organisation as a whole, more and more of the players began to refer regretfully to the abandonment of the old policy of co-operation, and the fears of others that the nationalist ideals of the movement were in danger of being shelved were intensified.

The unfortunate matter that now developed took place at a general meeting of the company in the theatre when Yeats supported a motion that some leading members of the company, of which I was one, should immediately become professional players, devoting their time wholly to the theatre under the control of the directorate in return for salaries guaranteed by Miss Horniman.

The motion had a mixed reception. Some members supported it; others pointed out that the suggestion that players turn professional was premature since it had already been agreed to continue on an amateur basis for at least another year, independent of outside support. Regarding the suggestion that the company as a whole should be subsidised by Miss Horniman, it was pointed out that the old Irish National Theatre Society had been founded in 1902 on the understanding that its independence as a national movement was to be secured only through the efforts of its members.

It would be contrary to these ideals to accept a subsidy from an independent source. If such a subsidy were accepted, the individual character of the movement would be completely destroyed. In any event, it was added, the subsidy was unnecessary since the members were prepared to continue working as they were until the company became self-supporting. There was no reason why more money should be taken from Miss Horniman, who had already done enough by providing us with the Abbey.

Yeats was adamant. He stubbornly supported the motion. 'Miss Horniman offers to subsidise us; we will accept her offer.' The discussion went on. There was some fiery talk; a number of opinions were aired. The meeting split into two opposing factions: the directorate and some of the members on one side strongly advocating the acceptance of the subsidy; over two-thirds of the original Irish National Theatre Society members on the other.

Eventually, on the strength of shares, the motion was carried in favour of the directorate. Since most of the original player-founders were opposed to the decision, the inevitable happened: there was a secession of members. Only four player-members of the original National Theatre Society remained behind with Yeats and Lady Gregory. The rest of us, including A. E., withdrew. There was nothing else to be done. We could not see our way to remain.

Looking back, I can see nothing wrong with our decision. It was not made hurriedly without careful consideration. Although, for most of us who took the course of secession, the action meant the end of any progress we might have been making individually towards international distinction as Irish players—in my own case it virtually meant the end of a career on the stage, which might or might not have taken me away from Dublin altogether in the years that followed. I doubt if many of us had any regrets at the time.

For myself, I can only say that at that period I had no desire to act, professionally or otherwise, with any theatrical project unlike the one I helped to launch in 1902. In those days I never thought of the National Theatre Society as a purely theatrical enterprise: it was a part of the larger nationalist movement in which most of us were then participating. Even at the risk of its ultimate stagnation and death, I would, just then, have preferred the theatre to struggle on alone, administered solely from within itself, as a subsidiary part of that movement.

But perhaps that was not a practicable idea. If the Abbey had remained subordinate to nationalism, political as well as cultural, in those years, it might never have achieved the success it did. It had to stand outside the nationalist movement in order to make its mark on the theatre of the world.

Shortly after the secession, Lady Gregory asked me to stay with the theatre until the end of the year, until she could get someone to take my place. A short English tour had been arranged by Miss Horniman, she said, and as my name figured in the advance publicity, much inconvenience would be caused if I refused to travel. Also, I had already been cast for a part in her new play *The White Cockade*, due for production at the Abbey in December. Would I remain until then? As it would have meant upsetting the arrangements of months, I agreed.

On 15 December 1905, I left the Abbey Theatre for the first time. Willie Fay, who at that time disagreed completely with my decision, I saw only once again. In 1908, after a disagreement of his own with the directors, both he and Frank resigned from the theatre and left Ireland. Thirty years later Willie visited Dublin again, playing at the Gaiety in a production of an Irish comedy, *Spring Meeting*. He was an old man then, but still, on or off the stage, the same Willie Fay we had always known. He had carved a little niche for himself on the stage in America and England, where he had become well known as an authority on theatrical matters. I was happy to renew his acquaintance.

We never met again. Not long after his visit to Dublin, he made a successful film appearance in Carol Reed's production of *Odd Man Out*, playing opposite the late F. J. McCormick. Unfortunately, like many actors of his generation, his genius as a cinema star was realised too late. This was one of his last appearances. Less than a year later, he died.

Part Two

The Theatre of Ireland

Chapter Nine

1906
A New Beginning

OUR WITHDRAWAL affected the progress of the Abbey little. The promotion of a few hitherto small-part actors, and the addition of some new, non-professional members, soon filled any gaps our departure created, and the theatre continued without us. In January 1906, William Boyle gave the theatre his second play, a three-act farce on municipal politics, called *The Eloquent Dempsey*, which achieved instant success and was hailed in its own particular field for its richly diverting dialogue and humorous plot.

Boyle was a master of comedy, and this play was amongst the most popular he wrote, although the three or four others that he gave to the theatre in the years that followed were far above the ordinary run of comedy presented anywhere else at that time. Later, when the Fays left the Abbey, and Arthur Sinclair, who had been discovered in 1904, became first comedian, all Boyle's leading characters were given to him with complete success. They suited his style particularly, and although he had only a small part in *The Eloquent Dempsey*, the title being taken in the first production by Willie Fay, he almost outshone the more experienced actor.

It was probably this play that marked the beginning of Sinclair's ascent to the position of leading Irish character comedian, which, with Fay, he held for many years afterwards, both here and in America and England. When he accompanied the Abbey on its first American tour in 1911, he refused several fine offers from leading companies in the States, his desire being to remain in Ireland, where he gradually created a style of Irish character comedy peculiarly his own.

During the first months of 1906, whenever former members of the Irish National Theatre Society met, talk frequently turned towards the stage and the possible formation of a group similar to the organisation founded in Camden Street in 1902. The probable amalgamation of the National Players—the title of the city dramatic society then connected with Inghinidhe na hÉireann—with the five or six who were interested in continuing a national theatre project was mentioned. Although the suggestion was an attractive one, little heed was paid to it at the time.

Our withdrawal from the Abbey had meant the parting of the ways for many of us, and there seemed little prospect of getting a sufficient number together to start again. Consequently, it was a pleasant surprise when, the following May, a letter was circulated inviting interested parties to attend a meeting to consider the possibility of establishing a society 'to further dramatic work in Ireland'. A sum of money was available, it added, and Edward Martyn had consented to act as president. The letter was signed by Thomas Keohler and Padraic Colum.

There was a good attendance at the meeting. Stephen Gwynn was in the chair, and the speakers included Keohler, Colum, Eoin MacNeill, Pádraig Pearse, Maurice Joy, Edward Martyn, George Roberts, Brian Callender and Cathal MacGarvey. All were members of the politico-cultural clubs, and all were interested in the theatre. The proposed formation of the group, when its ideals were outlined, met with considerable opposition, and it was suggested that its establishment was at once unnecessary and presumptuous, since the Abbey was working towards the same end.

The whole subject received a full measure of detailed and at times rather fiery discussion, but after a long debate a resolution was passed in favour of starting a new amateur company. Its ideals were to be similar in many ways to those of the old National Theatre Society for the advancement of drama in Ireland through the production of plays by Irish writers in Irish and in English and such works of foreign dramatists as might be considered advisable. It was to be a non-profit-making organisation; its funds were to be used only to further these objectives.

Deputations from other city dramatic clubs promised they would co-operate in every way possible with the new group, and a provisional committee was formed. A few weeks later, in a room at the back of a house in High Street, acquired as temporary headquarters, the society was formally named 'The Theatre of Ireland' (Cluithcheoiri na hÉireann), and a permanent board of officers was elected, which had Edward Martyn as president, and included Padraic Colum, Thomas Keohler, George Nesbitt, Dermot Trench, James Cousins, Helen Laird, Pádraig Pearse and Thomas Kettle on the committee. As one of the conditions in our secession agreement with the Abbey had been the rental of the theatre for productions by any society that we might establish, the premises in High Street were held only as rehearsal rooms and no attempt was made to convert them into a public hall. It was just as well: they were smaller and in an even worse condition than the Camden Street hall had been.

The Theatre of Ireland for six years ran parallel (although not always in concord with) the Abbey. During the few years of its existence it rivalled and sometimes outshone the work in Miss Horniman's theatre. Its members were all amateurs, young men and women, typical of the period, who strove first for a national ideal, secondly for a theatrical one. It began to decline in 1912 only because its members were absorbed into the wider, and at the time more important, work of the Irish Volunteer Movement.

Early in August some members of the new society made an appearance at the Gaelic League Oireachtas with an Irish version of Colum's *The Land*, translated by Professor Tadhg O'Donoghue (Torna). It was not an official appearance—the society was nameless on the occasion—but it was a success. *The Land* took well in Gaelic, and if the dialogue was a trifle ponderous at times, it made up in colour what it lacked in vitality. Even the most commonplace English statement sounds picturesque in Irish.

For our first real appearance, which was arranged for December, we chose a triple-bill that seemed fairly representative of the aims of the society as set out at our inaugural meeting. The programme consisted of the formerly successful *Racing Lug* of James Cousins; an extract from Ibsen's *Brand*; and, as a demonstration of our policy for the production of plays in Gaelic, Dr Hyde's *Casadh an tSúgain*, the piece that had inspired Fay to found the original dramatic society. The productions took place, not in the Abbey as had been expected, but in the Molesworth Hall. These were the casts:

THE RACING LUG

Johnny, an old fisherman	George Nesbitt
Nancy, his wife	Honor Lavelle
Bell	Maire Nic Shiubhlaigh
Bob, a young fisherman	Frank Walker (P. Mac Shiubhlaigh)
The Revd Mr MacMeekin	Seumas Connolly

BRAND (Act IV)

Agnes	Vera Esposito
Brand	Joseph Goggins
Gipsy Woman	Maire Nic Shiubhlaigh

CASADH AN TSÚGAÍN

The Poet	Diarmuid Trench
Una	Maire Nic Shiubhlaigh
Seumas	Frank Walker
Maire, Una's mother	Sheela Hallissy
Sheila	Honor Lavelle

Our production of part of *Brand*, Ibsen's most famous tragedy, was probably one of the first times the play had been given in these islands. We found it impossible to give the piece in full—in its original form it takes four or five hours—but we fixed on a scene from Act IV that was almost self-contained. It dealt with the gradual readjustment to life of Agnes, Brand's wife. It may be worth mentioning here that my part as the gypsy woman was strikingly like that of Moll Woods, the Shuiler, in *The Shuiler's Child*, the play that Seumas O'Kelly, the Loughrea dramatist, wrote in 1909. When I mentioned this to O'Kelly years later he admitted that it was as a result of seeing the scene from Ibsen that he wrote *The Shuiler's Child*.

The productions were a success. If we had any doubts about our acceptance by the Dublin public, they were soon dispelled. Curiosity, mingled perhaps with a little admiration for our independence, attracted an audience representative of most sections of the writing world. The productions were by no means flawless—we missed the guiding hand of Fay—but, good or bad, it would probably have made little difference. We had a following.

Chapter Ten

1907
The Playboy

THE NEXT year, 1907, was a memorable one for everyone connected with the theatre in Dublin. It has gone down in theatrical history as the year of the first Abbey Theatre riots. In January, the theatre produced a new Synge piece, *The Playboy of the Western World*, a play that was followed by a series of remarkable scenes that shook the Dublin theatre world, and began a controversy that was to continue for many years, not only in Ireland but in America and elsewhere.

I will, I suppose, be accused of dwelling unnecessarily on a regrettable occurrence by telling what I know of this affair, but I feel that I am justified in doing so. The 'Playboy riots', as they came to be known, indicate very clearly some of the difficulties that the Abbey was called upon to face during its first years, and they show how the theatre, under Yeats, managed to surmount them. When this play is produced in Dublin now it is recognised and enjoyed as a work of art. In 1907 it drove a number of people into such a frenzy that they nearly wrecked the Abbey. I am in rather a good position to describe the riots because I was in the audience during some of them. Curiosity had taken me into the theatre, as it had taken many another person that week.

It was about the end of 1906 that Synge finished the *Playboy* after, it is said, rewriting it several times at the suggestion of Yeats, principally to conform with the limitations imposed by production on a stage. Yeats later mentioned that Synge took considerable trouble over the piece and scrapped a number of earlier versions before he fixed on the one that was eventually produced. Originally it was said that he had had an outdoor setting, but that he subsequently rewrote parts of the play for the interior when it was pointed out that the presentation of the original scene was impossible. Yeats never tired of recounting the care that Synge lavished on the piece.

This, indeed, may have been indirectly responsible for the reception accorded the play by some sections of the public, whose main argument against it was that it was 'a slander on the peasantry of Ireland'. As in the case of *The Shadow of the Glen*, its realism gave offence. The only difference between it and any other play that did not take was that the public, instead of showing its lack of interest in the accepted way—by its non-attendance—displayed its disapproval by rioting in the theatre throughout the play's run.

The most unusual feature of the affair was that although the players appeared on the stage and acted their parts for a whole week, the uproar caused by the audience was so great that the play was never really heard on any night but the first, and those who took part in the demonstrations on subsequent occasions were dependent on the opinions of the first-night audience and a few rather hysterical newspaper reports. As the week progressed, the trouble, instead of lessening, increased, and before the run of the play was half over, the management felt compelled to call for the assistance of the police to preserve order.

The explanations put forward by the rioters during the week were many and varied, and it is worth remarking that no two people appeared to base their objections on exactly the same thing. Some objected to the piece because it 'made a hero out of a murderer' (the play deals in part with the welcome accorded by a west-of-Ireland village to a weak-willed boy who believes he has just killed his father); others claimed that the language used was too strong; more contented themselves by saying that the play was 'vicious, untrue and uncalled for'—a 'hideous caricature' in fact; while a considerable number based their objections on the assumption that the piece was a deliberate attack by Synge on Ireland in retaliation for the manner in which *The Shadow of the Glen* and *The Well of the Saints* had been received.

The latter theory may have been near the truth. It is possible for a writer unconsciously to express resentment through his pen.

Synge had been deeply hurt and annoyed by the reception of his earlier plays, and it is just possible that when he wrote *Playboy* he let his personal irritation influence him, which resulted in each of his characters having a nasty streak. Imaginative production on the first night, however, less emphasis on tragedy and more on comedy, would have hidden this. Produced nowadays, the play is done as a comedy, and is invariably successful. When it was given for the first time it was played seriously, almost sombrely, as though each character had been studied and their nastiness made apparent.

The idea of any Irish man or woman making a hero out of someone guilty of parricide completely enraged the first-night audience and the press. The uproar raised in the papers was enormous. The people in the play, it was said, were vicious caricatures born of the writer's imagination and completely untrue to life. The whole thing was 'an unmitigated, protracted libel on Irish peasant men and, worse still, upon Irish peasant girlhood.' 'Enough!' howled one man in an excess of self-righteous indignation, 'the hideous caricature would be slanderous of a Kaffir kraal!'

During the week, Synge said that the play had been suggested to him by the fact that a few years earlier a man who had committed a murder was kept hidden by the people of the Aran Islands until he could get away to America, and also by the case of Lynchehaun, who brutally attacked a woman and yet, with the help of Irish peasant girls and men, managed to conceal himself from the police for several months and evade capture. These comparisons, however, coming at the height of the trouble were useless. Nothing could have changed the public's opinion of what was really a fine dramatic work. It was taken as a personal insult.

The Playboy of the Western World was first produced on Saturday, 26 January 1907. It was an all-Synge programme, and the curtain-raiser, *Riders to the Sea*, was listened to attentively. The climax brought long and appreciative applause.

The *Playboy* scene, laid throughout in the main room of an inn on the western coast, was typical of Fay. He achieved the effect of brightness against the lime-washed walls of the set in a pleasantly unobtrusive manner. The fittings were a lovely deep brown, the colour of turf, and helped to show up the bright peasant costumes of the characters. The scene will remain long in memory, although it is not the best that Fay designed. The impression it leaves is of course bound up with the events that took place in front of it.

As Christy Mahon, the weak-willed playboy who strives for the admiration of the community and the love of the girl, Pegeen Mike, Willie Fay was a revelation. He broke completely new ground as the weak-willed, poetic Christy. Never will there be a playboy to equal his. One forgot his diminutive figure and sharp features in the utter mastery of his playing. His love scene with Pegeen (played exquisitely by Maire O'Neill) was one of the most beautiful pieces of acting I have ever seen. One remembers too the jaunty Widow Quinn of Sara Allgood, her bright eyes and rich, gurgling laugh.

The first act went well. There was laughter at the right places, and the correct degree of solemnity when it was demanded. But during the second act I began to feel a tenseness in the air around me—I was sitting in the pit—and there were murmurs from the stalls and parts of the gallery. Before the curtain fell it was obvious that there was going to be some sort of trouble. Faint calls like 'Oh, no! Take it off!' came from various parts of the house, and the atmosphere gradually grew taut. In the third act things really came to a head, and those around began to stamp the floor and shout towards the stage, the noise gradually increasing until the voices of the players were drowned. People stood up in their seats and demanded the withdrawal of the play, and when it became clear that the cast was determined to see the thing out to the end, tempers began to fray. The auditorium became a mass of people pulling and pushing in all directions.

By the time the curtain fell on the last act, the crowd were arguing and fighting among themselves. People in front leaned over the back of seats and demanded quiet—a lot of people seemed to be doing this—and those at the back responded by shouting and hissing loudly. The crowd that eventually emerged into the street was in an ugly mood.

After that, it was generally accepted that the play would be withdrawn, if only to prevent further trouble. It came as a surprise when the directors announced that they would do nothing of the sort. Yeats said that the theatre would continue to give the play for the advertised time—a week. This attitude did not help matters when the press reports of the first night appeared. In fact, it only served to stir up a premature antagonism amongst those who had not yet seen the play.

Many were the protests entered against the piece in the papers. Wrote one man: 'No adequate idea can be given of the barbarous jargon, the elaborate incessant cursings of these repulsive creatures' (this in reference to the use of the word 'bloody' and once or twice of the word 'shift', meaning chemise, when Christy in one of the finest speeches of the play, says: 'It's Pegeen I'm seeking only, and what'd I care if you brought me a drift of chosen females, standing in their shifts itself, maybe, from this place to the eastern world?'). Other reviews were as bad. The voices of the few who did say an intelligent word of the piece were completely drowned.

On the third night, Yeats addressed the audience before the curtain rose. If anyone had anything to say against the piece they would be welcomed at a debate that he would be glad to arrange in the theatre at some other time. He was interrupted several times. He asked the interrupters at least to listen to the play so that they would know to what it was they were objecting. People had a right to hear the play and object to it if they pleased, but they had no right to prevent others from hearing it. The rest of his remarks were drowned out by the voices of a number of people who stood up and addressed the stage. A few moments later the house lights went out and the curtain rose.

As on the first night, the opening passages were listened to quietly, even getting a little laughter. Halfway through the second act, however, a murmur arose in the pit, and a man a few rows away stood up and, without any apparent reason, hit the person beside him. A gasp ran round the whole house and the lights went up. All around him the crowd was breaking into disorder.

Within minutes, the audience in the pit and stalls was completely disorganised, and the crowd in the back and side galleries was almost as bad. Almost everyone was standing. The noise was deafening. Yeats appeared on the stage and pleaded with the sensible members of the audience to remain quiet. His voice was drowned by catcalls, cheers, much stamping of feet, and from somewhere at the back the notes of a toy trumpet, which came from the centre of a group of young men who looked like university students. He continued to speak, but his words were apparently objected to by those in front, for a howl of protest went up from the stalls and parts of the side gallery, which increased in volume as those behind joined in or tried to cheer the protest down. On the stage the players stood in little knots discussing the occurrences amongst themselves.

As the noise increased, and several arguments broke out around the theatre, Yeats left his place on the stage. A few minutes later the doors into the auditorium opened, and to the horror and surprise of most of those present, a party of police entered. At the same time the curtain came down and a semblance of order was restored—partially due to the sight of the uniforms. Although the arrival of the police was only to be foreseen in the circumstances, to many of those present their appearance was totally unexpected. The summoning of the guardians of British law, no matter for what reason, into what was ostensibly an Irish national theatre, was the last thing anyone anticipated. After a brief speech by Yeats, and the ejection of the more truculent members of the audience, peace was partially restored, and everyone sat down again. At this stage it would have been impossible for anyone to get out. After everyone had been quietened, and the greater part of the audience reseated, it would have been dangerous for anyone to stand up. Those who did so were immediately surrounded by hefty policemen and shepherded, not too gently, in the direction of the vestibule.

Meanwhile, the orchestra, a recent addition to the theatre, began to play. The music seemed to help matters somewhat, and things almost returned to what they were before the play began. There was much discussion and gesticulation going on, however. The affair was still far from settled.

After some time the orchestra retired, the lights were lowered, and the curtain went up. Almost immediately the audience reverted to what it had been before the arrival of the police. Not a word of the play could be heard. The cast eventually gave up speaking altogether and went through the piece in pantomime. As the play progressed, the noise increased. Men and women stamped the floor, banged the backs of their seats with their fists, shouted and sang alternately. On the stairs from the stalls a man stood, dramatically addressing no one in particular.

The players courageously went through the whole piece. During this time several arrests were made, and the police were kept busy operating between the doors and the hall. Just before the play ended I saw an opportunity to escape, and took it. Almost everyone in the row where I had been sitting had vanished. I was able to make a dash for the door at the rear of the pit while the police were busy in the front of the house. My last impression of the scene was the sight of a figure standing on a seat somewhere about the centre of the stalls and the sound of a few bars of 'God Save the King', which were quickly stifled as someone pulled the singer down.

Yeats spoke freely through the press. He referred to the play as Synge's masterpiece, but would only discuss it incidentally to the larger and more important question of the freedom of the theatre, upon which he spoke long and fluently. He spoke about 'young men and women who came down to the theatre, not to judge the play, but to stop others from doing so.' The directors, he added, fully intended to continue with the play until it had been heard sufficiently to be judged on its merits.

His attitude was courageous, but foolish. Although he was right in his estimation of the play as a dramatic masterpiece—time has proved this—it seemed foolish to expect those who had so forcibly demonstrated their dislike of it to change their opinion by its mere repetition. At the time, most of us were inclined to believe that he was wrong in keeping the play on. It can be argued that he was right: Yeats was not fighting a mere battle of wills; he was fighting for freedom of expression for the theatre.

But his attitude had repercussions. The remaining nights were repetitions of the ones just described, with slightly more spectacular variations such as threatened street demonstrations. What was probably the greatest blow to the theatre came early in

February when William Boyle withdrew his plays publicly from the Abbey's repertoire. He protested against:

> ... the present attempt to set up a standard of national drama based on the vilification of any section of the Irish people in a theatre ostensibly founded for the production of plays to represent real Irish life and character.

This was a significant setback for the Abbey. Boyle's plays were a sure money-spinner for any theatre that ran them. It was not until about 1911 that he returned his plays to the theatre where they had been first produced.

Local Galway councils passed resolutions of protest against the *Playboy.* The whole chain of events culminated with the public debate promised by Yeats and held in the theatre after the play's run. It served no useful purpose, breaking up in disorder.

As 1907 drew on, the riots, although they affected the prestige of the Abbey, did little to harm the Theatre of Ireland. It was perhaps an ironic fact that while Abbey audiences dwindled, and isolated arguments over Synge's play still continued, the greater part of the theatre-going public began to turn towards the society we had founded in 1906, many people seeing it for the first time as an important part of the dramatic movement. Yeats's attitude over the production of Synge's play, while it had not exactly antagonised more people than it pleased, had nevertheless resulted in a noticeable falling off in attendances at the Abbey. Even people who had seen nothing objectionable in the *Playboy* were perhaps chary of attending a theatre that had for a week been the scene of a series of such violet disturbances unfamiliar to the city.

In a roundabout way, those who had opposed Synge's play, although it was believed that they were in a minority, were having the better of the argument. In a theatre, rows of empty seats can be very eloquent.

The Theatre of Ireland, still less than a year old, now had the nucleus of a following in excess of anything for which it had hoped, but it was still not altogether a competent dramatic society. Its first appearance in 1906, although a success, had shown that the company lacked the guidance of an experienced producer. The society's second appearance in March 1907 was a ragged one, unworthy of the plays presented. We gave the first production of *The Fiddler's House*—a rewritten version of *Broken Soil*—and revived Alice Milligan's *The Last Feast of the Fianna*.

What the Theatre of Ireland needed was a good stage manager and producer who could take the material constituted by the society's members and mould it into a good company. Several of us had experience of the stage, but a number of our new members had never acted before and needed someone to train them as the Fays had trained us. Luckily, such a person was forthcoming. In 1907 the Ulster Literary Theatre came to Dublin and brought the Morrows of Belfast with it. The Morrow brothers, Jack and Fred, especially Fred, 'made' the Theatre of Ireland, much as the Fays had made the original National Theatre Society.

The Ulster Literary Theatre, which was then about three years old, had been conceived in the Protestant National Club of Belfast. In 1902 this group, with the assistance of some members of the National Theatre Society, had produced *Kathleen Ni Houlihan* and *The Racing Lug*, and some time later had made an appearance with A. E.'s *Deirdre*. After this, the Ulster Literary Theatre had appeared, established on a basis somewhat similar to that of the original National Theatre Society. Actors and playwrights had been forthcoming. The society gathered about it an excellent company. It appeared in Belfast, produced plays by Bulmer Hobson, Lewis Purcell, Joseph Campbell and Rutherford Mayne. It visited the Abbey on 30 March 1907.

The appearance of the company in the city excited some comment, since the work of the players was not unlike that of our own. The plays produced were Rutherford Mayne's *The Turn of the Road*—his first folk-drama—and Lewis Purcell's *The Pagan*, a very original comedy set in the sixth century. Naturally, the visit attracted the attention of the Theatre of Ireland, which arranged a reception for the players. The most notable result of this meeting of the groups was that it excited the interest of Fred Morrow in the career of the Theatre of Ireland.

Not long after the Ulster Theatre's visit he returned to Dublin, where he set up an interior decorating business at D'Olier Street, and offered us his services as stage manager. This was a remarkable stroke of good fortune, for Fred, whose skill as a producer had been shown by the success of the northern group, which he had directed, brought with him his brother, Jack, who designed scenery.

He was also in direct touch with another brother, Harry, a playwright and amateur actor whose plays are amongst the most excellent examples of the Ulster playwrights' early trend towards dramatic satire. Harry, although he lived in Belfast, became associated with the Theatre of Ireland through several plays that he contributed to its repertory in subsequent years. Nowadays most amateur groups are familiar with a play of his that is frequently revived and has been broadcast several times. What dramatic society does not know his delightful satire on northern life and manners, *Thompson in Tir na nÓg*, the story of the Orangeman who wandered into the land of the ever-young?

The first appearance of the Theatre of Ireland under the direction of Fred Morrow took place in the Abbey on 13 December 1907 with a revival of A. E.'s *Deirdre* and the first production of a new play, *Matchmakers*, by Seumas O'Kelly. It was a success. The productions were vastly better than the society's earlier ones. Morrow had original ideas, and his interpretation of *Deirdre*, although completely different to Fay's in 1902, was nonetheless praiseworthy.

We had a good press. Seumas O'Kelly's *Matchmakers*, which supported, was a lively little comedy of rural life; a racy little piece of not very great distinction, although slightly better than some of the Abbey productions during this period. Oddly, despite its inoffensiveness and the cleverness of its construction, it annoyed some hasty members of our public, who, because the story dealt with a 'made marriage', came prepared to register their disapproval on the first night. Happily, however, the surprise of both the cast and the greater part of the audience itself was so apparent that the objectors, a few of whom had begun a faint hissing, realised the folly of their attitude and retired abashed. There were congratulations and apologies afterwards.

Had any of us been discerning enough we might have remarked, as we did in the case of Synge, that talent—or genius—is seldom accepted on its first appearance. Seumas O'Kelly, although he does not bear comparison as a dramatist with Synge, became one of the most distinguished literary figures of this period, and one of the most gifted young playwrights the Theatre of Ireland produced. He came from Loughrea and was at that time living at Naas, County Kildare, where he worked as a journalist. Before *Matchmakers*, which was his first play, he had become widely known as a short-story writer and political commentator, and had published a small collection of stories, *By the Stream of Kilmeen*. This volume, which subsequently achieved wide success both here and in America, was the first of a number of books to come from his pen. *Waysiders*, which followed, is a larger and better-known collection of his tales, and includes the famous 'Festus Clasby' short story, *The Can with the Diamond Notch*.

It is as a novelist, short-story writer and political journalist, rather than as a playwright, that Seumas O'Kelly is best remembered, but at least three plays, later produced by the Abbey, established him as a dramatist of power and imagination. In recent years he has come to be recognised, especially in America, as the writer of one of the greatest short stories written by any Irishman: 'The Weaver's Grave'. Not long after his introduction to the Theatre of Ireland he settled in Dublin, where he worked for many years with Arthur Griffith. Of the four early plays of his first produced by the Theatre of Ireland, one, at least, achieved great recognition: *The Shuiler's Child*—the most successful play presented by the society.

Despite a bad heart, which his doctors warned him would not stand undue strain, he worked extremely hard in nationalist circles before and after the 1916 Easter Rising. In 1918, after a short but fruitful life, he died, literally at his post, as editor of *Nationality*, the immediate successor of Griffith's newspaper, *Sinn Féin*.

Chapter Eleven

1908
Fays Depart, and the Cracks Appear

THE KINDEST thing that can be said of 1908 is that it failed to fulfil anyone's hopes of being a prosperous year for the Irish theatre.

It began badly, and ended on the sourest of notes. The first weeks brought further dissension in the Abbey Theatre company, resulting in the departure of Frank and Willie Fay. The year then closed with an unprovoked attack by Miss Horniman on the Theatre of Ireland, and a refusal to admit the society as an acting group to the Abbey stage.

Dublin learned little of the events that led up to the resignation of the Fays from the Abbey. As was natural, the brothers were reluctant to discuss publicly what was essentially a matter between them and the directors. But to the Theatre of Ireland their departure was merely the result of the policy that had been introduced into the theatre in 1905. In any event, whatever it was, the Fays had resigned. It was easily the saddest blow the theatre suffered.

It did not pass unnoticed that the society, which had started the movement of which the Abbey was a part, now had no real connection with the theatre. The Fays had been amongst the only members of the original company to remain with Yeats after 1905, and their resignation meant, in a sense, that the Abbey company was now almost entirely a new group. Their departure was the theatre's loss. It could ill afford to lose Willie Fay as an actor-producer or Frank as an elocution instructor. The loss of the latter was something from which it never really recovered. As a teacher of verse, Frank Fay was never replaced.

Although it must have touched them deeply forever to leave the movement for the foundation of which they were mainly responsible, their resignation did little to harm the Fays. Frank went back to his first love, his elocution lessons, and Willie departed to England, where his name was sufficiently established to get him the best of parts. There he made arrangements with a syndicate to produce some of the early Irish plays in New York. Early the following February, with a little company consisting of him, his wife, Bridget O'Dempsey, a former member of the Abbey company, as well as Frank, he sailed to the United States, where he introduced audiences to the wit of Lady Gregory and William Boyle with fair success. After that it was a short step to the top rung of the British theatrical ladder. He subsequently appeared with most of the bigger English companies. He played with Tree for a season in London.

Frank Fay carved his own little niche on the professional stage. Eventually, however, he returned to Ireland, where he began to practise extensively as an elocution teacher. He became adviser to numerous Dublin dramatic companies and taught voice production at a number of ecclesiastical colleges in the provinces. He trained a select number of private pupils, most of whom, by their success on the stage, have since displayed the care their teacher lavished upon them. The most famous pupil whom Frank Fay tutored during this period is probably the late F. J. McCormick.

With the passage of the years, Frank, although he was still doing more for Irish acting than any other man of his generation, slipped quietly out of the public eye. When he died, one of the greatest personages of the Irish theatre passed. It is ironic that few of those who patronised the Abbey throughout the years realised that the quiet-looking dark-eyed man whose image gazed across the little vestibule was the one to whom every Irish player for the past fifty years owed his reputation. Not only the Irish theatre, but Ireland, owes a debt to Frank Fay, which it has still done little to repay.

*

The Abbey opened its 1908 season in February with a new play, *The Man who Missed the Tide*, by a Dublin writer, W. F. Casey. This is worth passing mention, not for the quality of the play itself but because it was the first piece given in the Abbey that had a Dublin setting.

It drew full houses. For the first time Dubliners were able to see themselves on the stage, and they took happily to the idea. The play is notable also because it brought forward a young Dublin actor, Fred O'Donovan, new to the Abbey, who was later to enjoy distinction as the theatre's juvenile lead. O'Donovan's acting was reminiscent of the work of Dudley Digges, whose place had never been filled since his departure in 1903. His work had all the quiet power Digges's had: the naturally clear enunciation and clean, straightforward method.

O'Donovan remained for many years with the Abbey before he followed his predecessors to the English stage, and from 1908 onwards filled a variety of parts too numerous to mention. Of the many characters he created, three stand out. His careful, almost painfully realistic portrayal of Hugh, the idealist son, in T. C. Murray's *Birthright* in 1910; his Maurice Harte in the play of the same name; and—a totally different type of part—his bumptious, much- misunderstood Denis in the original production of Lennox Robinson's *The Whiteheaded Boy*. One remembers his Playboy too, during the stormy days of the Abbey's 1911 American tour. His interpretation of the part came closer to that of Willie Fay's than any before or since.

Early in the year, Miss Horniman, who since the establishment of the Abbey had been concentrating on the development of drama in her native Manchester, opened in one of the larger Dublin theatres with a company of English professionals, which she had formed some months before with William Poel and Ben Iden Payne. The play was Shaw's *Widower's Houses*, and the production probably marked the appearance of the group that was later named the Gaiety Repertory Company and established in Manchester with the Gaiety Theatre there as headquarters.

During its first English season, some months later, Sara Allgood appeared with this company opposite Basil Dean.

Subsequent productions included *Candida*, and Poel's production in the Elizabethan fashion of *Measure for Measure*. This venture also introduced several new dramatists to the British public, a number of them young Manchester writers, and was directly responsible for the bestowal of an honorary degree of Master of Arts on Miss Horniman for her contribution to the English theatre.

Meanwhile, in face of all this progress, the Theatre of Ireland continued on its modest way. In April, with a rapidly growing membership and an uncomfortably small bank account, we forsook our quarters in High Street and rented rooms over a shop in Harcourt Street. These, although small, were adequate for our rehearsal needs since it was understood that from then on all our productions would take place at the Abbey. The Morrows decorated them throughout in artistic and appropriate fashion and provided the necessary bohemian atmosphere by the judicious distribution of old posters and odd scraps of scenery. We settled in, and as on a somewhat similar occasion in 1902, prayed quietly but fervently that the future would provide some means by which we could pay the rent.

We began rehearsals for our next appearance, arranged for 22 May at the Abbey. The plays chosen were Colum's short one-act *The Miracle of the Corn*; *The Enthusiast* by Lewis Purcell; and a revival of Edward Martyn's *Maeve*. The production was an odd mixture of good and bad. Considerable chopping and changing during rehearsals, the dropping out of players and the holdups that ensued until suitable substitutes were found—there was always a shortage of understudies—told in the performances of the two shorter plays.

The only redeeming feature of the appearance was *Maeve*, the cast of which had managed to stay together. It is a play that might have taxed the resources of a better group, but this production received praise in the proper quarters and, what was more important, from its author, who paid a special visit to Dublin to offer personal congratulations.

The most unpleasant feature of 1908 developed about the middle of November. That month the Theatre of Ireland gave a performance at the Abbey of a new play by Seumas O'Kelly, *The Flame on the Hearth*, a short but effective little piece, subsequently retitled *The Stranger*, which dealt with an incident during the Fenian rising of 1798. With this was given a special performance of Rutherford Mayne's *The Turn of the Road*, in which the author himself took part. Both plays were well accepted, particularly the Belfast one.

The following week, at the invitation of William Mollison, who, with Mayne, was giving a season of plays in Dublin, we appeared with even greater success at the Gaiety. It was the first time an Irish company had appeared with an Irish play outside the Abbey, or any of the downtown halls in the city. 'No more significant event,' wrote one man, 'has taken place since the production in the Gaiety of Dr Hyde's *The Twisting of the Rope*.'

The unfortunate matter that now developed was the result of our Gaiety appearance. Through a mistake on the part of our hosts, the advertisement announcing the Theatre of Ireland production titled us 'The Abbey Theatre Company'. It was an error that was soon corrected through the letter columns of the next day's newspapers, but the damage was done. Miss Horniman, who had learned in London of the error, wrote a letter to the press disclaiming all connection with the Theatre of Ireland and forbidding it, for its 'discourtesy', from using the Abbey again for any of its productions.

A series of letters from the Theatre of Ireland committee followed in which the company apologised for any inconvenience that might have been caused, pointed out that the matter had been put right within a matter of hours, and asked Miss Horniman to reconsider her decision. She refused to accept any of the explanations or the apologies. For the few years of its lifetime that remained, the Theatre of Ireland never again appeared in the Abbey Theatre. Miss Horniman's action caused a fracture between the two companies that was never completely healed.

Chapter Twelve

1909–1910
Gipsy and the Countess

THE ABBEY suffered most as a result of the break-up. The publicity that the affair received resulted in widespread comment on the part of followers of both companies. To the majority it appeared a petty affair that could have been easily settled. Unfortunately for the Abbey, the Theatre of Ireland had the greater support, and its subsequent appearances flourished as a result. In March 1909 we repeated the programme that had caused the break, this time appearing before a distinguished audience at the Rotunda in Parnell Square.

For me, this production is chiefly memorable because it gave my youngest sister, Gipsy—'Betty King'—her first grown-up part. As Jane Graeme in *The Turn of the Road* she displayed all the talent that was later to make her a popular member of the Abbey number two company.

Her arrival as an actress meant that four members of the Walker family were now on the stage: Frank and I had both been playing continually since 1902, Gipsy, and Annie, my second youngest sister, who had joined the Abbey a year earlier. Here as 'Eileen O'Doherty', Annie was playing leads with success and had already been mentioned as one of the most promising character actresses in the company. Within a year her name was to move to the top of all the theatre's programmes for her interpretation in T. C. Murray's *Birthright* of the mother, Maura Morrissey—a part she created.

Seumas O'Kelly gave the Theatre of Ireland his third play in April 1909. *The Shuiler's Child* has since been described as one of the most memorable Irish plays produced in Dublin during these years. It is a work of great power and intensity, and its theme is a powerful one—the love of men and women for a child—and definitely placed O'Kelly in the front rank of the younger Irish dramatists. It tells of Moll Woods, an itinerant, who has abandoned her only child to the workhouse, from which he is taken by Andy and Nannie O'Hea, a childless couple living in comfortable circumstances.

The shuiler, calling by chance at the O'Heas' farmhouse, sees the child, and her feeling for him is reawakened. Her desire to have him back is aggravated by the visit of a government inspector who mistakenly considers that the child would be better cared for elsewhere. To prevent him being taken where she may never find him again, the shuiler reclaims the child and goes back with him to the workhouse. Her action breaks up the O'Hea household.

She later leaves the workhouse again and takes to the roads with the child. Realising the comfort that has been his with the O'Heas, she finds her way back to the farmhouse, bringing him with her. After the child has been restored to the O'Heas she finds that a warrant has been issued for her arrest for desertion. The play ends with her wild denunciation of the circumstances in which she finds herself, and she departs with the police, leaving the child behind her in the comfort of a home.

A bare outline of the plot does not do justice to the play, which paints a harshly realistic picture of an abandoned woman torn by circumstance. The figure of Moll Woods is clearly and painstakingly drawn. One sees a woman, once respectable, fighting wildly but vainly against the circumstances that have almost killed her maternal instincts, turning her into a vagrant and an outcast, despised by even her own child. She is a woman of wild moods and sudden fancies, longing for her own restoration, overwhelmed as she sees her only possession slipping away from her towards another woman whom she hates because she is all that she herself desires to be.

From a review in *Sinn Féin*:

Cluithcheoiri na hÉireann has produced its best play, and produced it well. *The Shuiler's Child* is the finest character study seen on the stage in Dublin for several years, and the only play written by a living Irishman about the life of our day that can be called tragedy. [...] We have now got a dramatist who is not afraid to face life, and he has given us a tragedy such as the author of *Widower's Houses* might have written if he had stuck to his country. [...] Seumas O'Kelly has shown that our selfishness and our stupidity have much more to do with our tragedies than Fate has. It was not Fate that made havoc of Moll Woods' life, but remedial causes. Why these causes exist is not explained by the figments we invent to cover our sins and our cowardice, but by our own selfishness. [...] If a hundred men had conceived the idea of *The Shuiler's Child*, ninety-nine would have failed in Moll Woods, and we would have had but another of those unconvincing sketches which pass for drama. Seumas O'Kelly is the hundredth man. His Moll Woods is a woman, and *the* woman. The dramatist has projected himself into the woman's mind—the woman's soul—and given us tragedy.

For this production of *The Shuiler's Child*, Morrow assembled a most interesting cast. Austin Martin, who played Andy O'Hea, the young husband, was a clever actor who had done some work with different companies in the city, and the part of Sara Finnessy, the gossiping neighbour, was taken by Lady Nellie O'Connell, the wife of Sir John O'Connell of Killiney, an eminent legal man, and I think some relative of Norrys Connell, the playwright-manager of the Abbey at that time, whose play *The Piper* had aroused almost as much controversy as the *Playboy* when it was produced in 1910.

The part of Tim O'Halloran, the poor law relieving officer, was played by James Stephens, at that time a young and comparatively unknown writer, for his great novel, *The Crock of Gold*, had still to be written. He was an enthusiastic follower of the theatre in Dublin. He was keenly interested in the Theatre of Ireland and, gleefully, as was his way, he had offered his services as a player.

There were those who said that he was no stranger to the stage. I heard it said that at some time during his earlier days he had been a member of a travelling company or a circus, and that he had once appeared as a clown. Indeed, it might have been true: he was game for anything; he was a gay little man, always making jokes and laughing. When he rehearsed for a play he chuckled his way through his role, and he was full of quaint mannerisms and sayings. When programmes were being written he always had the order of his names reversed to Stephen James. I never knew why.

He would go off alone to some quiet corner of the room and hunch his little figure over the script, emerging only now and then to take up a cue or make some joke. He was a bit of a practical joker in his own way. I remember a joke he played on the first night of this play. He must have hidden himself away while he made up for his part; none of us saw him until he walked onto the stage. I still recall the shock I got when he appeared. He wore a stubby grey beard and bushy eyebrows, trousers too long, and an old body-coat. To crown this he had a battered half-tall hat that he removed at intervals in the course of the action and held clasped to his breast. He was a remarkable sight, and I think he must have enjoyed himself immensely. Someone said later that he looked like one of his own leprechauns dressed up for a day in the city.

The most interesting member of this whole cast was Countess Markievicz. She played a small part as a visiting government official. Madame was a memorable soul. To everything she did she brought much of the vigour that had made her one of the most colourful figures of the whole national scene; the idol of every young girl with a spark of nationalism; the colleague in later years of the Labour leader, James Connolly, during the great industrial strike and lockout of 1913, who was to march with the Citizen

Army in 1916 and later to be the first woman elected to a seat in an Irish Parliament.

Madame was an early member of the Theatre of Ireland— she had played my old part of Lavarcham in Morrow's revival of A. E.'s *Deirdre*—but she was rather unpredictable as an actress. On stage, her enthusiasm for the work occasionally carried her away. She could never quite sink her own vivid personality in a role. She had been a follower of the old National Theatre Society from the beginning. She had often visited us at Camden Street. I can remember her still—I could never quite forget her, for she was, I think, the most remarkable woman I ever knew—coming down to rehearsals in her brown tweeds, a dog always at her heels.

She would have been in her late thirties then, a lovely woman. It was said that as a young girl presented at court she had dazzled a distinguished gathering of nobles. But she seldom made any attempt to show off her beauty; she was completely indifferent to her appearance. I saw her in evening dress only once, and I can still remember my surprise: it was like looking at a different woman. A few touches to her hair, a Paris gown, and she was completely changed. Her beauty had character. It was easy to imagine her as Constance Gore-Booth, the young girl who had ridden to hounds, been presented at court, and been sought by every eligible young man of standing in the country. She had thrown all this away for her work as a nationalist in Dublin.

Madame always came down to meetings and rehearsals by motor. She had an old two-seater car, well known in Dublin. She used to drive this around the city as fast as it would go. Its joints rattled and clanked, but Madame sat at the wheel, every bit of her enjoying it. Sometimes the dog sat beside her, sometimes there would be a passenger or two, maybe some of her Fianna boy scouts. The scout force she founded in 1909 was one of the first of its kind in the world. It was a purely national movement, and its inspiration was the ancient Fianna Éireann of Finn McCool. It was in the old Camden Street Hall that Madame launched it a few years after the National Theatre Society went into the Abbey.

Madame Markievicz was a light to us all. There never was anyone like her. When she came to Dublin first, in 1900, she was one of the most active workers of Inghinidhe na hÉireann, and it was there that I met her first. Around her and her husband she gathered a most interesting circle. The theatre took its place in it. Madame attended all the first nights, discussed plays, acted in them, and later produced some when she began a dramatic company of her own in the city. She wrote a lot for the stage too, and all her plays were successful, even if they weren't masterpieces. They were all on national topics, and most of them had enormous casts: when Madame wrote a play she wrote parts for her entire company. There would be five or six changes of scenery, and usually a spectacular climax. She loved a play that was vigorous and full of action.

The latter part of 1909 is chiefly memorable for the production of a Gaelic version in four acts of the story of Deirdre. The author, Father Thomas O'Kelly, who was the fourth Irish writer to dramatise the story since 1900—Yeats's version had been produced at the Abbey in 1906, and Synge was completing his own *Deirdre of the Sorrows*—was then a professor at Summerhill College, Sligo, and had just won the Gaelic League Oireachtas drama prize with the play in manuscript form. The work had aroused so much interest that the Ard Craobh or head branch of the Gaelic League meeting at Parnell Square had approached Fred Morrow and offered to supply a cast if he would produce the play for it with some of us in the leading parts.

The production took place on 12 December at the Round Room of the Rotunda, and was an immediate, and it must be added a surprising, success. Every performance of the play, which ran for three nights, was well attended, the audiences were enthusiastic and the press was flattering. All of which was surprising, for Gaelic plays, although frequently produced in the city then, were seldom successful. Father O'Kelly's *Deirdre* proved the exception, and should receive special mention because its cast was the direct forerunner of what was probably the first important Gaelic theatre company in Dublin. Its success proved that plays in Gaelic could be popularised if promoters concerned themselves not with original subjects but with translations of former Irish theatre successes.

This theory was borne out in 1913 when the Gaelic League formed a permanent company and produced translations by An Seabhac, Father O'Kelly, Seán Mac Giolla an Atha, and Mrs MacDonagh-Mahoney in Dublin. Before 1916 this little company flourished, and at times rivalled the Abbey and kindred companies in popularity with translations of *Birthright*, *Kathleen Ni Houlihan*, *The Shuiler's Child* and *Spreading the News*. Unfortunately, like many other enterprises founded during this period, it faltered with the changes in political affairs after 1915, and did not survive the Easter Rising of the next year.

In April 1910, the Abbey took the first of a series of steps towards establishing itself as an independent theatre when a newspaper statement confirmed a rumour that Yeats and Lady Gregory had arranged to purchase the theatre from Miss Horniman. An experiment begun towards the end of the preceding month of keeping the theatre open for most nights in the week had satisfied the directorate that it might be possible for the Abbey to continue without the subsidy guaranteed by Miss Horniman if it could depend on some small help from sources inside the country. An appeal was subsequently issued for subscriptions.

In May I received a letter from Lady Gregory asking me to rejoin the theatre as an actress. It was hoped, she said, to take the company on tour to America in the near future, and as soon as Miss Horniman handed over the theatre a second company would be formed. This, which would be something in the nature of a school of acting, would keep the theatre open while the original company was on tour. A semi-professional body, it would be under the direction of a new producer, Mr Nugent Monck, an Irishman who had studied under William Poel.

Now that the Abbey was about to establish itself as an independent unsubsidised concern, she hoped that old differences would be forgotten and that I would accept the position of leading lady with the new second company. Monck intended to concentrate on the production of verse-plays, and needed someone who was already trained to take leading parts. The new company would not be formed until about the middle of 1911. If I agreed to return to the Abbey I would have an opportunity of appearing in some of my old parts with the number one company before it left for America. A special production of *The Shuiler's Child*, in which I would have my old part of Moll Woods, would mark my return.

It was in many ways an attractive proposal, and one that the Theatre of Ireland urged me to accept. That was, of course, the most practical thing to do, if only because the offer constituted a permanent job. Although in almost ten years on the Irish stage I had earned some reputation as an actress, I had never drawn a salary for acting in my life. My position had meant that unless I wished to go on the English stage I had to earn my living otherwise in Dublin and make acting in Ireland a hobby rather than a profession. An offer to provide me with good parts in the city, and to pay me for it, was something worth considering.

In November 1910 I accepted the offer, and returned on the understanding that I would tour and act with the main Abbey company until the second group was formed the next year.

Playing again with the Abbey, one could not help noticing that the theatre had changed much in five years. New faces had come and gone, and the new plays that had arrived with the years had helped to create a slightly new style of acting to which it was rather difficult to become accustomed. Petty individual squabbles about stage-stealing were not infrequent. A brisker, more businesslike atmosphere was noticeable at rehearsals. Players had now become mere employees, and had no say whatever in the running of the theatre.

There were also many strange structural changes in the building. The old green room was gone; in its place was a modern coffee bar. The premises to the left of the pit entrance in Abbey Street had been acquired, and that portion of them which ran parallel with the Abbey stage had been converted into a series of dressing rooms. On that side, too, was the new green room—a specially built one, hung already with some of the theatre's trophies. Over the vestibule the rooms that had once been dressing rooms were now the offices of the directorate.

But more than anything else in this new Abbey one missed the Fays and A. E. It was remarkable how much a part of the theatre these men had been. A. E. had been the prop upon which the old National Theatre Society had leaned; the real leader under whose patronage we had worked, and whose place could never be filled.

One could never quite accept Yeats and Lady Gregory as the supreme directors. With the Fays had gone the personal atmosphere that had characterised the theatre of 1904 and 1905. The businesslike atmosphere that surrounds all well-run organisations was out of place in the Abbey to me.

Waiting for stage-calls in the green room, or moving behind the stage before making an entrance, one was conscious too of another loss. There was no Synge sitting in the wings or conversing quietly with the players. The author of the *Playboy* had died in a Dublin nursing home a year earlier.

Rehearsals for *The Shuiler's Child* began on about 7 November. Lennox Robinson produced O'Kelly's play. It was a pleasure to work with this tall, quietly spoken man, and good too to note that his work as a producer was very much in keeping with the traditions of the earlier Abbey. He slipped quietly into the auditorium, draping his long legs over a vacant seat and only occasionally raising his thin, rather tired voice to give directions.

The first Abbey production of *The Shuiler's Child* on 24 November received as much praise as had the earlier production by the Theatre of Ireland. It was the last production but one of the Abbey 1910 season. The theatre closed the year with Lady Gregory's *Coats*. In the intervening period, the application for the renewal of the Abbey patent came up at Dublin Castle. Lady Gregory applied, there were no objections by other theatres, and the matter, little more than a formality, went through quietly. On 29 November Miss Horniman officially relinquished her interest in the theatre, and the directorate in Dublin took over control for the next twenty-one years.

Late in January, Nugent Monck, a small, pleasantly spoken man, produced the first Abbey presentation of Lord Dunsaney's *King Argimenes and the Unkown Warrior* with a revival of Yeats's *The Land of Heart's Desire*. Shortly afterwards he began to gather personnel for the new second company. This temporarily released the permanent players, and as a last outside appearance before the suggested American visit, for which arrangements were then almost completed, we made a two-months tour of England, beginning on 1 May at Stratford-upon-Avon and working towards London, where the Court Theatre had been taken for the season.

At Stratford, in the Memorial Theatre, we presented the *Playboy*. Synge's play, produced now as a rapid comedy, went well with a distinguished audience. At Scarborough, which we reached two days later, we were unlucky to meet with the finest of summer weather—always fatal for the theatre at a holiday resort. On our first night here we gave the *Playboy* with *Kathleen Ni Houlihan* and Lady Gregory's short *Rising of the Moon*, and despite the fact that the audience was small, got a reception that was in marked contrast to that accorded to Synge's play on its first production in Dublin.

In the review of the play that appeared in the next day's press, a writer, after deploring the attendance, went on to say:

> The chief piece of the triple-bill, the late Mr J. M. Synge's three-act comedy, *The Playboy of the Western World*, is, no doubt, foreign in complexion to the average playgoer: its theme is so novel as almost to jar on ordinary sentiments. But with such delightful picturesqueness and natural charm, with life palpitating through every situation, is the play presented that the swagger of the 'young fellow' who has 'destroyed his da', the mingling of savagery and gentleness in the girl he wins, and the farce which resolves from the whole affair, all exercises a fascination that is quite out of the common. It is all so quaint and wildly romantic [...] and despite a bewilderment of peculiar phraseology, one reads right into the heart of the Irish peasant character.

Any hopes I had of playing leads with the Abbey in Dublin were dashed in September of this year, soon after our return from London. Maire O'Neill, who shared the position of leading lady with Sara Allgood, became ill, and since there was no one else to fill the vacancy created I was chosen to take her place on tour in America. The news came on the Friday before the company was due to sail. I found myself with little more than three days in which to prepare for a tour halfway across the United States.

Luckily, kind friends came to my assistance. The following Tuesday, 12 September 1911, with trunks hurriedly packed, I sailed with sixteen other members of the company for Boston.

Part Three

The Abbey in America

Chapter Thirteen

1911
The Western World Goes
Wild for *Playboy*

THE TOUR was expected to last for a little over two months. On 23 September, which was just over a week ahead, we were to dock at Boston where we might stay for about three weeks, afterwards going on to New York, Philadelphia and possibly Chicago. En route we hoped to touch several small towns in Massachusetts, New Jersey, Connecticut and Indiana. In Boston we were billed to open a new Leibler theatre, The Plymouth.

Lennox Robinson and W. B. Yeats led the company. The latter, although travelling with us, did not intend to remain in America for the whole tour. Lady Gregory had been delayed in Dublin, and he intended to look after our affairs until she arrived the next week to supervise the final rehearsals of the *Playboy*. We hoped to present Synge's play towards the end of our stay in Boston, since there had been rumours that some sort of trouble—not defined, from circles that, it was suggested, might have their headquarters in Dublin—might surround its production.

There were seventeen in the party: Robinson and Yeats, Sara Allgood, J. M. Dolan, Kathleen Drago, J. M. Kerrigan, Sidney J. Morgan, Agnes McGlade (Una O'Connor), Eithne Magee, Cathleen Nesbitt, Fred O'Donovan, J. A. O'Rourke, Arthur Sinclair, J. Weldon (Brinsley MacNamara), Dossie Wright, Annie, and me. None of the players had been in America before.

There were three newcomers to the company, all of whom had been picked up during the summer tour to England. Cathleen Nesbitt had some experience of the English stage, whither she had since returned with complete success; Una O'Connor was a North of Ireland actress whom Lady Gregory had interviewed at the Court Theatre in London, and who is now in Hollywood; and Kathleen Drago was a young but by no means untalented ex-amateur, whose work with the National Stage Company had attracted much notice in the Dublin press.

Despite her years—she was a little over sixteen—this girl had already been mentioned as one of the upcoming great Irish character actresses. She had a future before her that her death at an early age cut short. Although she came to the Abbey with little experience of the professional stage, she rapidly ascended to the top of all the theatre's programmes, and was one of the really great that the Abbey produced. Her greatest part during the years that followed was as the crippled girl in Lennox Robinson's *Patriots*, a play that excited considerable comment during its first production in Dublin.

It was an eventful trip. We were not due in Boston for nine days, but we made full use of the time with rehearsals, and on one occasion a public appearance with one of Lady Gregory's comedies for the benefit of the Seamen's Fund. We disembarked in a welter of high-pressure American journalism. The ship berthed and the gangways became thronged with photographers and reporters, young men who persisted in stopping us and writing everything we said, irrelevant or not, in gigantic notebooks. We were herded together on the quayside facing a battery of cameras almost before we knew we had stepped onto American soil.

There was a bewildering mixture of questioning accents, a confused impression of the customs, a glimpse of Yeats towering elegantly above a group of respectful reporters, and a brief moment of anxiety when I found myself estranged from the other members of my party in an overwhelming, steam-heated customs shed, then Annie and I were away from it all.

We stayed at a quiet hotel near Mount Vernon Street, within easy reach of the theatre, which was in Elliot, a few doors west of

Tremont Street. Before our evening meal the newspapers arrived, and there we were, most of us, spread across a prominent page, with an inset of Yeats. 'Irish players on steamer *Zeeland*' said a rather startling headline. 'Abbey company of Dublin reaches Boston'.

The press welcomed us enthusiastically—almost too enthusiastically, one might say: some of the reports were colourful in the extreme. One article described us as 'the only theatrical organisation in Dublin,' adding that we had 'the most elegant brogue, to be sure,' and that our names were well known 'all over the Emerald Isle.'

Another report, surprisingly, quoted a member of the company as saying, of the entertainment on board, that:

> ... all the ladies of the company danced Irish jigs and sang Irish songs for the ship's company. [...] They put so much Irish earnestness into their work that the officers found a few bars of *God Save the King* necessary, whereupon the ladies of the company sat down promptly on the deck so that their standing up during the singing of the British National Anthem might not become a political demonstration. In Ireland, you know, *God Save the King* at once resolves society into its original elements.

After this, Boston itself was something of an anticlimax. The popular conception of America as a land of rush and tall buildings was speedily dispelled. It was pleasant to find a city that resembled in everything except size one of the larger English university towns. Boston was full of beautiful buildings, quiet suburbs and well-kept commons; Franklin Park was restful, as serene as Phoenix Park in Dublin. It was like a breath of Stephen's Green to sit in the common that we crossed each day to rehearsals.

The Plymouth Theatre looked very solid, very big and very impressive to Dublin eyes. Although small in comparison with the other theatres in which we were to play, it was larger than anything we had seen outside the London West End.

The auditorium itself was little enough, but purpose-built to achieve a feeling of intimacy between player and audience. In this respect it was the intention of the lessees to have it as much as possible like the Duke of York's, or Antoine's *Théâtre Libre*, or the Abbey.

There was nothing very American, very ornate, about the appointments, but neither was there anything coldly formal. Backstage there was ample room for movement, and there was a magnificent scene-dock into which our simple scenery fitted easily, looking rather mournful. When the first box was erected, it was, as a critic later put it, 'there at the expense of a good deal of audience space.'

We opened on 23 September, a Saturday, with a triple-bill: *In the Shadow of the Glen*, *Birthright* and *Hyacinth Halvey*. All the leading citizens of Boston were present, and a large mayoral party occupied two boxes. If we had tasted sensational American journalism earlier, it was nothing to what we got after our appearance. The Sunday newspapers, resembling quarterly magazines more than anything else—some of them were at least an inch and a half thick—devoted much space to the plays. The opening of the new theatre, the attendance of the mayor and most of the leading citizens, coupled with the novelty of the acting, gave writers abundant material for long reports.

Reviewers extended themselves, and some of the more conservative publications went out of their way to congratulate us. Synge's play was undoubtedly the success of the evening, and much time was spent in emphasising the brilliance of its construction:

No one who knows the rural life of Ireland can fail to recognize the domestic scenes and personages seen at The Plymouth as types he knew in every hamlet of his acquaintance. [...] In both *The Shadow of the Glen* and *Birthright*, the spectator who knows his Ireland forgets the theatre for the time being, finds himself watching scenes that are as real and true as any he has seen himself in many scores of places.

Synge himself came in for quite a bit of comment, all congratulatory:

> Synge is freely granted recognition as the greatest of Irish dramatists. He must be given consideration as amongst the ablest of any nationality.

The novelty of the acting was almost too much for some writers, and they nearly ran out of superlatives:

> There is little suggestion of theatrical artifice in their work. [...] Simplicity and naturalness is what they strive for and what they accomplish.

> These actors remind one of the best traditions of the French school.

> It was a night of surprises [...] in a word, of unprecedented theatrical pleasure.

> The passionate sincerity of the acting provides a novel experience for the auditor in these days of polished stage artifice.

We were a complete success.

We repeated our first-night bill the following Monday, then went on to give *The Well of the Saints* and *The Workhouse Ward*, shuffling all five plays during the following days until the end of the week. With our second bill we scored again, although some writers professed to be at something of a loss to recognise Synge's motive in his three-act play. This puzzlement apparently extended to sections of the audience itself, and came in for some humorous comment from a few of the more popular writers. From one review:

> *The Well of the Saints* is, like all Synge's work, poetic in conception and speech, but the deepest of us scholars

can't tell you exactly what may be its point, its meaning. At a recent performance of it, a gentleman—a scholarly soul—sat in the darkened auditorium with a copy of the play and a little electric light—an intellectual dark lantern—with the aid of which he frequently compared the speech of the actors with the print of the book (Oh, Boston, Boston!) Perhaps he can tell you what the play means. Certainly as the performance advanced he threw light on the dark places.

We had a good laugh over this at the time, but it was not long before we were able to appreciate the significance of the lantern, and the reader's application to it, as I shall tell later.

On 2 October—the first night of our second week—I had my first taste of these audiences when we gave *Riders to the Sea* as a curtain-raiser for Boyle's *The Eloquent Dempsey*. As expected, they were mostly pleasant, at times unrestrainedly enthusiastic, and generally sympathetic. The lower portions of the house remained still, almost uncannily so, but throughout the whole week the galleries, which appeared to hold some of those who had come expecting to see either Irish vaudeville or plays of the 'begorrah' school, upset us with raucous laughter. Apparently, some of the lines were not understood; the most lyrical and dramatic passages were greeted with cheers against which it was difficult to act.

The press greeted *Riders to the Sea* with enthusiasm; *The Eloquent Dempsey* swept on to victory from its first curtain. The political flavour of Boyle's comedy struck a chord in the hearts of most Bostonians. As the sly provincial Irish shopkeeper who attempts desperately to remain loyal to nationalists and Unionists alike, Arthur Sinclair appeared at his best. Each performance was better than the last. It was in Boston, I believe, that the first of those offers from theatrical companies was thrust upon him, but he refused to accept any of these and returned with the Abbey company to Dublin, where he stayed for many years.

Towards the end of our first week, Lady Gregory arrived and took over rehearsals of the *Playboy*. The play had already received some mention in the newspapers: some writers had commented on the riots during its first production in Dublin. There had been some speculation as to how it would be received by Irish America. Our progress to date had overcome any fears we might have had regarding the production of the play in Boston—or elsewhere—and a few rumours that there would be trouble if it was produced, which had reached us in Dublin before we left, seemed unfounded.

Our surprise can be understood when, in an edition of a Boston paper on 5 October, a reader's letter appeared, condemning us and our work. This letter, containing the first real hint of opposition on the part of Irish-American audiences, was the beginning of a controversy that was to rage for the next weeks. Echoes of it were to follow us across the country for the rest of our visit.

It ran to the best part of a column, summarised our progress in Boston, mentioned the ideals of the company as set out by Yeats, then went on to wonder at 'the parrot-like praise of the dramatic critics,' adding that some of the plays were 'an abomination which outraged every sentiment and feeling of the Irish heart.' It continued:

> I know almost every hill and glen in Ireland and the people who dwell therein. For 35 years I have seen almost every so-called Irish play, from the absurdly romantic to the burlesque, in which the green-whiskered baboon played his antics. But I never saw anything so vile, beastly and unnatural, so calculated to calumniate, degrade and defame a people and all they hold sacred and dear as the plays of the so-called Irish players.
>
> Nothing but a hell-inspired ingenuity and a satanic hatred of the Irish people and their religion could suggest, construct and influence the production of such plays. On God's earth the beastly creatures of the plays never existed. [...] They are not alone anti-national, anti-Catholic, but anti-Christian. [...] I first thought Mr Yeats was playing a grim joke on Boston audiences. Next I thought him insane. But there is method in his

madness. Through every play one purpose runs. And that is to show that the Irish people are too savage, crude and unreliable to be trusted with Home Rule; in fact unfit for anything but fettered slavery. Secondly, to show their boasted morals and religion are a myth, for contempt of both is expressed many times in every play I witnessed Saturday night.

Lady Gregory's comedy, *Hyacinth Halvey*, is the silliest and most unmitigated rot that was ever called a play. The only human character in it is, of course, the representative of England—the peeler. A man in Charlestown was fined because a policeman said he uttered a blasphemy in calling him a d—mn liar. Cursing, swearing and blaspheming is the rule in these plays, and I have not heard of any arrests.

Irishmen of Boston, what are you going to do about it? Writing letters will not do any good. The time has come to call the Health Board of Public Opinion to coffin and seal up these festering plays and consign them to oblivion without a candle or a wake.

Yeats replied to all the accusations. Mentioning that they seemed to be based upon a single misunderstanding of the nature of literature, he spoke of Synge and realism in the theatre.

Synge was not photographing life; he was representing it as an artist. His accusers seem to believe that the characters in a work of art must be typical representatives of the people of the place where the scene is laid.

Don Quixote was typical of something in Cervantes' mind, as Macbeth or Iago or Shylock were typical of something in Shakespeare's mind. Art deals with the exceptional, and it uses local knowledge to make vivid to our senses personages who represented states of mind that are in some degree in the minds of all men. An artist brings terrible august persons and makes them inhabitants of some real or imaginary place. Only the fool takes them for villagers. He may have observed something like them, but he has so expanded and intensified that he has transformed what his eyes have seen out of all recognition.

By local knowledge the artist creates his illusion; it is merely a fiction that is mixed into his truth. When he represents his country he does so because he has intimately in himself a portion of its mind carried to its highest power and deepened by great knowledge. Even historical plays are not historic, for it was Goethe who said: 'We do the persons of history the honour of giving to our own minds their names.'

Synge's mind was Irish, but what he showed (full as it was of incidental truth, or traditional phrases, of profound observation of local character) was to perfect an expression of that mind to represent any one Irish locality. He was as Irish as Cervantes was Spanish. *Don Quixote*, a work of supreme intensity, is true of all human life, and it is the glory of Spain that one of its writers has been able to express a universal truth while seeming to be expressing a local one. But you cannot make omelettes without breaking eggs, and I can imagine a patriotic Spaniard who thought it did but poor justice to the gentlemen and peasantry of Spain.

Only the Irish and Jewish people are at present sensitive in this way, and it is very natural that they should be, considering their history. In Dublin, Synge's *Playboy of the Western World*, which at first seemed to offend the sensibilities of many, has overcome the hostility which greeted it at first: it has won its fight and now when we produce it it attracts large and enthusiastic audiences. It is not asking too much that what Irish Dublin accepts ought not to be rejected by Irish America without much thought, nor is it perhaps saying too much to suggest that Dublin might know its Ireland better than those for whom Ireland is but a memory or a tradition.

The press made much of the controversy. The following Sunday a newspaper devoted a full page to the case, giving the personal views of citizens of Irish extraction. From this it appeared that the Irish population was about equally divided over the plays. We learned that the Irish county clubs were active in the matter and that a committee had been appointed whose duty it was to attend every play and report any objectionable features that might appear. It was stated that if any features radically detrimental to the Irish race came to light, it was intended to hold a mass meeting, denounce the methods of the company and ask for the suppression of the plays by the authorities.

The newly formed committee had already waited on the management and talked the matter over. After the show it had a meeting and compared notes. As yet it had no report to make officially. A member of the committee was quoted as saying that all the plays witnessed up to and including Thursday of that week, while not heaping any abuse on the Irish race, 'did not elevate it any'. It was intended to continue attending the productions and to protest when the time was right.

On Monday, 9 October we gave a quadruple-bill consisting of *Falsely True*, a one-act play by Johanna Redmond (a daughter of John Redmond, the Irish politician); Lady Gregory's *Jackdaw* and *The Workhouse Ward*, and Yeats's *Hour-glass*. We had good audiences for all these plays, but now the press began to advise the company. The suggestion was to:

> … stick to the good plays done so well—the powerful, artistic Synge pieces, Lady Gregory's *Hyacinth Halvey*, *The Workhouse Ward*, *Spreading the News*, *The Rising of the Moon*, *The Building Fund* and Shaw's *The Shewing up of Blanco Posnet*, etc.

Some of the other productions did not impress, it was stated, and would not be popular.

Our week drew to a close. The following Monday we were due to open with the *Playboy*, playing for seven days. The drama committee of a council of Irish county associations published a statement regretting the necessity that compelled it to denounce the plays, which were described as 'un-Irish exhibitions'. This was followed on the fourteenth, two days before the play was put on, with more condemnations from New York.

When Sunday came we were all feeling a little nervous. It seemed to be the opinion of our friends in Boston that if there was going to be any trouble it would come to a head with the production of the *Playboy*, and would probably be engineered from Dublin. Going into the matter, few of us could see how there could be any trouble as most of the passages in Synge's play that had caused offence in Dublin had been eliminated. In any case, one felt that the play should first be produced before there were any objections.

It was with mixed feelings that we assembled behind the drawn curtains on Monday, but there was little cause for worry. Our reception, although it left much to be desired, never developed into a riot. Halfway through the evening there was a slight disturbance in the upper part of the house, a murmur of voices, followed by a prolonged hiss and some booing. Almost immediately there were sounds of movement, a few snatches of conversation too far away to hear, and a scuffling of feet. That was all.

Afterwards we learned that an attempt to cause trouble had been forestalled by the ejection of a number of people. The rest of the play went through satisfactorily. Although we did not know it at the time, the Mayor of Boston had sent an official from his department, Mr William A. Leahy, to judge the play and report any offensive passages in it. This man saw the mayor later and said that there was nothing in the piece, as he saw it, to offend anyone. He was later joined in this opinion by an official police censor who had also been present.

To our relief, all further attempts to make trouble in Boston fell flat. Towards midweek there was a further echo of protest from New York, which told us that feeling had far from died down there. A society protested against the performance of the *Playboy* in the States, 'seeing that that contentious play had been produced in Boston a few evenings ago amid booing and chuckling.'

The protest went on to say that there were many Irish people who had not seen or read the play and who thought the protests were based only on flimsy grounds. These people, it said, reasoned that in Ireland, as in every country, there were people with a criminal instinct, so why object to the portrayal of crime on the stage? The plea, it added, arose from pure ignorance of the play or the harm it could do.

> The Irish peasant community depicted in this play are wholly low and debased; the whole idea is bizarre and improbable. The language is lewd and suggestive as well as vulgar, and the people who, knowing the play and all it means, and still wish to set it before the public and other people who want the Irish people misrepresented, are so tangled up in aesthetic flap doodle as to have their ideas of truth and right blinded.

This criticism was at least acceptable since it put forward a definite argument, but there was no excuse for the diatribes published in a newspaper the following week. Both Lady Gregory and Yeats were singled out, and a number of personal gibes slung at them.

The rest of our Boston appearance was, financially, a success. The Plymouth was crowded for the remainder of the week. Our visit was so successful that the company was invited to remain for a fortnight longer, all advance bookings.

On 30 October, after five successful weeks, we left the city, closing on a successful note with Boyle's *The Mineral Workers* and Lady Gregory's *Gaol-gate*.

Chapter Fourteen

1911
Roosevelt to the Rescue

OUR WAY to New York, the next big stop, was a roundabout one. We spent the greater part of a week weaving in and out through several 'smalls', touching Washington and some university towns en route. Providence, Rhode Island, a pleasant town, was our first stop. We arrived there one autumn morning. To our dismay, we learned that opposition to the *Playboy* was being organised here and that feeling ran very high.

There was a very strong Irish society in the town, which had joined forces with fellow organisations in Boston and New York. A deputation had gone to the Commissioner of Police requesting that he make all efforts to have the *Playboy* withdrawn from our repertoire, but Lady Gregory forestalled this by travelling ahead of us and placing the full facts of our position before the authorities, with a request that we be allowed to go on subject to subsequent disapproval by any censor. This suggestion was agreed to, and we put the *Playboy* on that night.

There was no trouble of any kind. The Commissioner attended the performance himself and posted police about the theatre. We had no compunction to agreeing to this. There was no parallel between seeking the protection of American police in America and English ones in Ireland. As it happened, the precautions were unnecessary. We did a light enough business; there were more empty seats than full ones.

We stayed two days there, but had little opportunity of seeing the town properly since most of the time was taken up with rehearsals. Annie and I lodged with family friends—an elderly couple whom we had met through the Abbey in Dublin. These, who were connected in some manner with the local societies that were objecting to us, warned us against going on with the *Playboy*. There was little enough danger in the small towns, they said, but the New York position was getting more serious. We were asked to use our influence with the directors to have the play withdrawn.

Many people, outsiders of the societies who admired the work of the company and were concerned with the players' safety, were worried about what might happen on Broadway. They feared a repetition of the Astor Place Opera House riots when military personnel had to be called out to prevent a mob from lynching performers.

Our host said, 'Most folk admire your spirit and the way you stand behind your arguments, but you can have no idea what may happen if you go against the wishes of these people. The societies are not the worst; they follow only the lead of others who claim to be authorities, and they do what they consider the best thing when they ask you to take off the play. But each place you pass through on your way, and defy by putting on the play, means another notch in your account when you reach the big cities.'

'There was trouble in Dublin...' we began.

'I know there was. But trouble in Dublin is one thing and trouble in America another. Over here, mobs tend to become violent. You mark my words....'

We touched Salem and New Haven, where we gave the *Playboy* to big audiences. Matters were still at simmering point over Synge's play, but these nights were devoid of incident. We might almost have forgotten the earlier trouble if it had not been for the murmurs that still echoed through some of the newspapers. More New York periodicals had now taken up the cry, and occasional references to us still appeared in other city newspapers.

In Albany, which was one of the last stops before Washington, disaster overtook us when Sinclair, on his way from the dressing room to the stage, slipped on the iron stairway and injured his back. He was taken to hospital immediately, where after treatment he was stated to be not too seriously injured, but he was confined to bed for some days and we had to go on to Washington without him.

More trouble awaited us there. Before we opened we learned that some people had entered objections to the company and that a letter had been issued condemning Irish plays. The newspapers added that a number of societies had passed resolutions condemning the Abbey Theatre Company. The letter, published in the press, quoted portions of the first letter against us published in Boston. It attacked *all* the plays, which were described as 'vicious caricatures', and added that we came from Dublin followed by 'the hisses of an outraged populace', having virtually been kicked from the stage there. England, it added, gave us no reception.

On the other side of the question I learned from Lady Gregory that a branch of the Gaelic League in Washington had asked her to address a meeting, that she had done so, and was praised.

Inevitably, as soon as the letter condemning us was published the newspaper letter-writers joined in the campaign. Some of these—the less violent ones—were for boycotting the theatre at which we proposed to perform Synge; others contented themselves with lengthy, mostly unauthoritative reviews of the *Playboy*, of which most writers appeared to have a very slight knowledge.

Most of the attacks appeared to be directed at Synge's mind, which was taken to be a diseased one, drawing its sustenance from a decadent France rather than a godly Ireland. His characters were decadent puppets far from the haunts of their originals. One writer, in a long summary of the *Playboy* story, described all the men in the play as 'drunken sots', whose language, manners and actions were 'gross and barbarous', and whose only conception of enjoying life was by 'over-indulgence in liquor'.

This letter added that the defective moral sense of the Irish people was portrayed by 'the decadent author of the play' in the action of the heroine's father by inviting a 'black stranger' to remain alone in the house with his daughter while he went off 'to get drunk at a wake'. And Christy's phrase of the 'drift of chosen females' was interpreted by the writer as an insinuation that it was the custom in Ireland to line girls up in their underclothes in order to allow a prospective husband to pick a wife!

From the tone of most of the letters it appeared that few of those who were opposing us had even seen or read the plays they were condemning. Most of them seemed to have their information by word of mouth. They had little knowledge of either Synge or his work.

Lady Gregory—Yeats had since returned to Dublin—stood firm and apparently unconcerned. Her determination to carry on regardless of the result may have been mistaken policy, but watching her one could not but admire her.

So we progressed in the midst of a shower of verbal and written abuse, hurled at us from all sides, and in mid November we boarded a train for New York, where we were booked to play off Broadway, at the Maxine Elliott Theatre.

It was pleasant to discover that it was a comparatively small, solid building with a homely air about it. Backstage accommodation, as in other American theatres, was adequate, and the dressing rooms were well laid out, not too far from the stage. Altogether it was like a big Dublin theatre. Lady Gregory overcame the absence of a green room—few American theatres have these—by acquiring a small dressing room off the stage, which she fitted out with periodicals and books. This became something in the nature of a common room for the company, where we met friends and discussed the various situations that developed during our stay.

This first evening we met John Quinn, a lawyer friend of the company, to whom we had been introduced in Dublin some years before. He was a tall, quiet, easy-spoken man, deeply interested in our work, who had watched the theatre's career from the beginning. He took charge of our affairs, and although he did not travel on with us afterwards he followed our movements closely during the tour. He was to take a big part in the events of the next month when his advice and prompt actions saved us a lot of embarrassment in Philadelphia.

We opened successfully the first evening on 20 November with a triple-bill comprising *Spreading the News, The Rising of the Moon* and *Birthright.* There was a full house, enormous booking ahead and a representative audience. The plays went well. The national flavour of *The Rising of the Moon,* and Sinclair's whimsical performance as the patriotic 'Peeler' who turns a blind eye on a fugitive, went over with almost startling success, while the rapid farce of *Spreading the News* got loud applause. *Birthright,* in which Annie eclipsed all former triumphs as the peasant mother whose life is bound up in her two sons, went well until the closing scenes, when the brothers grapple on the floor.

There was a faint stir during this incident, and what might have been construed as the beginning of a disturbance, when voices were heard at the back of the auditorium. These sounds were followed by an indignant murmur from those in front and a few muttered words from the back and some footsteps. The rest of the evening passed quietly. There was no trouble for the rest of the week. As during our first week in Boston, the novelty of the acting and the beauty of the plays captured the attention, but in the background the growlings about the proposed production of the *Playboy* went on. Some of the Irish-American newspapers opposing us launched vigorous campaigns. Wrote one:

> The *Playboy* must be squelched as the stage-Irishman was squelched, and a lesson taught to Mr Yeats and his fellow agents of England that they will remember while they live. [...] There is no law in New York that sanctions indecency on the stage and gives actors a right to insult a whole race, even when they are themselves unworthy members of that race.

It was feared that articles such as this might incite otherwise peace-loving playgoers to actions for which they would later be sorry. The *Playboy* was billed for the following Monday.

For this first week I had little enough to do since I was not appearing in many of the plays billed. I spent the time in seeing the city, which was a constant source of surprise, and in visiting acquaintances. It was a stroke of good fortune that threw me in the way of Dudley Digges, who was working only a few doors away from the Maxine Elliot with George Arliss. I spent many pleasant hours remembering old days with him and Máire Quinn, who had since become his wife. Dudley said he had temporarily abandoned acting and was then concentrating on stage management. Later, of course, he returned to the stage and found his way to Hollywood.

I was staying with cousins and an aunt at Brooklyn. The youngest cousin's husband was a policeman, and we spent some time discussing the position that had arisen over the *Playboy* with him. He said it was hard to say what might happen if the play was produced. The antagonism of the New York Irish had been aroused not by the play, of which few of them knew anything, but by the persistence of the company in keeping it on. Most of the Irish folk would have liked to see it and judge it for themselves, but were afraid of a section that seemed determined to cause trouble.

The bewildering denunciations of these people, although displaying complete ignorance of the play and of its value as a dramatic essay, had to be taken seriously: it seemed certain that there would be trouble. The attitude of certain Irish-American periodicals he described as 'disgusting', adding that few Irish or American people agreed with them.

These opinions were confirmed to some degree towards the end of the week, when leaving the theatre I met Father Michael O'Flanagan of Roscommon, a Catholic priest we knew in Dublin through the nationalist clubs. He was accompanied by the secretary of the New York Gaelic League, for which he was organising in America at the time, and he wanted me to ask Lady Gregory to have the play struck out of the repertoire for the rest of the tour. Like our police friend, he believed that trouble would ensue if the play was produced, adding that the position was much more serious than we might believe.

Over a supper table within reach of the theatre, he said that feeling over the play was running high, and that earlier reports from Boston and Washington, coupled with the editorials of a New York newspaper, had caused arrangements to be made for a riot in the theatre on the first night. He did not know anything of the play, but thought it would be wise to withdraw it.

A strong follower of the Irish nationalist clubs and an admirer of the Abbey's work himself, he felt it would be a pity if our reputation suffered as a result of any public demonstration. The objecting element, though it was in a minority, could do us more harm than we might realise. It was set on causing trouble if the play appeared, and the least that could be expected was a repetition of the Dublin riots of 1907. He did not know what form the riot would take other than the fact that it would be serious, probably resulting in broken heads.

The Gaelic League did not object to the play, but thought for the sake of our prestige, and the prestige of all peace-loving Irish-Americans in the city, that a compromise should be reached. It would be a pity to mar our success by an unnecessary demonstration that it lay with us to avert. He said:

> You must remember that I am a follower of the Abbey Theatre in Dublin. I do not want any rowdyism over the Irish plays here. These people won't even sit the piece out; they won't allow it to be heard.

One could hardly answer an argument like that. While we had been told often enough that there would be trouble if we went on, this was the first concrete information that there would be a demonstration in the theatre. It was irritating to think that it was all being caused by a minority. Every author has a right to be heard and judged before he is rejected. The wisdom of putting the play on, and risking any trouble that might follow, was another matter, although there did not appear to be any reason for a demonstration now, when the play was being given simply as a comedy with which no one could reasonably find fault.

In addition, considerable trouble had been gone to on the technical side of the production to tone down any sequences that might give offence. Even Christy's now-famous 'shift' phrase had been temporarily deleted. I pointed out that in any case there was nothing I could do about having the play withdrawn since I had no influence with the directors. Even if I had, it would have made little difference.

Yeats was in Dublin, and Lady Gregory could not take off any play without first consulting him. All the programmes had been arranged by Leibler's, who stipulated, even before the tour began, that the *Playboy* was one of the plays to be produced. It lay with the sponsors to withdraw the play from the New York stage, not with the Abbey directorate. I could only offer to arrange for him to meet Lady Gregory, who would certainly listen sympathetically, but could do little to help.

The next day I saw Lady Gregory, told her what I had learned, and arranged for her to meet the priest. I do not know what passed at that interview. The following Monday, 27 November, the *Playboy* went on.

We were down at the theatre early that night. I was playing the young wife in Lady Gregory's *Gaol-gate*, the curtain-raiser, and spent the greater part of the evening in the dressing room making up, so I was unable to watch the auditorium. From the sounds it appeared to be filling up rapidly, and Annie, who had gone stagewards earlier, brought back word that everything looked quiet and well organised.

Gaol-gate went over well. The short, three-character tragedy of the peasant woman whose son 'dies for his neighbour' was a favourite with every type of audience, and is one of the best things Lady Gregory wrote. There was a round of polite, sincere applause after the curtain. The audience seemed a particularly well-ordered one.

I was taking a small part in the second act of the *Playboy*. A few minutes later, standing in the wings before we started, I took the opportunity to look out across the auditorium. There was nothing very odd-looking about this crowd. In front were the usual idlers, leaning back in seats or studying programmes, and farther back parties chatted together in what might or might not have been loud voices. High in the gallery the crowd stirred and shifted, and heads bobbed occasionally as people returned to seats. The many quiet figures occupying positions at the end of rows could have been plain-clothes detectives, for we had heard that the management had arranged for police to be present.

The play opened quietly to the accompaniment of the usual scattered coughs and shiftings about the house, and, as in Dublin, appeared to go well for several minutes. But after Christy's entrance there were signs of increasing restlessness, some loud coughing, and a few faraway murmurs reached us. Then there was a scuffling sound from the direction of the gallery, a lot of coughing and muttering, and finally a long, low concerted hiss that swept downwards out of the darkness, gathering in force all the time until the voices of the players were almost drowned. This was followed by a sound—which might have been a signal—a scraping thumping noise, and what can only be described as a ragged shout as voices rose in protest.

It was difficult to see what was taking place, but it sounded as though members of the audience had risen to their feet and were yelling anything and everything that came into their heads. We caught a few snatches of the now-familiar slogan, 'It's not Irish!' and an occasional cry of 'God save Ireland!', most of which seemed to come from above.

Less than a minute after the first shout reached us, the side-pieces of our scene shuddered and rocked dangerously as something struck them, and a variety of missiles rattled onto the stage around Sinclair and Eithne Magee. Almost immediately the noise from the auditorium swept towards us in a huge roar as portion of the less-violent onlookers panicked or cried for order. There were sounds of running footsteps, seats slamming back into position, a few feminine cries or screams, and a rhythmic stamping or shouting from the upper portions of the house as the first troublemakers continued to bombard the stage.

An extraordinary collection of objects thudded about the footlights: rolled-up balls of paper, pieces of sticks, a variety of not very fresh vegetables, half loaves of bread, well-ripened cabbages and a shower of big knobbly potatoes, heavy, dusty and hard. We had a confused impression of ducking figures, a glimpse of Lady Gregory, rotund, thin-lipped and very determined-looking, her voice crying (rather unreasonably) 'Keep playing!' to those on the stage before the lights in the auditorium came on with a suddenness that was startling.

A dozen figures rushed from the dressing room towards the wings, half of them under the impression that the stage was being mounted. There were loud sounds of movement from the stalls. People who were taking no active part in the disturbance stood in the aisles or scrambled nervously out of their seats. In the orchestra stalls a man in a dinner jacket danced in fury and waved his fists. High up across the gallery, standing figures shouted and fought. It was from here that most of the noise seemed to come.

When the lights came on, the doors into the stalls and the balconies burst open and scores of uniformed police poured in, spreading out and taking up positions at the command of an officer. This man appeared to be asking the first troublemakers to stay quiet. He called across the seats and ran down a few steps from the door at the extreme back of the gallery. He was ignored, and after some hesitation he turned and waved his arm.

The police, who by this time had lined up along the walls and barred all exits, rushed amongst the audience, dragging the noisiest people from seats, swinging batons. This seemed to quiet the troublemakers in the stalls, but had the opposite effect on those in the gallery. People who seemed to have been quiet during the earlier episodes rose and clambered over the backs of seats to the assistance of friends, throwing themselves on the police, biting, spitting and clawing. A number of the noisiest and most savage attackers were women. The whole gallery became a heaving mass for a few minutes. Screams floated down to us; figures struggled dangerously near the gallery rails. At this point some thoughtful soul lowered the curtain. We saw no more.

Lady Gregory had been conferring with someone on the other side of the stage. In a few minutes she reappeared and told us to 'keep our heads'—everything was all right. The police were empowered to make arrests, and when order was restored the whole of the first act would be played again. A few seconds later the curtain rolled up and Fred O'Donovan made a courageous appearance. Ignoring the missiles, and kicking the refuse on the stage out of his way, he shouted that we would continue with the first act until all was heard. This brought another roar from the gallery, which was soon drowned by what we gathered were shouts of admiration from the stalls. A few minutes later the beginners reassembled on the littered stage and the play started all over again.

The noise now wavered somewhat and died away as more people were ejected. The first-act players carried on until the house was almost quiet again. By about the middle of the second act, things were almost back to normal.

It transpired later that the riot could not be pinned down to any one body or gang. A number of arrests at the expense of torn clothing and loosened teeth had been made. As the troublemakers left the theatre with the police, their shouts attracted a crowd of New Yorkers, who gathered outside, holding up traffic. Police rushed to the scene, and the area was cordoned off. Inside, although a number of seats in the gallery and stalls were now empty, the rest of the evening passed uneventfully. There was a faint murmur during the third-act argument between the Playboy and the villagers, nothing more.

Afterwards, however, a force of police waited near the stage door, and each of us had a bodyguard to escort us home.

As was natural, the next day's papers carried long reports. The riot was dealt with in detail. Most reviewers recognised the play as a literary achievement, and did not hesitate to say so. It was amusing to read the cause of the sneezing and coughing that had taken place during the first act. It appeared that a number of men had stationed themselves quietly near the gallery rails, blowing handfuls of pepper across the stalls.

The *Playboy* lasted the length of its advertised run: four nights. On the second night, Lady Gregory invited Theodore Roosevelt to the theatre. A packed house was the result, the former president, occupying Lady Gregory's box near the stage, laughing the most heartily at the humour of Synge's play. As soon as he made his appearance a few moments before we began, the whole audience stood up and cheered loudly. He accepted the applause silently, then turned and handed Lady Gregory forward to take a share.

It was a gallant gesture. The audience took its cue from him and cheered every line for the rest of the evening. A few people in the gallery who attempted to cause a disturbance during the second act lost no time in making themselves scarce when they saw the futility of it.

Halfway through the evening Roosevelt himself asked to be taken backstage to meet the players and congratulated us all personally for our performance and what he called our courage. Here again was a gesture that the audience did not allow to pass unnoticed.

We were seven weeks in New York, and played our entire repertoire during the stay. We were so successful that the tour was extended again to take in Chicago and four or five extra one-night towns before returning to Dublin in March, almost two months later than we had arranged. For the last week in New York, having run ourselves out of plays, we gave the *Playboy* again, this time for seven days. There was no trouble from audiences. Monday, the first night of the play, was Christmas Day. I have no memory of any celebrations in the city, and the fact that we were to work that night took all the pleasure out of the festival. I don't think I really missed Dublin until then.

Going down to the theatre on a brightish winter afternoon and preparing to go on that night was one of the hardest things I ever did. It is odd how absence from home can colour sentiment. We gathered together on the stage before the curtain rose, a forlorn little group of exiles feigning unconcern. There was no mail, no Christmas cards, no gifts from Ireland. Then Lennox Robinson, tall and a little shy, came down from the theatre office, his arms loaded with parcels, and handed us all something from himself: books, cosmetics, handkerchiefs for the girls, pipes, walking-sticks, and ties for the men. It was one of those things that are remembered.

We left New York on 31 December 1911.

Chapter Fifteen

1912
Under Arrest in Philadelphia

PHILADELPHIA WAS the next stop. We arrived on 12 January and—to our surprise, in view of the collapse of the New York opposition—more trouble awaited us there. A number of people, inflamed by the remarks of a newspaper, were organising opposition on a grand scale. We learnt that anything resembling stage-Irishism would not be tolerated.

But despite reports, and a number of blood-curdling threats, our first week was a success. Philadelphians were every bit as enthusiastic as New Yorkers or Bostonians. Nevertheless, the first night of the *Playboy* in the second week brought trouble. Halfway through the second act a fight broke out somewhere at the back, and there was an attempt to stop the play when a figure jumped out into the aisle and registered a noisy protest before being finally ejected.

As in New York, the troublemakers came armed with missiles and littered the stage in the course of an uproar that lasted for several minutes, then stopped abruptly when the police, who had been called in by the management, used strong-arm methods. A number of people were taken from the theatre and the play continued quietly to the end. Luckily, this aspect of our reception died out almost as soon as it had begun. There were no more riots.

The opposition was still far from at an end, however. The next step taken in the campaign against us was perhaps the most spectacular of the tour. A law passed in Philadelphia about a year before our visit forbade the production in the city of any stage play that might be deemed immodest. Under the ruling, any citizen was entitled to bring a charge of indecency against theatrical companies appearing within the city boundaries. It was a privilege that had never, as far as we knew, been availed of, but on 18 January a citizen of Irish extraction brought the charge against us in respect of the *Playboy*.

There was an attempt to stop the production of the play altogether by withholding the warrants for our arrest until a few minutes before we were due to begin in the evening, but Lady Gregory, who had apparently heard beforehand of the affair, had forestalled this by seeking legal aid and arranging for the issue of bail-bonds. As a result, before the curtain rose that night we found ourselves technically under arrest and on bail to the extent of five hundred dollars each, pending the result of a hearing fixed for the next day.

Early on Friday morning we gathered at the theatre and set out for the magistrate's court, where charges were to be formally made against us. This, it appeared, was merely a formal procedure and took little time. Our principal accuser was the man who had been ejected for making the speech on the first night of the *Playboy* there. He admitted that he had not seen all of the play, but he felt that the indecency of the opening passages was enough to warrant any charge.

Other witnesses had similar stories. We were allowed no witnesses at all, save in the later stages, when Fred O'Donovan gave evidence that we had appeared with the play in other cities and never had a legal charge made against us. I like to think, however, that public opinion was with us. We were returned for trial that afternoon.

There was quite a big attendance of public and press at the trial. Long passages of the play were read from the published book, produced some years earlier in Dublin, but as most of the so-called offensive speeches contained in the volume had been deleted for the American stage, this was rather ridiculous.

The most extraordinary feature of the whole affair was that those who brought the charges based their accusations principally upon these passages, even though they had not been spoken. Some of the witnesses carried the affair even further by mangling some of the Playboy's most innocent statements out of all recognition. One witness declared that the play was degrading because it held up to admiration a parricide, and it was blasphemous because of the unnecessary use of the word 'God' in the mouths of Irish peasants. He added that the play was immoral, indecent and sacrilegious, and was a travesty.

Some of the evidence fell flat when the Director of Public Safety testified that he had been to the theatre with his wife and had found nothing of an immoral or corrupting nature in the play.

Halfway through the trial, John Quinn, Yeats's lawyer friend from New York, put in an appearance and took charge of the company's interests. From the time of his arrival things took a different turn. When one of the witnesses for the prosecution asserted that the fact of Christy and Pegeen being left alone in a house implied immorality, he asked: 'Did anything take place on the stage to make you say that?'

'Well, no,' said the witness, 'it wasn't anything that went on on the stage.' After a pause, he added: 'But we all knew what happened when the curtain fell!'

In the course of a clever cross-examination, Quinn pulled the prosecution to pieces. There was an answer to everything that our accusers said. One of them registered an objection to Pegeen making an exit before the end of the first act, leaving a door to an inner room open for, it was alleged, Christy to follow her. There was consternation when it was revealed that the company had gone to some trouble to have a special lock fitted to this door so that the audience might hear a key being turned. The whole trial was farcical.

After about two hours the court adjourned for the judge to consider his verdict. In the meantime we were granted permission to fulfil our engagements in the city. It was as well. It was five or six days before we learned that the whole thing had been dismissed, and by then we were at Pittsburgh, our last stop but one before Chicago. The remainder of our stay in Philadelphia had proved the general attitude of audiences there. Every show was well attended. The reports of the trial had filtered through the newspapers, and if the events in court had not been sufficient to dampen their ardour, the comments of some writers were sufficient to put all further thought of opposition out of the heads of our accusers and their friends. Ironically enough, the trial had happy results for us. People came to see us who had never even known we existed, and liking what they saw, came back for more. We had a good week.

We stopped at Pittsburgh for an evening show about midweek, travelling on that night to Indianapolis. Here we learned that more trouble awaited us: further ahead, in Chicago, people were stirring up opposition on a grand scale. We passed into Chicago in the coldest of winter weather. The snow lay thick on the highways. A glimpse at the preceding week's papers told us that someone had indeed been working against us there. Amongst other things, an 'Anti-Irish Players' Association' had been formed, the mayor had been petitioned privately, and a local council had made representations to have the *Playboy* suppressed. The papers were making the most of what reports had preceded us, and there was quite a lot of speculation about what might happen when we arrived.

Very little did happen. Despite a few sensational articles in the newspapers, and some rumours, which we lost no time in denying—one of these was that none of us was Irish at all and that some of us came from France, where Synge was supposed to have written his plays—the whole thing died away. The mayor, after repeated complaints, read the play and issued a brief statement that he would do nothing to stop its production. Right up to the date set for our appearance with the piece, a verbal controversy raged. Lady Gregory received an anonymous letter threatening her life if she persisted in 'forcing the play on the people'.

Of all the cities we were in, and all the threats we received, those we got in Chicago were probably the most melodramatic. Troublemakers there were very definitely in a minority. Most Chicago people we met were pleasant and sociable, and usually amused by the actions of the small sections that opposed our appearances. The latter apparently came to realise the futility of their opposition: after a week or so all opposition to us and the plays vanished with the production of the *Playboy* itself. Synge's play got quite a good reception, although the favourite appeared to be St. John Ervine's *Mixed Marriage*, which was later repeated with success.

We left Chicago on 5 March on the first stage of our journey home. In New York we made a brief appearance with a triple-bill, then left for Boston, where, at a personal benefit show, we netted over five thousand dollars. Two days later we sailed home.

Dublin welcomed us with open arms. The first person we saw at Kingsbridge Station was Joe Holloway, bowler hat firm on head, a smile spreading over his face. Being Holloway, what he wanted was news. Was it true we were kicked off the stage in New York? And what was this about being arrested in Philadelphia?

In the Abbey, where the new school under Nugent Monck had been doing good work, we made a successful return appearance to a good house. On 14 March, eight days after our return, I had an opportunity to appear in my old part of Nora Burke in *The Shadow of the Glen*. This was the first time I had acted in the play since its initial production in 1903.

As it happened, it was one of my last appearances with the Abbey Theatre Company. There is no need to dwell upon the reasons for my departure from the theatre. To a great extent they were personal and have little to do with the story. Just then, although I loved the theatre and hated to leave it, my interest lay in the nationalist movement, in the little politico-cultural clubs like Inghinidhe na hÉireann, where, for me, the theatre had begun in the first place. I was like hundreds of other young men and women in Dublin then: my great desire was to work in every way I knew for the complete national independence of Ireland—that above all. It was my great aim in life. Anything that threatened to occupy me to its exclusion I considered a danger.

The professional theatre is a heartless taskmaster. It will not tolerate a divided allegiance. It demands time, energy and concentration to the almost complete exclusion of everything else. There is truth in the saying that acting is a vocation. The rudiments of playing may be learnt, as any craft may be learnt, through study, but unless the actress possesses the little extra that springs essentially from a deep, authentic love of the stage, she will never really make any of the characters she portrays live.

You often hear of the player whose entrance is immediately felt by an entire theatre, even though the part he or she plays is small. 'Electrifying' is, I think, the term most used here—the impact of a personality upon a crowded auditorium. What comes across the footlights is not so much, I think, the personality of the player in question as the depth of his or her sincerity for the work. The actress has put herself completely into the character she is playing; that character stands out because it really lives.

Alas, there are too few who are capable of this—what a theatre we would have if there were more. Contributory to this sincerity there is the actual work of acting, the mental toil that goes into the preparation of a part. The actress, if she is sincere in her work—if she really wishes to succeed—must study every character she is given, she must learn its every turn and whim, even before she begins to rehearse it. She must create a living personality out of the material that the author has supplied.

Frank Fay put it better to me in 1903: 'The author only makes suggestions which the player enlarges upon.' When she plays her part, she creates from her study of it and her observation of the life around her. She is working all the time, in the theatre and out of it. Always there is a part of her that stands outside the ordinary work-a-day world. Somewhere, at the back of her mind, the theatre, her work, must always be. Everything else must be incidental to it.

I knew this from experience. I knew also in which direction the path I should follow lay.

I suppose it was only natural that I should find the Abbey changed in 1910. Perhaps my earlier association with it had something to do with this. The businesslike atmosphere of the well-run theatre seemed alien somehow to the building into which the National Theatre Society went in 1904. The Abbey was full of memories. I could not pass through any part of it without recalling some incident of its first year. I would keep remembering the excitement of the opening night, the long discussions we held in the green room, and before that in Camden Street. I was being sentimental, of course. I missed A. E., I missed the two Fays, and above all I missed the old National Theatre Society.

Sometime in March 1912 I learned that my contract had expired. By agreement, it was not renewed. There is no more to tell. I need hardly say that it was just as difficult to go out of the Abbey in 1912 as it had been in 1905. I left a little of myself behind when I said goodbye to the new friends I had made, and passed through the doors into Marlborough Street.

Apart from a few engagements I fulfilled in Dublin in later years, I never acted professionally again.

But I never regretted it. Life had much to offer in those years. There were plenty of interesting things to be done. And I never left the theatre completely, although it always remained secondary to the other work I was given.

Until the eve of 1916, I was playing with amateur clubs in Dublin. There were plenty of these in the city then—indeed, the amateur theatre was never as strong—and all of them were interesting.

Part Four

The Rising

Chapter Sixteen

1912–1913
Setting the Stage for
Pearse's Passion Play

DUBLIN WAS a drama-mad city. Almost everyone was a playgoer, for there were not many other kinds of entertainment available. The kinematograph had arrived at the Rotunda, but it was not then sufficiently developed to divert attention from the legitimate stage. And the legitimate stage had plenty to offer. In 1912—the year I left the Abbey—the Queen's had an established reputation as the home of melodrama and old-time Irish patriotic plays, and the Gaiety and Theatre Royal presented good English and continental plays and European opera.

With such widespread affection for all things dramatic, it was hardly surprising that most of the younger folk were dabbling in the amateur theatre. Almost all the national clubs, literary, political or otherwise, were associated with theatrical groups in the young years of the dramatic movement. Many young nationalists appeared as players with amateur companies, and a lot of the political clubs, led by Arthur Griffith's Cumann na nGaedheal, had dramatic societies attached, either as a means of gathering funds or of disseminating propaganda.

All over Dublin, in small halls and concert rooms, and when they were available for hire in the Abbey or the Rotunda or the Queen's, little amateur stage groups of the most varied kinds were always appearing, and although not all of them were important, either because of the plays they produced or the standards they achieved in presentation, they were at least interesting to watch, if only because of the people whom they managed to enlist as members, players, writers or producers.

At that time the most unexpected people in Dublin, poets, writers, artists, revolutionists, were interested in the theatre; everyone was ready to discuss a new play or the work of a player. The arrival of a new Irish dramatist—and most of the young writers at this period wrote for the stage at some time or other— would create quite a noticeable stir, and a controversial play was always certain to cause widespread discussion. And sometimes, as was the case with Synge, it would cause a lot of bitter argument and ill-feeling.

From the point of view of variety, individual amateur productions in the city during these years left little to be desired: the most diverse types of plays could be seen on almost any night in the small halls, all the way from peasant pieces in Irish and English by groups influenced by the work of the National Theatre Society, to dramas and farces produced by companies unconcerned with national movements.

There would be occasional revivals of Irish Literary Theatre successes, like Alice Milligan's *The Last Feast of the Fianna* or Edward Martyn's *Maeve*, which the Theatre of Ireland produced in 1908; small independent societies would give dramatic adaptations from the classics or English drawing-room comedies; and, inevitably, amateur groups outside the national movement fell back on the old time-worn Irish and English melodramas, like *Arrah-na-Pogue* or *East Lynne*, which were said to be triply attractive to small companies since they usually called for big casts, absorbing the entire membership of a society, were sometimes free of royalties, and could always be sure of a certain following.

Then, when the weather permitted, amateur companies would give open-air productions of various sorts, and pageants. There would be repeats by small Gaelic League groups of Oireachtas prizewinning plays, sometimes musical productions like O'Brien-Butler's *Muirgheuis* (one of the first Gaelic operettas ever produced) and *Eithne*, written by Father Thomas O'Kelly to music by Robert O'Dwyer.

In about 1908 or 1909 there was even some talk of a bilingual pantomime, books and lyrics to be written by a group that included A. E. and Susan Mitchell. But this was probably never produced, although it was certainly discussed by members of the Theatre of Ireland, and a scenario drafted by Fred Morrow, who was mentioned as producer. The story was based loosely on a legend of Balor of the Evil Eye, and that was to be the title. There was to be a distinct political flavour about it.

Although revivals were frequent with little amateur companies, the emphasis, naturally, was on original works, the more patriotic in character the better. Plays about the Fenians, about '48 and '98 came from many pens—pieces liberally sprinkled with propaganda and usually successful despite the fact that most of them were variations on a set theme. Plays of this sort found their way into the repertories of most groups, big and small, and, as was sometimes the case, passed from one company to another, a popular success standing the test of numerous revivals over a number of years before fading away.

One of these was Count Casimir de Markievicz's *The Memory of the Dead*, a play about the insurrection of 1798, the sentiments of which are best expressed by the title itself. Its production at the Gaiety launched Count and Countess Markievicz's 'Independent Dramatic Company', one of the better known groups, which was responsible for a lot of good work during the few years it remained in existence. Madame Markievicz was its moving force, and doubtless it was due to her popularity in nationalist Dublin that the company enjoyed the success it did, although its work was consistent with that of most good companies of a kind in the city.

It produced an odd mixture of plays, some good, some not so good: at least one by George A. Birmingham, *Eleanor's Enterprise*; a few by Madame Markievicz herself, *His Invincible Mother*, *Who Fears To Speak? Blood Money*; and it did some work by Kathleen Fitzpatrick, who also wrote for the Theatre of Ireland.

One of its successes was a production of Shaw's *The Devil's Disciple*, given at the Gaiety, which was remarkable for an outstanding performance by a young actor, Breffni O'Rourke, who up to the time of his death many years later, was working in English repertory and films. He was probably the best actor the company had. His stepson, Cyril Cusack, has more than fulfilled hopes as one of the most promising Abbey actors of recent years.

Breffni was cast, too, for a leading role in the Independent Dramatic Company's production of *John Gabriel Borkman*, but although this certainly went into rehearsal by the group, it was never produced. The company began to die soon after 1912 when Count Markievicz left Dublin and the Countess's work with the Irish Citizen Army began to absorb most of her time. The Rising of 1916 and her subsequent imprisonment as a Citizen Army leader definitely killed it.

The work of the Gaelic League, which influenced every side of Irish life, affected the amateur theatrical movement too. Productions of original works in Irish were frequent in Dublin during the young years of the National Theatre Society and the Abbey, but were not always successful despite the earnestness and hard work of various groups.

A number of promising Gaelic theatre companies were founded between 1900 and 1912, but few survived for long, or, if they did, suffered from a lack of appreciation even worse than that experienced by the National Theatre Society at the beginning. Perhaps it was that the Gaelic theatre movement lacked the determination necessary to interest the general play-going public in plays in this medium. But there was no lack of plays. There was an abundance of Oireachtas plays, but few that, despite their merit, evoked more than passing notice during these early years.

The greatest success achieved by Gaelic plays in regular play-going circles was achieved by Dr Hyde's one-act pieces—which themselves had such an influence on the early folk-drama of the movement in English—*Casadh an tSúgáin*, which was revived with success after its first production by the Literary Theatre in 1901; *An Naomh ar Iarraidh* (The Lost Saint); *Tigh na mBocht* (The Poorhouse), and the other pieces translated into English by Lady Gregory and produced later at the Abbey. But generally speaking, the reception of plays in the Irish language left much to be desired.

The titles that were mentioned with anything approaching enthusiasm by ordinary playgoers might be counted on the fingers: Dr Hyde's plays, those by established writers like Father Dineen, Father O'Kelly, 'Torna' (Tadhg O'Donoghue), and by Pádraig Pearse, whose plays in Gaelic began to be produced in 1909 with pupils of his boys' school in Ranelagh.

It was not until after 1912 that a really satisfactory attempt was made to produce Gaelic plays on a level with those good pieces that were given in English. One attempt was made by *Na Cluithcheoiri*, the little Gaelic League company that produced translations of Abbey, National Theatre Society and Theatre of Ireland plays after 1910; another by Piarais Béaslaí's Gaelic Company, *Na hAisteori*, which concentrated on the production of original plays.

Of the two, *Na hAisteori* lasted the longest, and after a hard struggle during its early years began to achieve a certain degree of success, before it came to an end with the outbreak of civil war in 1922. Nevertheless, it did something for Gaelic in the theatre, for out of it came *An Comhar Drámaíochta*, whose work the Abbey carries on now. The founders of both these companies laid the foundations of a Gaelic dramatic company in Ireland, but full success can hardly have been known until after 1928, when Micheál Mac Liammóir and Hilton Edwards founded *Taibhdhearc na Gaillimhe* simultaneously with their establishment of the Dublin Gate.

An Taibhdhearc comes closest, perhaps, to the national theatre ideal than any similar enterprise launched in Ireland since the beginning of the dramatic movement. It produces plays in the national language; it does not confine itself to any specific type of Irish play, peasant or otherwise, but mirrors every aspect of life in the country; it gives translations of worthwhile European dramas; its players are enthusiasts, drawn together for a common purpose; and the standards it achieves in production and acting are excellent. The success it enjoys is heartening.

Probably the most outstanding Gaelic production seen in Dublin before 1916 was Pádraig Pearse's Passion play, produced at the Abbey with pupils of his boys' school, St Enda's, in 1911. In its own way this created something of a minor sensation in Dublin, reports of it travelling across the Atlantic, and some of them finding their way into the continental press.

One leading critic wrote: 'It has root power. It gives the emotion out of which a true Gaelic drama may yet arise,' and added that if its production were ever made an annual event it might create a tradition of acting and dramatic writing in Irish. Unfortunately, it was never seen again, nor was it ever published. It passed out of the minds of Dubliners after 1916, and nowadays seems to be forgotten, although it was probably the first really serious piece of Gaelic dramatic writing produced. It had been Pearse's intention to present it triennially, but when 1914 came he was too engrossed with his work in the Irish Volunteers to arrange for its revival. After his execution, it was never repeated.

The Passion play was one of the most successful plays that Pearse's pupils at St Enda's produced, and was one of a long list of remarkable productions for which the school was responsible. St Enda's school productions usually aroused widespread interest in Dublin. The eldest member of the company could have been no more than fourteen or sixteen years of age, but the work bore comparison with that of many top-rate companies in Dublin producing good Irish plays.

The results achieved as far as acting was concerned were remarkable. There was a freshness about the work of the young players. Many held that the acting of the school company was surpassed in the city only by that of the Abbey players—a rather sweeping statement that was not quite true—but certainly the acting was of a high standard. Pearse's plays have already taken a place with the best of Irish literature.

St Enda's was the first of the two schools founded and run by Pearse and his brother between 1909 and 1916. St Enda's was a secondary school for boys; St Ita's a school for girls. They were the first bilingual schools in Ireland, and were a practical expression of all Pearse's own ideals of what Irish schools should be. He said he wanted to found a school that would be more Irish in spirit than any school opened in Ireland since the Flight of the Earls.

He put the theory into practice at St Enda's. He combined all the usual college subjects with many of the ancient theories of education, which aimed at fostering the growth of a personality along its own lines, influenced by the personality of a teacher. He believed that the work of the teacher was not merely to prepare a pupil for examinations, but, as he put it, 'to foster the elements of a character already present.'

He was completely successful in the six or seven years he gave to the work. St Enda's has since been described as the soundest and most determined attempt ever made to reform Irish education.

The school began in a big double-fronted house standing in its own grounds at Oakley Road, Ranelagh, with about thirty or forty pupils. A few years later it moved to a bigger house at Rathfarnham because the original building could not accommodate all who wanted to join its classes. Pearse interrupted his work only to lead the Rising, which resulted in his own execution by a British firing squad in a Dublin barrack yard.

I met Pearse frequently before 1916, but I never knew him very well—not so much as an individual as a member of a family. I knew his mother, Margaret, intimately, and of the two boys it was Willie with whom I was best acquainted.

Pádraig appeared an ordinary enough person, but he was one of the most remarkable men of his generation. His whole life was dedicated to a cause. One of his pupils wrote that the only tragedy in his career was the resolute pursuit of an ideal. In his speech at his court martial he told of how as a boy he went down on his knees and swore that he would devote his whole life to setting Ireland free.

No one who knew him would say that he was completely the legendary figure, the man of the popular ballads. Neither was he the unbalanced idealist drawn by some of his critics. In fact he was a quiet, rather shy young man in his thirties, stockily built, not very impressive in appearance despite the high forehead and clear profile.

Pearse filled so many different roles. He was a leader of men, a writer, a soldier, an inspired orator, and—this is how one remembers him best—a schoolmaster. Those who knew him at his home with his family, or alone with his pupils or his brother, would never remember him as anything other than the quiet young man, full of nothing but the business of his school.

But outside, some might have said Pearse was vain—a bit of a poseur. He was very neat; a lot of people said he was finicky about his clothes. His hair was always sleeked down, never out of place. He liked to make an impression through his appearance. In St Enda's he was always the soberly suited schoolmaster, his tie always at the right angle. At other times, when he wore his green Volunteer uniform, which was perfectly tailored, his slouch hat with the brim bound to the crown was always firm and straight on his head, never rakish. It made him look very intense and serious.

There was never any restriction to speak of on the boys of St Enda's. To the casual observer, the pupils ran wild. Inside the school gates was an empire of their own, administered by themselves. Over it all hovered the Pearse family: Pádraig and Willie, Mrs Pearse and the two girls, Margaret and Mary Bridget. With his boys, Pearse himself was transformed. He knew all their separate traits and was keenly aware of their attitude towards him. When he was in their company he had a sort of boyish enthusiasm that set him on a level with all of them.

He really loved his boys. Once, at a pageant organised by the school at Croke Park, he was leading parties of pupils onto the field, heavily made up in the character of CúChullain or some such legendary hero. One of the stands was full of boys who were not taking part in the pageant. The stand caught fire. Pearse was off the field in a moment and had flung himself into the flames almost before anyone knew what was happening. He was shaking all over, not from fear but from anxiety for the safety of the boys who were trapped, yet he climbed to the top of the flaming structure, handing the smaller children to safety and calling for an orderly withdrawal.

The boys heard his voice, lined up, and walked quietly to the ground through the flames. When it was all over he leaned against a nearby railing, the grease-paint smeared down his face from the heat, his head bowed. In a moment he was back with the boys on the field, clapping his hands for order, calling names, making jokes. That was the Pearse his pupils knew.

In St Enda's the school dramatic company took up a lot of the boys' time outside classroom hours. Most of the plays produced were written by Pearse himself for performance at a prearranged place and time by certain people. When he wrote a play he wove each character around the individual characteristics of the person who was going to play it. Those were the 'masterpieces to order' he used to joke about in his writing.

Most of the performances took place in the school theatre or in the school grounds. Only occasionally did he permit a play to be given elsewhere. Only about three St Enda's performances took place at the Abbey—the Passion play, a programme of short pieces, one by Padraic Colum, *The Destruction of the Hostel*, which was written specially for the school company; and later, about 1913, a revival of Pearse's own *An Ri* (The King), which accompanied what was the first performance in Europe of Rabindranath Tagore's *The Post Office*. This performance was given at the suggestion of Yeats, who had a deep admiration for Pearse.

At that time Yeats was very full of Tagore's work, which was only recently becoming known in an English translation. He said the poet was one of the greatest then living, and was doing all in his power to bring his work before Dublin. It was one of the highest compliments he could pay Pearse to refer to Tagore's school for eastern boys as 'the Indian St Enda's'.

In the circumstances it was natural enough that when he contemplated the production of one of the Indian's plays, he should ask Pearse to produce one of his own with it, played by his pupils. The event aroused great interest, and was held in aid of St Enda's school fund. Pearse spoke afterwards of it himself, referring glowingly to Yeats, whom he greatly respected. He often said that Yeats was one of the few men in Ireland who was doing something useful for Irish nationalism.

Willie Pearse, like his brother, was deeply interested in the stage. He was a sculptor and had a small studio at Brunswick Street, but from about 1910 he gave most of his time to St Enda's, where he taught art and, more significantly, drama. When the Theatre of Ireland started he was one of the first to offer his services, and often afterwards appeared in plays with the company.

Some of us from the Theatre of Ireland used to go out to Ranelagh to help now and then with the school's plays. Willie acted as producer, and the performances were usually given in a little corrugated iron shed, which was also used as a gymnasium. Invariably they were well attended; indeed, the hall seldom held all who wanted to get in.

Apart from his school work and his preoccupation with his family, drama appeared to be his great interest in life. He gazed at the stage and its actors with a sort of awe.

It seems a hard thing to say that he was not successful as an actor himself. He never lost his self-consciousness on a stage. He was acutely aware of the unsuitability of his speech, and though he worked hard to perfect it, his voice never completely became his servant. But what he lacked in ability he made up in enthusiasm. At rehearsals he obeyed every command with humility. Often he would take you aside and whisper: 'Do you think I was good? I'm doing my best ...'. One could always gain his gratitude with advice.

Willie was a slight figure in the fitted suits and long poet's cravats he favoured. He had the same fine profile as Pádraig, the same high forehead and heavy hair sleeked back. But here the physical resemblance ended. He had high cheeks and dark gentle eyes and was better-looking than the other, not so powerfully built, but with a little more height, which his slimness accentuated.

He displayed none of the personality traits of his brother. Altogether, he seemed to be overshadowed by Pádraig and agreed to his every decision and seldom put forward an argument of his own. This submission could be irritating, but Willie's deference was not lack of character. To those who knew them the most remarkable thing about these two was the similarity of their views on all subjects. What Pádraig thought, Willie believed; whom Willie liked, Pádraig admired.

Before 1916, Gipsy and I had many opportunities of acting with him. Apart from our visits to Cullenswood House and our work with him in the Theatre of Ireland, we were able to watch his development as an actor with the short-lived 'Irish Theatre', which Edward Martyn, Thomas MacDonagh and Joseph Plunkett founded after 1914. It was the most interesting of all the theatrical companies that appeared in Dublin immediately before 1916, and probably the most important that appeared in Ireland since the beginning of the dramatic movement itself, for it indicated the path Mac Liammóir and Edwards later took with the Gate.

Later, when Willie and his sister founded the Leinster Stage Society, we appeared with him in Dublin, and once visited Cork, where we played for a week at the Opera House in *The Cricket on the Hearth*, *The Chimes* and other adaptations from Dickens.

We had a nice little company in this, which included Gipsy, Desmond Ryan, one of Pearse's closest pupil friends, Maire Hughes and James Crawford Neil, the young poet best remembered for his unique child studies of Dublin life. Crawford was engaged to Gipsy and an avowed pacifist. Tragically, he was killed by a looter's bullet in 1916, and my sister never fully recovered from his death.

Chapter Seventeen

1914–1915
The Irish Theatre, Tom MacDonagh and Joe Plunkett

WILLIE PEARSE was one of many interesting people whom Edward Martyn drew into his Irish Theatre after 1914. The small company was drawn greatly from amongst people who had former experience of the stage, and its work was generally of a high standard. Martyn suggested it and probably financed it during its early years, for it could not have existed for long on the support that it got from Dublin audiences.

His intention was to have it run parallel with the Abbey producing plays of a non-peasant character by Irish authors, translations of foreign masterpieces and plays in Gaelic. It had a fair share of success at first, but as time went on, and a lack of interest on the part of Dubliners became apparent, the movement faltered. Playgoers, who were still being catered for by English stock companies and cheap British variety troupes, found it hard enough to work up an interest even in the Abbey. They ignored the Irish Theatre. Its performances came to be attended mostly by those who were interested in the work of its players rather than in its ideals.

It produced several interesting plays in its short life: plays in English by the two MacDonaghs, Thomas, and his brother, John; Martyn, H. B. O'Hanlon; plays in Irish by Douglas Hyde, and some fine Gaelic translations by Mrs MacDonagh-O'Mahoney and Liam O'Domhnaill. It also gave translations of Chekhov,

Ibsen and Strindberg. Its work invariably excited great interest in the press and dramatic circles, but the general public, which is necessarily the breath of life to all theatrical enterprises, was not enthusiastic. It died. It was a pity, because at the time it filled a great need, which the Abbey, in its role as a purveyor of peasant drama, did not meet.

It made its first appearance on 2 November 1914 at the Crane Hall, Upper O'Connell Street, with a performance of Edward Martyn's *The Dream Physician*. The cast included Una O'Connor—who had then left the Abbey—John MacDonagh, Nellie Gifford and Eric Gorman. Later the same year it produced Martyn's *The Heather Field*; Douglas Hyde's *Casadh an tSúgaín*; H. B. O'Hanlon's *The All-Alone*; and Chekhov's *The Cherry Orchard* and *Uncle Vanya*.

Rehearsals of the Irish Theatre were interesting affairs. The directors gathered a company that was the best of Dublin talent at the time. There was 'Nell Byrne' (Blanaid Salkeld), Daisy Cogley—who later helped with the foundation of the Gate—Angela Coyne, the two Reddin brothers, Kerry and Norman; and Paul Farrell. Frank Fay, who had come back from touring in England with Willie, joined the company and played with it for a time. There were Gaelic League players, Art Ward, Padraic Sheehan and Sean Mac Coilte, who were associated with *Na Cluithcheoiri*. Pat Hayden, who was one of the pioneers in later years of Irish broadcasting, played with it too.

One young man, who was in a modest way making a name for himself as an actor and as a comedian, merged unobtrusively into the background at most gatherings. Very retiring indeed was Jimmy O'Dea.

But the most interesting members of the company were the directors themselves: Edward Martyn, Thomas MacDonagh and Joseph Plunkett, particularly the last two, for it is doubtful if many of us who appeared only occasionally with the group ever got to know Edward Martyn well. At that time he was already well into middle age, tall, courteous, but rather reserved at most times, whereas MacDonagh was already well known in the city through his work as a writer with the Gaelic League, and as the assistant headmaster of St Enda's; and Joe Plunkett came of a well-known and highly respected Dublin family. His father was a Papal count, a collateral descendant of the Catholic martyr, Blessed [Saint] Oliver Plunkett, a cultured gentleman and a fervent nationalist. Both the Count and Countess were interested in the theatre and had done much for the amateur dramatic movement in Dublin.

In about 1911, the Countess, who owned property in the city, had given the Theatre of Ireland a quaint old building at Hardwicke Street that was formerly a Jesuit chapel. The society used to appear there in company with other little dramatic groups that had the use of the place. It was small but well equipped as a theatre, and proved a boon to struggling companies.

Fred and Jack Morrow had worked wonders on the interior, turning the main room of the building into a dainty little theatre, rather in the French style. Like the old Camden Street rooms in 1902, it became a recognised meeting-place for the dramatic clubs. Later, the Irish Theatre produced its plays there.

Although they shared many interests and were close friends as well as colleagues in the theatre, and later in the Irish Volunteers, Plunkett and MacDonagh were opposites in appearance and manner. Joe Plunkett was quiet and delicate-looking; MacDonagh carried with him a vivid gaiety at all times. He was always busy at Irish Theatre meetings, either watching a rehearsal or talking animatedly with some visitor in the auditorium, emphasising a point with his hands or making jokes.

Tom was a gay spirit; he seldom remained serious for long. In appearance he was a well-built, fresh-complexioned man in his mid thirties, not very tall, with light-brown curly hair and eyes that lit up easily with wit. Neatly dressed, sometimes in dark suits, sometimes in kilts—which many men in Dublin affected at that time—he was always the debonair man of affairs, very brisk and businesslike; a popular figure everywhere in the city.

At St Enda's, where he taught languages, he was greatly admired by his pupils, for he was boyish in appearance and manner, enthusiastic about most things, and a gifted teacher, deeply interested in his work. His good humour never faltered under any circumstances. I can never forget how he carried himself two years later during his command of the Irish Volunteer garrison in Jacob's factory in Easter Week. Although his own arrest and execution as a leader of the Rising was inevitable, he kept his courage and good humour until the end.

In contrast to MacDonagh with his brisk efficiency was Joe Plunkett, at this time about twenty-six, who was quiet, tall, and slightly built. His pale earnest face and heavy spectacles gave him a studious look. He was a gifted young man: a capable artist, musician and actor, he had travelled widely in Europe and the East, sometimes visiting America as a Volunteer emissary to the republican clubs. But his frequent trips to Europe were mainly for health reasons: he had spent most of his time outside Ireland. He was a gently spoken shy young man, yet easy to speak with on acquaintance, for he had a quiet wit of his own. To the stranger he might have appeared distant and rather mysterious with his dark hair, long tapering hands and penetrating eyes.

His youth, his heroism two years later in the burning General Post Office, and the manner in which he carried himself through the bullet-swept streets during the Rising, created a colourful picture of a young man who, despite his ailing health, helped to plan an insurrection, then threw himself into the thick of the fighting. His memory was venerated only a few years later when his name was swept into the street ballads and folk-songs of the countryside.

Edward Martyn's Irish Theatre suffered its greatest loss after the speed-up in political affairs in Dublin in about 1915. Both Plunkett and MacDonagh were drawn away from it as the Irish Volunteer movement expanded, and many of the young people who had played with it turned temporarily from the stage, or at least began to give less of their time to acting.

The changes taking place politically, or rather the reawakening of an interest in politics, affected most of the small clubs, theatrical and otherwise, working in Dublin. To some extent an interest in the theatre, and in the arts generally, began to fade in face of a growing interest in affairs at Westminster. There was much theorising about whether Home Rule, which promised a degree of autonomy for Ireland, would become a fact instead of a mere theory. Most people in Dublin, even those who had formerly shown little interest in politics, had an eye on the new bill that had been put before the Commons in 1912.

The Home Rule Bill had passed its first reading, but the opposition of the Lords and the vacillations of the Liberal Government in face of fierce opposition by Orangemen in the north, led by Sir Edward Carson, had rendered the prospects of its success doubtful. Carson, who had the support of the Tories, had begun to uphold what were called 'the rights of the Ulster Unionists', and had succeeded in raising a small rebel army. The Ulster Volunteers had begun to parade openly and noisily. When they announced that they would oppose by force any attempt to govern Ireland from within, it was a direct threat to constitutional authority. There was a lot of irony in the fact that they were responsible for making nationalists in the rest of Ireland take up arms.

The administration made a show of suppressing the Ulster Volunteers, and when this failed proceeded to ignore them altogether. There was then talk of importing guns into the north. Carson said that if necessary his followers would march from Belfast through Ireland to Cork. There was a great deal of indignation in Dublin when the administration made no further effort to put an end to these threats. People began to ask why, if an illegal organisation in the north could threaten to oppose Home Rule by force, nationalists in the rest of Ireland could not organise to defend it.

When Professor Eoin MacNeill wrote in the official journal of the Gaelic League recommending the formation of the Irish Volunteers, the situation was seized upon by the old separatist party, which had been kept alive by the activities of the IRB.

Then, late in 1913, the Irish Volunteer movement was launched at a mass meeting in the Rotunda, Parnell Square. It was a force of young men drawn from amongst all classes to 'defend and maintain the rights and privileges common to all the people of Ireland'. And a few months later, a women's organisation, Cumann na mBan, was founded as an auxiliary.

You could see the effect that all these events had on members of the various clubs in the city. The formation of the Volunteers caused a great deal of discussion: many people were interested. Still, there were those who disapproved of the new organisation, including the Irish Party, led by John Redmond.

Many of the younger folk, however, had begun to be stirred by the turn events were taking, just as, in a different degree, they had been moved by the events that had preceded the formation of the Irish Citizen Army. Before the establishment of the Irish Volunteers, the new Irish Labour movement had been struggling against an attempt by Dublin employers to kill it. A strike had precipitated a situation in which several hundred workers were locked out because they would not resign their membership of the new trade unions. Many workers were close to starvation, and unemployment figures had reached an alarming height, but the workers had made a gallant stand.

It is hard to believe now that this dispute made international news. Almost all sections of life in Dublin had protested, including writers, artists and people who had nothing to do with politics at all. A. E., who was a champion of justice everywhere, had written a brilliant open letter to the employers in which he revealed the terrible conditions under which the workers laboured. There had been meetings and public protests of various kinds. When several innocent people were seriously injured in a baton-charge by police on workers in O'Connell Street early in 1913, James Connolly and James Larkin, the two Labour leaders, had organised the workers in Dublin into an unarmed body, the Irish Citizen Army.

After the outbreak of war in Europe the following year, Dublin was in a ferment politically. The Ulster Volunteers had landed arms at Larne, and nothing had been done to stop them. When the Volunteers in Dublin unloaded rifles from Erskine Childers' yacht, the *Asgard*, at Howth, police and military turned out in force to confiscate the guns. They had not been successful: the Volunteers had escaped with empty rifles, but the event had a tragic sequel when the British soldiers returning to Dublin fired haphazardly into a crowd of civilians at Bachelor's Walk. Three people were killed, thirty-eight were injured, and one man later died of bayonet wounds.

When war was declared it looked as though the Home Rule Bill might become law. The Irish Party had finally recognised the Volunteer movement and had some of its members elected onto the executive of the organisation: it was felt that, with all the nationalists in Ireland behind them, they would be able to force the bill through. To everyone's surprise, the opposite happened. No effort was made to have the bill passed, and it was announced that Home Rule would be shelved until after the war. It was understood that it might become law then, with any modifications that the faction in the north might want.

This raised a storm of protest. John Redmond, whom many felt was out of touch with feeling in Ireland, offered the strength of the Volunteers to the British Army in France. After the news of the suspension of Home Rule, it was a shocking blunder. The young men were outraged. The Volunteer movement split in two, one side standing for the original policy of independence, the other following Redmond.

Recruiting for the British Army began all over the country. Dublin was flooded with propagandist literature of every sort; there were eloquent speeches and recruiting rallies. In Dublin there was a great deal of counter activity by the Volunteers and the Citizen Army. There were meetings and public parades. Everyone seemed to be affected in some way by the events that were taking place.

Chapter Eighteen

1916
The Eve of the Rising at the Ceannt Household

AFTER 1914, I used to go to meetings of the Ard Craobh, the headquarters branch of Cumann na mBan. This branch met in rooms at Parnell Square and controlled the activities of other sections working in Dublin. Essentially, Cumann na mBan was founded to help in establishing the Volunteers. At the beginning, before belief in the wisdom of insurrection rather than debate became widespread, it was not the military organisation it later became.

Apart from classes in first-aid, stretcher-bearing and, occasionally, field signalling, a great deal of the time was given over to the gathering of funds in support of the rapid expansion of the Volunteer organisation. Since there was a certain degree of opposition to the movement in some circles—after the Volunteer 'split', many looked upon the refusal to join forces with the British in France as a treacherous 'stab in the back'—the most effective way of doing this was by arranging entertainments. Door-to-door canvassing was almost certain to meet with failure. A number of Cumann na mBan members, like myself, had been associated with theatrical clubs in former years and were able to get the help of artistes for the entertainments that the organisation sponsored.

The emphasis was now not upon players and dramatists, but upon singers and instrumentalists. In an effort to assemble parties for concerts and what were called *aedhireachtanna*—open-air festivals of music and singing—the executive of the Ard Craobh used to send out regular appeals for artistes. The calls were answered. Many people who at that time were not Volunteers or members of Cumann na mBan replied readily to the appeal for voluntary help for entertainments. The 'republican concerts', as they were called, began to achieve considerable popularity in Dublin. They were well-planned entertainments, usually ending with an address by a prominent nationalist speaker.

The pattern followed by the established music hall was carefully avoided. All the music, songs, verse, even the scripts of comedians, had a nationalist flavour. The appeal of the concerts spread outside Dublin and served a dual purpose. Money poured into the Volunteer fund, and the special character of the entertainments created an interest in the work of the organisation. Audiences responded readily to national airs and traditional music. Patriotic verse was always popular. Indeed, enthusiasm for *anything* national was easily awakened just then.

Before 1916 I did a lot of 'national concert' work for Cumann na mBan. By that time I had an extensive repertoire of patriotic verse, and I spent a lot of spare time travelling with concert parties. But at some time about the beginning of 1916 my family moved house from Dublin to Glasthule, a suburb about seven miles from the centre of the city, and I had to suspend my membership of the Ard Craobh. I was teaching elocution at a school in Dundrum, and could never find the time in the evenings to go to meetings at Parnell Square.

I had begun a small branch of Cumann na mBan at Glasthule—about twenty members, whose homes were in the vicinity. There was little for us to do locally at the time, but we occupied the evenings with first-aid lectures and occasional visits from Ard Craobh visitors. Most of the time during the early months of 1916 was taken up with the endless preparation of first-aid kits for Volunteers, which were sent to areas throughout the country.

During Holy Week 1916 I spent the days making up these kits at the Volunteer headquarters in Dawson Street. Most branches in the city had been notified of a coming route march to the country on Easter Sunday, and preparations for this were underway.

On Easter Saturday I visited some friends, the Ceannts, at their home in Dolphin's Barn. Both Mrs Ceannt and her sister, Lily O'Brennan, were active members of the central branch of Cumann na mBan. They had both spent the afternoon assembling equipment for the 4th Dublin Battalion of Volunteers, of which Éamonn Ceannt was commandant. Lily asked me what arrangements I had made for the proposed route march.

'None as yet,' I told her, adding that the Glasthule Cumann na mBan had not, to my knowledge, been notified of its part in the arrangements, and might not go at all. She said that she was moving off with Eamonn's battalion the following afternoon and asked if I would like to go with her. I said yes. 'Be here at three o'clock tomorrow afternoon … and bring your bicycle,' she said.

We made no further reference to this arrangement. I never thought to ask where the battalion would meet, or where it would go afterwards. It was natural to assume that we would move off to the hills and spend the day there in manoeuvres. No one knew that the route march was really a covert manner of mobilising for an insurrection. On Monday morning this ignorance of the whereabouts of Ceannt was to leave me uncertain of what was taking place in the city, and cut me off completely from his battalion, which took the South Dublin Union buildings at Mount Brown, and held them with many skirmishes and bitter fighting until the surrender.

Easter Sunday morning put all thoughts of my engagement at Ceannt's out of my head. The newspapers carried an order countermanding all arrangements for Volunteer movements, cancelling all parades and marches. It was signed by Eoin MacNeill as chief of staff.

I brought the paper to my father, Matthew, at the breakfast table. He was puzzled when I read out the order to him. At some time before this, a little after the foundation of the Volunteers, he had emerged from retirement as a compositor-printer to publish several covertly distributed republican newspapers. I did not know until later that in this position he either knew or suspected that an insurrection was planned and was due to take place that morning at noon. He told me to ignore the order. 'Get the next tram to Ceannt's,' he said. 'See Lily O'Brennan yourself and ask her if this is genuine. Make sure you see her and don't ask anyone else.'

I hurried out to Ceannt's house. Lily opened the door herself. 'Yes, it's true enough,' she said when I asked her. 'Don't ask any questions. The whole thing is off for the moment.'

I stayed with the Ceannts all day. That evening at tea, Éamonn, dark, quiet, reserved as he always was, seemed preoccupied with thoughts of his own. He did not join in the talk that went on during the meal. Afterwards, he asked for a fire in a separate room and withdrew. Later, Mrs Ceannt joined him. I wondered a little at the time about this, but had the sense to ask no questions. Instinctively I felt that something important was taking place, but I could not guess, of course, that Ceannt, as one of the seven who were to lead the fighting the next day, was probably trying to straighten out the upset that the countermanding order had caused to the carefully laid plans for the Rising.

I sat with Lily in the dining room, talking of general things. She was very full of an idea she had for a new play she thought of writing. Apart from her work with Cumann na mBan, she ran a small private school and contributed to Irish and American periodicals. She was the author of a number of books, and had written a short play, *May Eve in Stephen's Green*, a fantasy inspired by the statue of Mangan there. Together we had staged this at the Father Mathew Hall, where it had aroused considerable interest. Afterwards, the script had been lost, and she thought of writing it out again with some changes. This was the main topic of our talk. The postponed route march never entered into the conversation again.

In the nearby room, Ceannt and his wife wrote industriously. Occasionally a knock came to the front door, and he answered it himself. There were murmurs in the hallway and rustling of papers as though documents were changing hands. Later on, Mrs Ceannt joined us before the fire. She didn't mention anything about what Éamonn was doing. We were an ordinary little party, passing what seemed a quiet, not very eventful Sunday evening.

At about ten o'clock I rose to go. At the door Lily asked me: 'Is there anywhere I can get you tomorrow; any place I can send a message?' I said I would be at home all the next day.

As I shook hands, Éamonn came out of the front room. He looked tired and strained. 'Goodbye, Maire,' he said. I never saw him again.

The next morning I went to ten o'clock Mass in Glasthule. Halfway through the service I felt a touch on my shoulder. It was my father. He had a telegram for me from Lily O'Brennan. 'Come at once,' it said.

I changed quickly into uniform, slipped on a heavy topcoat and caught a tram. All vehicles leaving the city were full of Easter holidaymakers before they reached College Green. I travelled on to O'Connell Street. There was a long wait at the Pillar. The city was thronged with bank-holiday crowds and racegoers making the best of the warm weather. Crowds heaved and pushed under the porticoes of the GPO. Long queues lined the street to the tram stops. At the O'Connell Bridge junction, traffic was held up by streams of cyclists.

As the tram turned the corner of Dawson Street, the end rank of a body of Volunteers flanking the College of Surgeons came into view. Not all the men were in uniform. Some wore slouch-hats and trench coats criss-crossed with bandoliers; a few of them had picks and shovels; most of them carried rifles. On the footpaths little groups of officers conferred. A few moved backwards and forwards between the ranks. The tram stopped for a moment and a figure standing at the junction of King Street and Grafton Street turned its head. It was Joe Plunkett. He was in uniform. His hat-brim, bound tightly to the crown, displayed a white surgical bandage swathing his throat and chin. Farther on, at the corner of York Street, Tom MacDonagh stood talking with a man in civilian clothes. This was Major John MacBride.

I had left my bicycle at a house in South Richmond Street, from which I now collected it and cycled out to Dolphin's Barn.

Ceannt's house was locked up, the blinds drawn. Although I hammered on the door I could get no reply. I then realised that I had forgotten to ask in which direction the battalion would go. The silent house was puzzling. Though Éamonn and Lily had gone on a route march, someone should have been left behind, yet even then the possibility of a rising never struck me.

I cycled down through Dolphin's Barn, across the top of Cork Street, then into the South Circular Road. It should have been possible to get back to the Green and join up with the Volunteers. I might easily have managed it too, but I was delayed for more than half an hour on the way and had an irritating and painful experience into the bargain.

Passing Wellington Barracks, a motor car skidded out of a side street and shot across the roadway. I stopped suddenly and swerved towards the kerb. The impact threw me off the bicycle and I stumbled over the footpath, tearing my knee on the concrete. The car stopped and the driver got out. He was a British officer. He was little more than a boy, and looked frightened out of his wits. He muttered an apology and asked if I was all right.

I said I was a little shaken, and pulled the heavy coat around my uniform. My knee was throbbing.

He lifted up the bicycle, which, miraculously, had escaped serious damage, began to fix it on the luggage rack of the car, and offered to take me wherever I was going. He was surprised when I refused. Pointing out that I was limping, he offered to take me to a doctor. I took the bicycle off the car while he was still protesting and limped away. He followed, driving the car at walking pace and calling out of the window until we reached the corner of Longwood Avenue. Though my knee felt badly bruised, I mounted the machine and rode off. 'I say! You can't do that!' he called. I glanced back. He was standing in the centre of the road, his cap tilted over one ear, scratching his head. He seemed anxious to help, but from what I was beginning to suspect he would have been little use where I was going.

Passing down Richmond Street, the pain became almost unbearable, and I decided to leave the bicycle and go the rest of the way on foot. I stopped at a house, the home of Paddy Morgan, a dentist, whom I knew through his association with Sinn Féin.

Paddy opened the door himself. When he saw my leg he became excited. 'Were you fired on?' he asked.

I asked what he meant. The pain from my knee was spreading down into my foot.

'It's the Volunteers,' said Paddy. 'They've taken Davey's pub at Portobello…. You'll be shot if you go any farther!'

Just then, from the Rathmines direction, there was a rattle of gunfire. It stopped almost as soon as it started.

'The Volunteers!' cried Paddy. 'They're taking the city!'

I leaned the bicycle against the wall and stumbled down the street as fast as my leg would allow me. I had an idea now that I might get into Camden Street and see Mrs Paudeen O'Keeffe, a Cumann na mBan officer, sister-in-law of Mrs Wyse-Power, who had a shop, Irish Farm Produce, there. It was only a few yards away. The shop was shut, but Mrs O'Keeffe came to the side door herself. I told her what had passed and asked what I was to do. She said: 'Go to 6 Harcourt Street, Sinn Féin. There should be some girls there. Get them together.'

In Harcourt Street, the door of the Sinn Féin office was open and five girls stood in the hallway. One, Sara Kealy of the Fairview Cumann na mBan, I knew by sight; another was named Kathleen Lane. There were two sisters named Pollard and a girl named Annie McQuade.

A man ran down the street. Passing the door, he called over his shoulder: 'The Citizen Army are taking the Green! The Volunteers are breaking into Jacob's factory!' Sara, who did not look very old—about seventeen—said: 'I've been to Jacob's. I saw one of the Volunteers. I think Tom MacDonagh's there!'

The factory was about three minutes' walk away. We set off down the road. In Cuffe Street, people looked at us out of windows, men and women ran along the footpaths. Near Mercer's Place a crowd of ragged little boys ran out of a laneway. They had paper bags pulled down over their ears. Discordantly, they chanted something about 'the Volunteers'.

As we turned the corner opposite Jacob's, a huge crowd of poorly dressed men and women, some of them shouting and screaming and waving fists, came into view. We later learned that this was a mixed crowd of Jacob's factory employees and Separation Allowance women—the wives of British soldiers fighting in France. They were quarrelling together on the footpaths. As we pushed on we saw the caps of Volunteers bobbing over the heads of the crowd, and caught the glint of steel. Then we were under the side of Jacob's.

The Volunteers were lined along the outside of the building, some of them holding the crowd back with rifles. A crowd of men and women in civilian clothing swayed across the footpaths, shaking fists and shouting at the Volunteers, daring them to enter the building at the risk of their skin. Down the Bishop Street side of the factory a few apparently unarmed men in uniform had gathered, while a large body of men with rifles and picks poured into the building through a shattered gateway. The crash of glass and splintering wood sounded from farther along the street as other parties effected entrances of their own. An armed guard stood at the gate ignoring the shrieks of the crowd. We went up to him and told him who we were. 'I don't know what you should do,' he said. 'You'd better go over to that gate and get inside.'

Just inside a door, in a passageway that appeared to lead to the main bakery of the building, I met Tom MacDonagh in the full uniform, cloak cap and accoutrements of a Volunteer commandant. He was talking to Major MacBride, who was still in civilian clothes, a navy-blue suit, grey hat, a malacca walking-cane on his arm.

MacDonagh said: 'My God … It's Maire Walker! How did you get in?' He put down his head, shaking it from side to side. A typical gesture. He seemed very much at ease. After a while, he said: 'We haven't made any provision for girls here …'.

I explained that we could cook for the garrison and look after casualties. He asked how many of us there were. 'Only six,' I told him, and asked if I should go and see if any others had arrived in Sinn Féin. 'Yes,' he said, 'but hurry.'

There were no more girls at Harcourt Street. Most of the Cumann na mBan members had already moved off with their respective companies. I returned to Jacob's. The Volunteers were all gone from the street. There were groups of them at windows, knocking out the jagged ends of glass that still remained in the frames, barricading with white flour sacks. When we got inside again, MacDonagh and MacBride had vanished.

Looking out towards the Peter Street side of the building, near the Adelaide Hospital, we were just in time to witness a striking incident. A group of Volunteers were letting the remainder of their comrades into the building. Down the street, swaying from side to side, came an open two-seater car. As it drew abreast of Jacob's, a figure in Citizen Army uniform stood up in the front seat and waved its hat above its head. It was Madame Markievicz on her way to Stephen's Green.

'Go at it, boys!' she yelled. 'The Citizen Army are taking the Green! Dublin Castle is falling!'

There was a pause amongst the figures on the street. Everyone looked after the noisy vehicle. In the hush that followed, the shouts of its occupants could be heard distinctly. There was then a cheer and a doffing of caps, and the remainder of the Volunteers scrambled through the windows and took up positions at the command of an officer.

In a room near the centre of the building, Tom MacDonagh unrolled a copy of the Proclamation of the new republic. We gathered around and read the words that Pearse had already spoken to crowds outside the barricaded GPO an hour before:

POBLACHT NA HÉIREANN.
THE PROVISIONAL GOVERNMENTOF THE IRISH
REPUBLIC
TO THE PEOPLE OF IRELAND.

IRISHMEN AND IRISHWOMEN: In the name of God and of the dead generations from which she receives her old tradition of nationhood, Ireland, through us, summons her children to her flag and strikes for her freedom.

Having organised her manhood through her secret revolutionary organisation, the Irish Republican Brotherhood, and through her open military organisations, the Irish Volunteers and the Irish Citizen Army, having patiently perfected her discipline, having resolutely waited for the right moment to reveal itself, she now seizes that moment, and supported by her exiled children in America and by gallant allies in Europe, but relying in the first on her own strength, she strikes in full confidence of victory.

We declare the right of the people of Ireland to the ownership of Ireland and to the unfettered control of Irish destinies, to be sovereign and indefeasible. The long usurpation of that right by a foreign people and government has not extinguished the right, nor can it ever be extinguished except by the destruction of the Irish people. In every generation the Irish people have asserted their right to national freedom and sovereignty; six times during the past three hundred years they have asserted it in arms. Standing on that fundamental right and again asserting it in arms in the face of the world, we hereby proclaim the Irish Republic as a Sovereign Independent State, and we pledge our lives and the lives of our comrades in arms to the cause of its freedom, of its welfare and of its exaltation among the nations.

The Irish Republic is entitled to, and hereby claims, the allegiance of every Irishman and Irishwoman. The Republic guarantees religious and civil liberty, equal rights and equal opportunities to all its citizens, and declares its resolve to pursue the happiness and prosperity of the whole nation and of all its parts, cherishing all the children of the nation equally, and oblivious of the differences carefully fostered by an alien government, which have divided a minority from the majority in the past.

Until our arms have brought the opportune moment for the establishment of a permanent National Government, representative of the whole people of Ireland and elected by the suffrages of all her men and women, the Provisional Government, hereby constituted, will administer the civil and military affairs of the Republic in trust for the people.

We place the cause of the Irish Republic under the protection of the Most High God, Whose blessing we invoke upon our arms, and we pray that no one who serves that cause will dishonour it by cowardice, inhumanity or rapine. In this supreme hour the Irish nation must, by its valour and discipline, and by the readiness of its children to sacrifice themselves for the common good, prove itself worthy of the august destiny to which it is called.

Signed on behalf of the Provisional Government:

THOMAS J. CLARKE, SEAN MAC DIARMADA, P. H. PEARSE, JAMES CONNOLLY, THOMAS MACDONAGH, ÉAMONN CEANNT, JOSEPH PLUNKETT.

A little later, a cheer from the street brought us hurrying through a doorway, and we saw, from a little enclosed yard, the figure of a Volunteer on the roof hoisting the republican flag.

Although I didn't know it then, my sixty-eight-year-old father, Matthew—who was a master printer and publisher—was walking from Glasthule to Dublin to take part in the fighting. He entered the GPO and volunteered his services to Pearse, whom he knew well, not least because of their IRB connection. Pearse took down some heavy telegraph paper and began to transcribe what would be become the *Irish War News*. He entrusted my father with its printing.

Father then discussed with James Connolly the possibility of taking over the *Irish Independent* offices on Abbey Street, but the latter was not in favour of this. My father was instructed to find a printing press outside the immediate vicinity of the GPO James O'Keeffe's on Halston Street was chosen. For the duration of the week, my father, brother, Charlie, brother-in-law, Joe Stanley, and two compositors, James O'Sullivan and Thomas Ryan, produced the *Irish War News* and four bulletins under the noses of the British Army as Dublin blazed.

As I said, I was unaware of this. I was also unaware that the man I would marry in 1925, Major General Eamonn 'Bob' Price

(Director of Organisation IRA GHQ)—then a captain—was close by fighting on the Green.

As for my little sister, Gipsy, she was frantically cycling into town and was to carry despatches for Cathal Brugha during the fighting. Her fiancé, Crawford Neil, was to be mortally wounded the following day.

Chapter Nineteen

Inside the Jacob's Garrison

JACOB'S BISCUIT FACTORY stands in a warren of small streets and laneways roughly in the centre of Dublin, in one of the busiest shopping centres in the city. It is difficult to fix its position exactly. A little to the west of Stephen's Green, its long frontage travels back through dozens of byways and commands an extensive view of the city, looking across Camden Street and Aungier Street on one side; Bride Street and Werburgh Street on the other. Running on opposite sides of it and linking up the main thoroughfares are two small side streets, Peter Street and Bishop Street, where the gate by which we entered was situated.

On all sides its façade is lined with windows, and from the highest point of the building two ornamental towers of wrought-iron and turreted brick look out over miles of streets. From there it is possible to look on all sides across the neighbouring rooftops, and the streets and intersections in the vicinity appear to be laid out like a map. A maze of backyards and blackened chimney pots stretches out on all sides. To the north, hidden in a cluster of fancy rooftops, is Dublin Castle; farther ahead in the same direction are the GPO and O'Connell Street.

About a mile to the east, Boland's Mill was occupied by de Valera during the week. To the west was the South Dublin Union and Marrowbone Lane Distillery, held by Ceannt. Portobello Barracks, in British hands, lay immediately to the south.

All around the factory within easy cycling distance the Volunteers held major positions, stemming any British approach through the streets. In such a position, strongly built and practically impregnable to anything but heavy artillery, the garrison was never in any immediate danger of close hand-to-hand fighting. As it happened, most of the bitterest fighting carried out by the garrison during the week was done by cycle patrols and raiding parties despatched to relieve other Volunteer points in the vicinity.

There were from 130 to 150 men in the building, members of the 2nd Dublin Battalion Volunteers; a few members of Madame Markievicz's Fianna boy scouts, and the Cumann na mBan girls. Major MacBride immediately assumed the position of MacDonagh's second-in-command; the latter had met him at Stephen's Green before the battalion moved off and asked him to come along. It is believed that the Rising took MacBride somewhat by surprise, but from his first knowledge of it he displayed a willingness to take part. This, despite the fact that as a former officer of the Irish Brigade in South Africa during the Boer War, and a marked man by Dublin Castle detectives, his execution was inevitable if he were taken prisoner.

He was without uniform throughout the week, and he carried no rifle, although he may have provided himself with a revolver during his occasional excursions through the bullet-swept streets on succeeding days, directing troops in the neighbourhood to new positions.

We spoke with him frequently in MacDonagh's room at Jacob's, and once when he visited us as we prepared meals. He fulfilled all expectations as a soldier of courage and resource, a gentleman, quiet, witty and always unruffled. Without exception, the Volunteers in the building admired and respected him.

With Major MacBride, MacDonagh's personal staff included Michael O'Hanrahan, the quartermaster, who was executed within a day of his commandant; Captains T. Sleator, T. Meldon and D. Riordan; Lieutenants Arthur Cahill, a chemist subsequently appointed medical officer; and John MacDonagh, Tom's brother. This was in addition to the minor commands scattered throughout the other rooms and in adjoining buildings.

We arrived back at Jacob's at about 12.45, arranged the storage of our equipment and began a tour of the building.

It would be impossible now to give an exact picture of the inside of the place. Its several floors were honeycombed with rooms and passageways, one leading off the other. There were staircases leading upwards to offices, small bakeries and dough-rooms; a huge kitchen, several rest-rooms and a canteen. A lot of the ground floor appeared to be given over to the main factory bakery—a huge place of ovens and pastry-benches with yards of steel piping.

Light came from windows looking out on adjacent streets. Volunteers were posted at each wall, so many windows to each man, and commanded all the street approaches to the place. Off this room on one side was a small forge, which we used as a kitchen, electricity and gas power having been cut off to prevent fire. There was an immediate danger of this.

Despite the activities of the Volunteers on the roof, British snipers succeeded in occupying a few positions in the streets outside our cordon, and their bullets occasionally ricocheted off the outer walls. As the Cumann na mBan spent the greater part of the week in this room, the sound of these bullets, the constant crack of rifles overhead, and later the explosions during the bombardment of the GPO, were the only hints we had of activity in the neighbouring streets. In the upper rooms and in one of the towers that we visited, bullets entered more often.

On the first or second floor, reached from the bakery by a steel staircase, we found a perfectly equipped but useless kitchen, formerly equipped by gas and electricity. Three Volunteers disconnected a couple of immense copper boilers and carried them down to the forge, where we set them on the fire. They made excellent urns for boiling meat and vegetables and brewing tea.

Despite constant foraging through the building, this first day no food suitable for hungry men could be found. There were biscuits in plenty, 'plain and fancy'—mostly fancy—slabs of rich fruit cake, some shortbread and a few tons of cream crackers. But there was nothing of which to make a hot drink. Eventually, one of the girls found a gross or two of slab cooking-chocolate. It was grated into the biggest boiler and stewed until it melted. The result was a dark-brown cocoa-like syrup, taken without sugar or milk. It looked horrible, but at least it was sustaining.

Within an hour, all the interior defences had been built up. Sacks of flour lay waist-high across the windows, loop-holed at convenient points, figures crouched behind these peering down silently into the streets. A few leaned against the walls, looking out sideways, rifles beside them. Small groups of officers clattered down the stairs through the rooms, trying to estimate the size of the place. Some Volunteers passed through the bakery carrying piles of equipment. The little force seemed to have been swallowed up into the vastness of the place. Although calls could be heard from the upstairs rooms, the sound of footsteps, an occasional clatter as a rifle fell, there was an eeriness about the place; a feeling of being cut off from the outside world.

Towards one o'clock, there was some movement in the streets, and a sudden burst of firing rattled over the rooftops from the Camden Street direction. This was an ambush organised by ten Volunteers who had learned that a party of British under an officer was making its way towards Redmond's Hill, near the Bishop Street corner. This walked straight into the Volunteers, who were lined over the street. The shots accounted for most of the British force, the rest of it breaking in disorder as the soldiers ran for safety. It was the first major skirmish in the vicinity of the factory.

Dublin soon acclimatised itself to the new situation. Outside, the crowds of sightseers although they thinned by about six o'clock, seemed quieter now, less truculent than before. People had at last begun to realise what was happening. Their reaction, surprisingly, was one of curiosity rather than fear. Figures crossed the street occasionally and stared at the windows.

Inside the building and on the street, everyone seemed to be waiting for something to happen. Now and again during the afternoon, Volunteers who had not been mobilised that morning clattered round the Bishop Street corner and stood on the footpaths, calling to those in upstairs rooms to let them in. As the evening drew to a close, a hush settled on the factory, broken only by the occasional crack of rifles overhead or in the distance.

When darkness settled, a group of Volunteers entered the bake-room with candles, which they set about the room in empty biscuit boxes. The boxes faced inwards, away from the windows, forming a huge circle, intensifying the darkness beyond. There was a murmur of voices from the doorway, and men started to shuffle into the light. The whole garrison, with the exception of those on sentry duty, gathered inside the circle and knelt. Someone started the Rosary.

As those in the bake-room responded to the prayer, the men on the stairs took it up, the sound passing slowly from room to room until the whole building vibrated with the rise and fall of the mumbled voices. The candles threw an uncertain light on the faces of the Volunteers, catching the glint of the rifles they had laid beside them. Now and then you could hear the noise of firing through the prayers; a strange background sound you could never, never forget.

We saw Tom MacDonagh often during this first day and throughout the week. He visited the bake-room on his rounds, for he seemed to be keeping a personal check on different parts of the garrison. He would appear at the door with a cheerful word or a smile and ask how we were managing on the rather mixed rations. Sometimes he would pause for a moment or two to talk before passing on to some other part of the building. Although his visits were brief, he always managed to pass on some of his own enthusiasm and optimism.

Later in the week, I found that his conversation relieved much of the strain we had begun to feel, even where we were quartered, away from the danger-points. Our isolation and occasional periods of inactivity were not pleasant. We heard many of the rumours that travelled around the building as the days passed, and we had no means of telling whether they were true or not.

He had set up headquarters in a room near the centre of the building on the second or third floor. From there he could command all points of the garrison. He carried his usual competent businesslike air with him, and was an excellent leader, hiding his worries behind his good humour, and never allowing anyone to think other than that the fighting was going well. He never tired of repeating that we might be in Jacob's for months, and that the position was so well in hand that nothing could stop a republican victory.

It was afterwards that we realised how much he must have had himself under control: he must have known that surrender could mean nothing less than his own execution. He showed no signs of worry.

Throughout this week he was the same unruffled MacDonagh most of us had always known. It was only when news of the surrender became fact that his good humour faltered slightly. Even then, he bore himself with dignity.

There was plenty for our garrison to do. The factory was an important link in the republican chain, and its great height made it an excellent vantage-point. Though the fighting never quite extended to its doors, the frequent vicious outbursts of firing in nearby streets during the early part of the week was evidence that the smaller garrisons established at MacDonagh's command were engaging approaching troops. Now and then parties of Volunteers returned to the factory and officers were closeted in the staffroom for long periods. Mostly these men looked tired and in need of sleep. Frequently they threw themselves down to rest after their interviews.

No one knew what was happening elsewhere. In many cases whole families taking part in the Rising were broken up; some of the men with the Citizen Army in the Green, where the fighting was fierce; others with the Volunteers; girls with the Cumann na mBan, some of them taking a part in the fighting; others administering first aid. It was rumoured that there were many deaths. Buildings in some of the main streets were completely destroyed by the British bombardment.

In Jacob's there was a constant feeling of isolation. The occasional shots in nearby streets, the sound of firing in the rooms overhead, and towards the middle of the week the thunder of heavy artillery from the north, made rest impossible. Despite MacDonagh's cheerfulness, and the occasional rumours of victory that passed through the rooms day after day, this ignorance of what was really happening in other parts of the city set nerves on edge.

Quartered downstairs, we had long, busy periods, for our party was small, and there was much to be done. As the senior member of the Cumann na mBan squad I assumed command of the group of girls, and reported at intervals to the staffroom. But events as they happened took place so quickly, and the strain and excitement that we all experienced was so great, that all that remains are brief, inconsecutive pictures, some of them vivid, others, in memory, dim.

In my position it would have been impossible to give at any time an overall picture of events inside the garrison. Everyone had their own work to do, and no one was certain of what went on elsewhere. For us downstairs the work would be broken by long periods of waiting, which were really the worst feature of our time in the building. Looking back, all the activities in which I took part are somehow blended together into one long, disjointed picture. The whole week seemed to pass like one long day.

Tuesday passed quickly. By then the garrison was firmly entrenched and the outposts established in the immediate vicinity kept the streets clear of approaching British troops. Snipers on the roof of the factory kept firing at intervals throughout the day. Occasionally the shots mingled with the crackle and crash of gunfire and bombing from Stephen's Green, where, we heard, Madame Markievicz and Michael Mallon, with the Citizen Army and Volunteers, had withdrawn to the College of Surgeons, and with something like a hundred men, rushed to occupy the Shelbourne Hotel and neighbouring buildings. We later heard the rattle of machine-gun fire as the English soldiers established themselves in the hotel and the United Services Club.

The main worry of our little Cumann na mBan squad—the provision of proper food for the garrison—was solved about midday when a party of scouts returned to the building laden with vegetables and provisions. There were potatoes, sides of meat and an assortment of groceries taken from neighbouring shops. In a little while we were cooking, stoking the fires and cleaning vegetables and meat. Our diet for the week consisted of tea, buttered bread or sandwiches, and at midday the principal meal was stew, which was the quickest and easiest to prepare.

I spent most of the day downstairs, for MacDonagh had forbidden us the freedom, unescorted, of the upper parts of the building, where a figure passing a window at once became a target. The only time we left the ground floor was to attend his headquarters for instructions. Later in the week he relaxed this order, and I climbed to one of the roof-towers, from where I saw the last of the burning GPO.

Rumour was one of the worst enemies the garrison had. It was the same elsewhere in the city, for no one could quite piece together a picture of the entire action. Wild stories sped through the rooms each day. We heard that German troops had landed at Wexford and were striking inland in thousands, routing British garrisons as they drove towards Dublin. It was said that the Volunteers were fighting bitterly along the coastline to Cork, where the city was supposed to be out like Dublin. British troops were being rushed from the Curragh camp and reinforcements were pouring into Dublin along the Naas road; Dublin Castle was on fire; the British were using explosive bullets and shooting prisoners; buildings all over the city were being burned indiscriminately; Dublin was almost in ruins.

Each rumour was more fantastic than the last, and one contradicted the other. Everyone was confused. Nobody knew the true state of affairs, or of the damage that Eoin MacNeill's countermanding order on the Sunday had done in the provinces, where the Volunteers still waited for the order to mobilise and wondered, as desperately as we did, what was happening elsewhere.

Many unpleasant stories reached us. There were rumours of civil riots, irresponsible civilian looting, and stories of outrages by British soldiers—for one of the things we heard was that most of the English soldiers rushed into the city during this week were fresh recruits, mostly unused to firearms and to a great extent bewildered by the street fighting against enemies they could not see.

After the Rising it was said that many of the British casualties were caused by young soldiers, not long in uniform, running amok and shooting their companions on barricades and in outposts. A number of similar incidents occurred behind the Volunteer lines, but not to the same extent, for there is a deal of difference between an untrained conscript and a man who goes willingly into danger and has prepared himself for death. I heard later of a hysterical man in the GPO who had to be forcibly restrained, and in another garrison a man succumbed to the strain of continuous attack, running wild and killing a companion before he was shot by a sentry.

One of the most appalling outrages of the week occurred within a few streets of Jacob's garrison on Tuesday when a man whom I knew personally as a non-combatant, a pacifist, Frank Sheehy-Skeffington, was brutally murdered by a British officer.

Skeffington carried no arms and had nothing whatever to do with the Rising. At some danger to himself he had been walking through the city in an attempt to organise a civil force to prevent looting. On Tuesday evening he was halted by the British as he crossed Portobello Bridge and was conveyed to the nearby barracks. A British officer flouted all military regulations and had him taken from his cell and conveyed as a hostage with a raiding party.

The officer led his squad spectacularly along the Rathmines Road, firing at the shadows and shouting defiance at the closed windows. Outside a church he met two boys, singled out one of them, then had him clubbed with rifles and afterwards emptied his revolver into the body. He bombed several houses in the vicinity, and pulled a man out of an empty building and shot him. All the time he threatened Skeffington with death and worse and referred with contempt to the 'Sinn Féiners.'

Later, when he returned to Portobello, he had Skeffington and two others shot without trial in the barrack yard.

I had known Frank Sheehy-Skeffington for many years. He was very closely connected with the suffragettes: his wife, Hannah, was one of the leaders of the movement in Ireland. He was a journalist and editor of *The National Democrat* newspaper. But he was a pacifist, a man opposed to war in any form, and although he sympathised with the nationalist movement he had no connection with the Rising.

He was a well-known and popular figure in the city; his courteous manner established him as a favourite. I knew him mostly through suffragette gatherings, which I used to attend at the movement's headquarters in Westmoreland Street, and through numerous public meetings, which he addressed in the city in protest against recruiting for the British Army.

A story told afterwards of how, in the midst of a street gunfight near Dublin Castle, he tried to rescue a wounded British officer, demonstrating his humanity and courage.

Dublin was outraged by his death. When it became known after the Rising, the affair raised such a storm of protest that a commission was hastily set up to enquire into it—a favourite device of the administration in those days, employed usually to save face. But the administration hardly regretted Skeffington's death: his shrewd pen had been an embarrassment, and his anti-recruiting activities had proved too effective to be pleasant. His absence was probably welcomed.

The days passed quickly. How can I describe how I felt this week? All the time I was divided between the excitement of being in Jacob's, and worries for those whom I had left at home. I had no means of knowing what was happening in Glasthule. It seemed likely to me that there would be fighting around that whole area; someone had said that the Volunteers would make every effort to prevent British troops landing at the harbour in Dún Laoghaire.

It was not until after the surrender that I learned that the district had seen no fighting. The Volunteer cordon did not go farther than Mount Street Bridge, where English troops attempting to get into the city were held back by a handful of men in Carisbrook House. But mostly I was conscious of a great excitement. I am sure everyone in the building felt the same. I seldom felt tired; I never felt the need of much sleep for the four days.

The great spirit of this whole period was all around us in Jacob's, the enthusiasm, the wonderful feeling that underlaid every worthwhile activity in Dublin in those years. No one had any regrets—why should they have had? Until the surrender there was not a word of complaint from anyone I met. You never thought much about what the result of it all would be. You never assumed that victory was certain, but neither did you think of defeat. What might happen if we lost meant nothing; life or death, freedom or imprisonment, these things did not enter into it at all. The great thing was that what you had always hoped for had happened at last. An insurrection had taken place, and you were actually participating in it.

The pity was that it ended so soon. The news of the surrender, when it came, was heartbreaking.

It was Thursday almost before I realised it. By then we had become used to the constant sound of rifles and machine guns; I hardly noticed it. The deeper note of artillery could now be heard. All night long there was the heavy thud of distant explosions. Still, I could not tell what was happening.

The truth was terrible enough. The GPO had fallen under the heavy bombardment of a British gunboat stationed on the Liffey and was abandoned by Pearse and the occupants. The garrison retreated through heavy fire to houses at Moore Street. One leader, The O'Rahilly, was killed by British machine-gunners as he led a charge across Moore Street armed only with a revolver.

James Connolly was carried out of the building on a stretcher in most heroic circumstances. We later learned of how he shouted encouragement to the Volunteers and urged a party of Fianna boys who formed a human shield around his stretcher to go ahead and leave him. Pearse was still uninjured as he directed the fortification of the new headquarters.

That evening I went up to one of Jacob's towers. Over in the north the GPO was blazing fiercely; it seemed as though the flames had spread the length of O'Connell Street. There were huge columns of smoke. Around us, in the turret, the Volunteers were still keeping up steady fire on British outposts nearby. In the distance the crackle of gunfire was accompanied by sudden little flashes. All around, through the darkness, bombed-out buildings burned. From where we stood, the whole city seemed to be on fire. The noise of artillery, machine-gun and rifle fire was deafening.

On Saturday there was a sudden lull, and the sound of the bombardment gradually died down. Pearse had surrendered to General Lowe, the British commander, that afternoon. On Sunday a member of the GPO Cumann na mBan called at Jacob's with the news.

I heard that MacDonagh at first refused to accept her despatch, maintaining that he would not take orders from Pearse as a prisoner, but after persuasion he agreed to meet General Lowe at St Patrick's Park and discuss the position with him and the prisoners. He left Jacob's with a priest, Father Augustine of Church Street Priory, who had attended the garrison the whole week. He had a very fixed expression, and little trace of his former good humour remained.

Inside Jacob's there was now much speculation. News of the surrender was not yet fully accepted. The almost uncanny silence that had hung over Dublin since the last shell was fired during the bombardment of the GPO made everyone uncertain. Everybody waited for MacDonagh to come back.

After his return he went straight to the staffroom. A few minutes later an order came for all Volunteer officers in the building to report to him. They were gone a long time; it seemed hours. Then he sent for me. When I went in, he was standing behind his desk, beside Major MacBride. He said, very simply, 'We are going to surrender.'

He seemed the same businesslike person we had always known, until he spoke: his voice was quiet, disillusioned. He said, 'I want you to thank all the girls for what they have done. Tell them I am issuing an order that they are to go home. I'll see that you are all safely conducted out of the building.' I started to protest, but he turned away. One could never imagine him looking so sad.

I went downstairs and into the bake-room. I will never forget that scene. Almost everyone in the building had assembled on the ground floor. The announcement of surrender had just been made. It had not been taken well. There were shouts of 'Don't give in … we can't give in now!' Everyone was talking at once. The noise was deafening. I saw a man throw down his rifle and put his hands over his face. Another was smashing the butt of a gun against a wall. Some of the men seemed confused, as though they could not believe it. The officers were calling for order and trying to explain why surrender was necessary.

Tom MacDonagh came in. He climbed onto a table and held up his hand. The noise died away at once.

'We have to give in,' he said. 'Those of you who are in civilian clothes, go home. Those in uniform, stay on. You cannot leave if you are in uniform.' He stepped down.

A Volunteer officer, Thomas Hunter, pushed his way through the crowd and climbed onto a bench. He held up his arms and shouted: 'All I say is, any of you who go home now ought to be ashamed of yourselves! Stand your ground like men!'

There was a murmur of approval. No one moved.

I gave the girls MacDonagh's order. They did not want to leave. I could understand their feelings. They were my own; I did not want to go myself. I told them what MacDonagh had said. He was anxious to have all girls out of the building before he surrendered. He feared that we would be arrested.

If this had been the only consideration I would have ignored his plea and stayed, but he thought that the sight of the girls being arrested might upset the men. He wanted everything to go as quietly as possible. On the other hand, Sara Kealy said that it might be useful for a few girls to stay behind. They could write letters for the men and take messages to relatives. She announced her decision to remain. I did not press the matter.

In the midst of much confusion, some women in Cumann na mBan uniform came in, amongst them Louise Gavan-Duffy and Min Ryan from the GPO. They were on their way home and asked me to go with them. MacDonagh came through the crowd and asked, 'Will you go now, please?'

'I don't know, Tom. All the girls insist on staying.'

MacBride was standing just inside one of the exits. 'It would be better for you to go,' he said. As we shook hands he asked that a message be taken to some friends at Glasthule. 'Tell them, too, that we had a good week of it,' he added.

Outside, a British officer was standing near one of the gateways. He said, 'I'll see you over the roadway, ladies.' We walked down the roadway and turned the corner into Camden Street. It was a route I had taken many times through the years. I cannot remember what we talked about, if we talked at all, for there did not seem very to be much to say. I felt confused and disappointed. All at once, I had begun to feel very tired.

Along Camden Street the shop windows were shuttered and dark. We passed few people on the footpath. Everything looked strange; even the street was different.

It was as though I had never seen it before.

Despite what was going on inside, Jacob's looked very dark, very empty. Dublin seemed unnaturally still.

Appendices

Appendix I

The Irish Literary Theatre

IN 1988, four years before Maire Nic Shiubhlaigh joined W. G. Fay's Irish National Dramatic Company, W. B. Yeats, Lady Gregory and Edward Martyn issued a public appeal for a guarantee to cover the expenses of performances in Dublin of Irish plays by Irish writers. They wrote:

> We propose to have performed in Dublin, in the spring of every year, certain Celtic and Irish plays which, whatever be their degree of excellence, will be written with a high ambition, and so build up a Celtic and Irish school of dramatic literature. We hope to find in Ireland an uncorrupted and imaginative audience trained to listen by its passion for oratory, and believe that our desire to bring upon the stage the deeper thoughts and emotions of Ireland will ensure for us a tolerant welcome, and that freedom to experiment which is not found in theatres of England and without which no new movement in art or literature can succeed. We will show that Ireland is not the home of buffoonery and of easy sentiment, as it has been represented, but the home of an ancient idealism. We are confident of the support of all Irish people, who are weary of misrepresentation, in carrying out a work that is outside all the political questions that divide us....[1]

---

[1]From the programme, Abbey Theatre Twenty-first Birthday Anniversary Performance, 27 December 1935.

265

The money was guaranteed by a group representative of all sections of literary and artistic life in Dublin, and later the same year the Irish Literary Theatre was founded. The guarantors were never requested to make any payment, Edward Martyn, during the three years of the theatre's career, defraying the cost of most productions himself. The Literary Theatre produced its first play, *The Countess Cathleen*, by W. B. Yeats, at the Antient Concert Rooms, Brunswick Street, Dublin, on 8 May 1899. The performance was accompanied by a demonstration in the theatre, with sections of the audience protesting against the ethics of the play on various grounds. W. B. Yeats wrote later of the occasion in an Appendix to the play published in 1912:

> They [the players] had to face a very vehement opposition stirred up by a politician and a newspaper, the one accusing me in a pamphlet, the other in long articles day after day, of blasphemy because of the language of the demons or of Seumas Rua, and because I made a woman sell her soul and yet escape damnation, and of a lack of patriotism because I made Irish men and women, who, it seems, never did such a thing, sell theirs. The politician or the newspaper persuaded some forty Catholic students to sign a protest against the play, and a Cardinal who avowed he had not read it, to make another, and both politician and newspaper made such obvious appeals to the audience to break the peace that a score or so of police were sent to the theatre to see that they did not. I had, however, no reason to regret the result, for the stalls, containing almost all that was distinguished in Dublin, and a gallery of artisans alike insisted on the freedom of literature[2].

The Countess Cathleen was followed immediately in 1899 by the first production of *The Heather Field* by Edward Martyn, and in the following two years five other original plays were produced,

---

[2]Appendix, *The Countess Cathleen* by W. B. Yeats (T. Fisher Unwin, Adelphi Terrace, 1912.)

one in Gaelic, *The Twisting of the Rope* (*Casadh an tSúgáin*) by Douglas Hyde. This was the first Gaelic play ever performed in an established theatre, and the cast was drawn from various Gaelic League branches in Dublin, the author himself taking the leading part of Raftery, the poet.

The complete list of Irish Literary Theatre plays, with dates of first performances, is as follows:

At the Antient Concert Rooms, Dublin:

8 May 1899:
The Countess Cathleen   W. B. Yeats.

9 May 1899:
The Heather Field   Edward Martyn.

At the Gaiety Theatre, Dublin:

19 February 1900:
The Bending of the Bough   George Mooie.
The Last Feast of the Fianna   Alice Milligan.

20 February 1900:
Maeve   Edward Martyn.

21 October 1901:
Diarmuid and Gráinne   Yeats–Moore.
Casadh an tSúgáin   Douglas Hyde.

Appendix II

W. G. Fay's Irish National Dramatic Company

THE FIRST production of *Deirdre*, by A. E., and *Kathleen Ni Houlihan*, by W. B. Yeats, took place at the Hall of St Teresa's Total Abstinence Association, Clarendon Street, Dublin, on 2 April 1902, and on the succeeding nights, 3 and 4 April 1902.

These were the original casts:

Deirdre

Deirdre		Maire T. Quinn.
Lavarcham (her foster mother)		Maire Nic Shiubhlaigh.
Fergus		P. J. Kelly.
Buinne	)	P. Colum.
Illaun	) Sons of Fergus	C. Caulfield.
Ardan	}	F. Ryan.
Ainnle	} Sons of Usna	H. Sproule.
Naisi		J. Dudley Digges.
Messenger		Brian Callender.
Concobar, Ardri of Ulla		F. J. Fay.

Kathleen Ni Houlihan

Kathleen Ni Houlihan	Maud Gonne.
Delia Cahill	Maire Nic Shiubhlaigh.
Bridget Gillan	Maire T. Quinn.
Patrick Gillan	C. Caulfield.

Michael Gillan   J. Dudley Digges.
Peter Gillan   W. G. Fay.

Excerpts from *The Freeman's Journal*, 5 April 1902:

If a crowded house—too crowded for comfort—an audience vibrating with enthusiasm and quick to seize every point and to grasp every situation, be any augury for the success of Mr W. G. Fay's experiment in the production of Irish drama by an Irish company, then the future of the Irish National Dramatic Company should be a bright one. Long before the time fixed for the performance of *Deirdre* and *Kathleen Ni Houlihan* last night, St Teresa's Hall was packed to overflowing, and later on all possible standing room was occupied.

Deirdre, the longer of the two plays, was placed first, an arrangement hardly to be commended. It is certain that Mr Yeats's little piece suffered by being placed last. The audience, tense with the excitement of the tragic situations of *Deirdre*, relaxed in the humour of Mr Yeats's opening scene, and were evidently unprepared for the deeper note which is struck when *Kathleen Ni Houlihan* enters. It would, we believe, do much to ensure a more perfect appreciation of Mr Yeats's play without in the least affecting that of *Deirdre*, were the order of their presentation reversed for the remaining performances.

We have already given the outline of the story round which A. E. has woven his dramatic poem of *Deirdre*. [...] It is evident that to A. E. the heroic past of Ireland is no mere storehouse of romantic legends, more or less authentic; for him, that past is a living reality and a source of spiritual inspiration. The old gods and heroes are, for A. E., the embodiment of everlasting forces, and their action is for no personal end, in his view, but tends towards the accomplishment of some Divine purpose. With this idea in his mind, A. E. evidently desires to make Concobar Mac Nessa not the jealous king [...] but rather the law-giver. But King Concobar, as a sort of Celtic Moses, is scarcely a convincing figure, so far, at least, as this story of the death of the Sons of Usna concerned; and he is, to our thinking, the least satisfactory character in A. E.'s play. Indeed, A. E. himself would seem to have wavered a little as to the real motive of King Concobar's treachery; for, while at one time he puts into his mouth the loftiest sentiments and makes him appear as the champion of the law, at another he shows him as the baffled victim of jealous passion, vowing vengeance on 'the Lights of Valour'. This inconsistency causes a certain obscurity as to the 'moral idea' of the play, and is a serious blemish to a work which is otherwise very beautiful. For in *Deirdre*, to a greater extent, perhaps, than in any other drama of the kind by a modern writer, the heroic past of Ireland stands revealed. A. E. has the power of imaginative creation to a very high degree, and his figures move with a dignity and a beauty which accord well with our ideals. The language, too, is throughout of the loftiest beauty, and some of the speeches are perfect little poems in prose. Of the three acts of the play, the second is, perhaps, the most completely satisfactory. The entrance of Fergus into the dun of Naisi and Deirdre in Alba is effective, and the farewell of Deirdre to the home where she has known so much happiness one of the most touching and beautiful passages in the play. The last act, though it contains some highly dramatic scenes—as, for example, the game of chess between Naisi and Deirdre—is somewhat wanting in tragic power at the close. The feeling of inevitability is too much forced upon one; there is not enough room left for regrets.

With regard to the acting of the play, the chief thing that must have struck the audience was the intense earnestness with which every member of the company had entered into his or her part. If there was failure—and such an attempt could hardly be an unqualified success—it was the failure of inexperience. The Naisi of Mr Dudley Digges was, undoubtedly, the most completely successful of all the characters. Mr Digges acted with real power and feeling, and spoke the beautiful words allotted to him with the greatest expression. The Deirdre of Miss Quinn was in many respects a most creditable performance, but the part—which is a difficult one—hardly suited her. Miss Maire Nic Shiubhlaigh, who acted with great intelligence, was more successful as Lavarcham; and Mr F. J. Fay was a satisfactory King Concobar, though his voice at times lacked passion. Fergus was well played by Mr P. J. Kelly, the two sons of Fergus by Mr P. Columb and Mr C. Caulfield; while Ainle and Ardan, the two brothers of Naisi, were played by Mr Fred Ryan and Mr H. Sproule.

[…] *Kathleen Ni Houlihan*, Mr. W. B. Yeats's one-act piece, which followed, was, for some unexplained reason, given with the hall, as well as the stage, fully lighted, and this injured the performance considerably, and it is to be hoped that such a mistake will not occur at any of the future performances. Of the piece itself it would be difficult to speak too highly. […] It is flooded with the beauty of 'old, forgotten, far-off things' and of ideals that are never quite lost. If this little play has a fault, it is that it has too much humour—'comic relief' would be too strong a term. […] The two old peasants who discuss their son's approaching marriage have their counterparts in hundreds of homes in Ireland; but, though this is so, we are inclined to doubt whether Peter and Bridget Gillan, practical persons though they were, would have remained so unmoved by the presence of the stranger within their gates. Surely, before she left the cottage, Kathleen Ni Houlihan would have stood revealed to them, however dimly, and Mr Yeats's faith in the spirituality of the Irish peasant would have been once more justified. The acting of Mr W. G. Fay, as Peter, was inimitable; and Miss Quinn was a capital Bridget. But it was with Miss Gonne, as Kathleen, that the honours of the performance lay. Her interpretation of the part was marked by a very high degree of histrionic power; and her beautiful voice was heard to advantage in the snatches of folk-songs with which her speeches were interspersed. We feel sure *Kathleen Ni Houlihan* will be a success wherever it is acted, and Mr Yeats is to be congratulated on the successful production of a singularly beautiful little piece.

Appendix III

Two Opinions of the Camden Street Theatre

THE LATE Joseph Holloway, in his diaries for 1902 and 1903, refers to two productions by the Irish National Theatre Society at the Hall, 34 Lower Camden Street, Dublin. Writing of the company's first performance in the theatre (4 December 1902), he praises the quality of the plays and the acting, but deplores the fact that, owing to 'insufficient advertising, the attendance numbered no more than twenty-five.' He later adds:

> It is a pity that the theatre is so placed that street-noises penetrate during the performances. [...] While it does not detract from the audience's enjoyment, it was no easy task for us either. [...] The hall in which the company intends to astonish the natives is a small one, and is approached by a very narrow hallway widening into an arena-like space immediately before reaching the Temple of Drama. Small beginnings often make great ends, but when the little play-house is discovered, I have no doubt that crowded houses will be the order, not the exception. [...] The more I see these players, the greater my admiration for them becomes. We wanted something really native of the soil to put some spirit into us. Here we have it now, and let us hope that we will not neglect making the proper use of it, and give it the support the movement deserves. As a mere playgoer even, these plays and players have given me quite a new sensation for

which I personally am truly thankful. After a lifetime of playgoing that is no easy thing to secure, yet I found it in the little 'theatre' in Camden Street.[3]

'R. M.', writing in the Dublin *Evening Mail* (5 December 1902), records some impressions of a performance by the company in the hall later the same month. The following excerpts from the review indicate the opinions of some other critics at the time:

> The ordinary playgoer is not the soundest critic of such an enterprise as that which has been undertaken by the Irish National Theatre Society in their 'very little hall' in unpoetic and uninspiring Camden Street. If at any period he has been blessed with a taste for the primitive and the simple—it is, perhaps, permissible to add, without discourtesy, the uncomfortable—it has been hopelessly vitiated by the luxurious ease of the modern playhouse, where he can sit without shivering and doze through a stupid piece without discomfort.
>
> To put it plainly, he lacks that divine warmth of soul which [...] enables some moderns to freeze with a sense of positive pleasure on a bitterly cold night in December in a draughty, ill-lighted, unheated hall. The limitations of endurance which afflict the modern playgoer are not his fault. [...] They are, perhaps, his misfortune. [...] Draughts offend him, he hates sitting on a wooden form without a back-rest, and he prefers even the crudest and most vulgar form of decoration to unrelieved whitewash or funereal black paint. This is not written in ill-will or even as a complaint. [...] It is simply intended to show that if the Irish Theatre Society wishes to make proselytes among playgoers, it must meet them at least half way; otherwise they will still turn to the jig of musical comedy and to the tale of bawdry society drama and the work of

---

[3] *Irish Playgoer's Impressions*, 1902/3. National Library of Ireland.

the Irish Literary Theatre goes for nothing. [...] Surely it would be possible to house more honourably the much-advertised Irish Dramatic Muse. She is now four years old, she has many friends and there must be many more waiting to be wooed. It may be, of course, that the mission of the society is not to the dramatic gentiles, that it preaches only to the elect, the chosen people. [...] If one may judge by last night's audience, the elect are few and strangely coy.[...]

Last night's audience was extremely small. [...] At eight o'clock the audience whiled away the time by discussing various subjects in an undertone and a half light. [...] One by one, the elect trickled in, each one bringing with him an icy draught from the regions outside, and at last, about a quarter past eight, three solemn knocks heralded the parting of the curtains. [...]

It would be unfair to apply the ordinary canons of criticism to either the plays or the players. The difficulties against which the latter strove were great. Their scenery, such as it was, was poor, and their stage was so small that one could not swing a cat on it. [...] Yet, in spite of all drawbacks, there was much earnestness and some very creditable acting. [...] If the Irish Theatre Society would keep free from fantastic dreams and insane ideals, if it would desert Scandinavia and evacuate Camden Street [...] if it would rally its friends and stage-topics of national—not merely nationalist—interest, creditably and with due regard for public comfort, it should not find it difficult to catch a public in Dublin and in Ireland.

Appendix IV

London Visit, May 1903

A. B. WALKLEY, then dramatic critic of *The Times*, wrote at length of the first appearance of the Irish National Theatre Society in the Queen's Gate Hall, South Kensington, London, 2 May 1903. The following excerpts from his review paint the attitude of other English critics of the time towards the work of the society:

> Stendhal said that the greatest pleasure he had ever got from the theatre was given him by the performance of some poor Italian strollers in a barn. The Queen's Gate Hall, if not exactly a barn, can boast none of the glories of the ordinary playhouse; and it was here that only a day or two ago, a little band of Irish men and women, strangers to London and to Londoners, gave some of us who are for our sins constant frequenters of the ordinary playhouses, a few moments of calm delight quite outside the range of anything which those houses have to offer. They were members of the Irish National Theatre Society, which consists, we understand, of amateurs, all engaged in daily work, who can devote only their leisure time to the stage. That was the case, it will be remembered, with the enthusiasts who helped Antoine to found his *Théâtre Libre*; but there is this difference, that while the French enterprise was an artistic adventure and nothing else, the Irish Theatre is that and something more. It is part of a national movement, it is designed to express the spirit of the race, the 'virtue' of it in the medium of the acted

drama. That is an excellent design. If the peculiarities of Irish thought and feeling can be brought home to us through the drama, we shall all be the better for the knowledge, and the art of drama too cannot but gain by a change of air, a new outlook, a fresh current of ideas. [...] Our present business is to record the keen pleasure which an afternoon with the Irish National Theatre has afforded us and to do our best to analyse that pleasure.

First and foremost, there is the pleasure of the ear. This, of course, is an accidental pleasure. [...] It has nothing to do with the aesthetic aims of the society—nothing to do with art at all; it results from the nature of things; from the simple fact that Irish speakers are addressing English listeners. It is none the less a very exquisite pleasure. We had never realised the musical possibilities of our language until we had heard these Irish people speak it. Most Englishmen, we fancy, get their notions of Irish pronunciation from Thackeray, and though, no doubt, Thackeray's version was always good-natured enough, yet the talk of Costigan, and the Mulligan and the O'Dowd tends to burlesque the truth. [...] The English of these Irish players gives us an impression, not of drollery at all, but of elegance. [...] We are listening to English spoken with watchful care and slightly timorous hesitation, as though it were a learned language. [...] These Irish people *sing* our language—and always in a minor key. [...]

The next pleasure is for the eye. These Irish gentlemen and ladies are good to look at; the men are lithe, graceful, bright-eyed and at least one of the maidens, with the stage-name of Maire Nic Shiubhlaigh, is of a strange, wan, 'disquieting' beauty. [...] As a rule, they stand stock-still. The speaker of the moment is the only one who is allowed a little gesture—just as in the familiar convention of the Italian marionette theatre the figure supposed to be speaking is distinguished from others by a slight vibration. The listeners do not distract one's attention by fussy 'stage-business', they just stay where they are and listen. When they do move, it is without premeditation, haphazard, even with a little natural clumsiness, as of people who are conscious of being stared at in public. Hence a delightful effect of spontaneity [...] Add that the scenery is of Elizabethan simplicity—sometimes no more than a mere backcloth—and you will begin to see why this performance is a sight good for sore eyes—eyes made sore by the perpetual movement and glitter of the ordinary stage. [...] The Irish Theatre is entirely of its own kind and of none other. Its sustained note of subdued gravity, with here and there faint harmonics of weird elfish freakishness ('harps in the air', Hilda Wangel would have called them) is entirely Irish and entirely delightful. [...] They are all from the outset to the end playing *pianissimo*, all hushed as in some sick room, all grave, and, as it were, careworn. [...] We are sincerely grateful to them for an hour or two of real refreshment, a train of curious suggestions, a series of new thrills. [...]

The plays given in London were W. B. Yeats's *The Hour-glass*, *Kathleen Ni Houlihan* and *A Pot of Broth*; Lady Gregory's *Twenty-Five* and Fred Ryan's *The Laying of the Foundations*. The casts were:

The Hour-glass

The Wise Man	J. Dudley Digges.
Bridget (his wife)	Honor Lavelle.
His Children	Geoffrey Dearmer.
	Síghle Ni Gúinn.
His Pupils	P. J. Kelly.
	Seumas O'Sullivan.
	G. Roberts.
	P. Mac Shiubhlaigh.
The Angel	Maire Nic Shiubhlaigh.
The Fool	F. J. Fay.

Kathleen Ni Houlihan

Kathleen Ni Houlihan	Maire T. Quinn.
Delia Cahill	Maire Nic Shiubhlaigh.
Bridget Gillan	Honor Lavelle.
Patrick Gillan	P. J. Kelly.
Michael Gillan	J. Dudley Digges.
Peter Gillan	W. G. Fay.

A Pot of Broth

A Beggarman	W. G. Fay.
Sibby	Maire T. Quinn.
John	P. J. Kelly.

Twenty-Five

Michael Ford	P. J. Kelly.
Kate Ford	Maire Nic Shiubhlaigh.
Christie Henderson	W. G. Fay.
A Neighbour	Dora Hackett.
Another Neighbour	P. Mac Shiubhlaigh.

The Laying of the Foundations

Mr. O'Loskin, T. C.	F. J. Fay.
Michael	P. J. Kelly.
Alderman Farelly	J. Dudley Digges.
Mr MacFadden, T. C.	P. Mac Shiubhlaigh.
Mrs O'Loskin	Maire Nic Shiubhlaigh.
Mrs Macfadden	Honor Lavelle.
Eileen	Maire T. Quinn.

Appendix V

The Abbey Theatre

IN APRIL 1904, Miss A. E. F. Horniman wrote formally to W. B. Yeats as President of the Irish National Theatre Society:

Dear Mr Yeats,

I have great sympathy with the artistic and dramatic aims of the Irish National Theatre Company, as publicly explained by you on various occasions. I am glad to be able to offer you my assistance in your endeavours to establish a permanent Theatre in Dublin.

I am taking the Hall of the Mechanics' Institute in Abbey Street, and an adjoining building in Marlborough Street, which I propose to turn into a small theatre, with a proper entrance hall, green room, and dressing rooms. As the company will not require the hall constantly, I propose to arrange to let it for lectures and entertainments at a rental proportionate to its seating capacity.

The company can have the building rent free whenever they want it, for rehearsals and performances, except when it is let. The green room I hope to arrange to be kept for their sole use. They must pay for their own electric light and gas, as well as for the repair of damages done during their occupation. The building will be insured, and any additions to the lighting for special occasions or plays, must be permitted by the insurance company, formally in writing.

If any president, vice president or member of the company wants the hall for a lecture, concert or entertainment, the rent must be paid to me as by an ordinary person. If a lecture be given on a dramatic or theatrical subject and the gross receipts go to the Irish National Theatre, then the president, vice president or member of the company can have the hall for nothing. But it must be advertised clearly as being for the sole benefit of the Irish National Theatre, pecuniarily, as well as in aid of its artistic objects.

The prices of the seats can be raised, of course, but not lowered, neither by the Irish National Theatre, nor by anyone who will hire the hall.

This is to prevent cheap entertainments from being given, which would lower the letting value of the hall. I hope to be able to arrange to number most of the seats and to sell the tickets beforehand, with a small fee for booking. The entrance to the more expensive seats will be from Marlborough Street, where there will be a cloak room.

The situation, being near to the tramway terminus, is convenient for people living in any part of Dublin. I shall take every possible means to ensure the safety and convenience of the public. I can only afford to make a very little theatre, and it must be quite simple. You all must do the rest to make a powerful and prosperous theatre, with a high artistic ideal.

A copy of this letter will be sent to each vice president and another to the stage manager of the company.

Yours sincerely,

A. E. F. Horniman[4].

On 11 December 1904, the society replied:

---

[4]Letters quoted Samhain: *An Occasional Review*, Edited by W. B. Yeats (Dublin: Sealy Bryers and Walker; London: T. Fisher Unwin).

Dear Miss Horniman,

We, the undersigned members of the Irish National Theatre Company, beg to thank you for the interest you have evinced in the work of the society and for the aid you propose giving to our future work by securing a permanent theatre in Abbey Street.

We undertake to abide by all the conditions laid down in your letter to the company, and to do our utmost to forward the objects of the society.

The letter was signed by W. B. Yeats, Thomas G. Keohler, F. J. Fay, Harry F. Norman, William G. Fay, Helen S. Laird, James G. Starkey, George Russell (A. E.), Prionsias Mac Siubhlaigh (Frank Walker), Maire Nic Shiubhlaigh (Mary Walker), Adolphus Wright, J. M. Synge, Marghreth Ni Gharbhaigh (Miss Garvey), Sara Allgood, Vera Esposito, Frederick Ryan, Dora L. Ainnesley, Padraic Mac Cuilim (Padraic Colum), George Roberts, Stephen Gwynne, *An Craoibhín Aoibhinn* (Douglas Hyde) and Augusta Gregory.

OPENING PERFORMANCE, 27 DECEMBER 1904

The casts of the new plays produced at the opening of the
theatre were as follows:

On Baile's Strand, by W. B. Yeats

CúChullain, The King of Muirthemne	F. J. Fay.
Concobar, the High King of Ullad	George Roberts.
	Daire, a King
	Arthur Sinclair Fintain.
A Blind Man	Seumas O'Sullivan.
Barach, a Fool	W. G. Fay.
A Young Man	P. Mac Shiubhlaigh.
Young Kings and Old Kings	Maire Ni Gharbhaigh.
	Emma Vernon.
	Sara Allgood.
	Doreen Gunning.
	R. Nash.
	N. Power.
	U. Wright.
	E. Keegan.

Spreading the News by Lady Gregory

Bartley Fallon	W. G. Fay.
Mrs Fallon	Sara Allgood.
Mrs Tully	Emma Vernon.
Mrs Tarpey	Maire Ni Gharbhaigh.
Shawn Early	J. H. Dunne.
Tim Casey	George Roberts.
James Ryan	Arthur Sinclair.
Jack Smith	P. Mac Shiubhlaigh.

A Policeman	R. S. Nash.
A Removable Magistrate	F. J. Fay

On 27, 29 and 31 December 1904, *On Baile's Strand* was followed by:

Kathleen Ni Houlihan, by W. B. Yeats

Kathleen Ni Houlihan	Maire Nic Shiubhlaigh.
Peter Gillane	W. G. Fay.
Bridget Gillane	Sara Allgood.
Michael Gillane	P. Mac Shiubhlaigh.
Patrick Gillane	U. Wright.
Delia Cahill	Maire Ni Gharbhaigh.

On 28 and 30 December 1904, and on 2 and 3 January 1905, *On Baile's Strand* was followed by:

In the Shadow of the Glen, by J. M. Synge

Dan Burke, farmer and herd	George Roberts.
Nora Burke, his wife	Maire Nic Shiubhlaigh.
Michael Dara, a young herd	P. Mac Shiubhlaigh.
A Tramp	W. G. Fay.

Appendix VI

Irish National Theatre Society Productions 1902–1905

At the Antient Concert Rooms, Dublin:

29 October 1902:
The Laying of the Foundations   Fred Ryan.
The Sleep of the King   James Cousins.

30 October 1902:
A Pot of Broth   W. B. Yeats.

31 October 1902:
The Racing Lug   James Cousins.
Eilis agus an Bean Deirce
(Eilis and the Beggarwoman)   P. T. McGinley.

At the Molesworth Hall, Dublin:

14 March 1903:
The Hour-glass   W. B. Yeats.
Twenty-Five   Lady Gregory.

8 October 1903:
The King's Threshold   W. B. Yeats.
In the Shadow of the Glen   J. M. Synge.

3 December 1903:
Broken Soil[5]   Padraic Colum.

14 January 1904:
The Shadowy Waters   W. B. Yeats.
The Townland of Tamney   Seumas MacManus.

25 February 1904:
Riders to the Sea   J. M. Synge.

At the Abbey Theatre, Dublin:

27 December 1904:
On Baile's Strand   W. B. Yeats.
Spreading the News   Lady Gregory.

4 February 1905:
The Well of the Saints   J. M. Synge.

25 March 1905:
Kincora   Lady Gregory.

25 April 1905:
The Building Fund   William Boyle.

9 June 1905:
The Land   Padraic Colum.

The Land was the last play produced by the Irish National Theatre Society; shortly after its production the society was dissolved and its place taken by the Irish National Theatre Society, Limited.

---

[5]Later rewritten as *The Fiddler's House* (1907).

The following is the list of player-members of the original society, 1902–1905:

Sara Allgood, Catia Nic Chormac, Maire Ni Gharbhaigh, Doreen Gunning, Dora Hackett, Honor Lavelle, Dora Melville, Maire Perolz, Máire T. Quinn, Eithne Nic Shiubhlaigh (Eileen O'Doherty), Maire Nic Shiubhlaigh, Padragan Nic Shiubhlaigh (Betty King), Emma Vernon (Vera Esposito), N. Butler, Padraic Colum, Brian Callender, C. Caulfield, W. Conroy, E. Davis, J. Dudley Digges, J. H. Dunne. F. J. Fay, W. G. Fay, P. Josephs, E. Keegan, P. J. Kelly, De Courcey Millar, R. S. Nash, Seumas O'Sullivan, A. Power, N. Power, George Roberts, Fred Ryan, Arthur Sinclair, H. Sproule (James Cousins), P. Mac Shiubhlaigh (Frank Walker), J. E. Sheridan, S. Sheridan-Neill and U. Wright (and others).

Appendix VII

Theatre of Ireland Productions
1906–1912

(asterisk indicates first productions)

At the Molesworth Hall, Dublin:

6 December 1906:
The Racing Lug   James Cousins.
Brand (Act Four)   Henrik Ibsen.
Casadh an tSúgain
(The Twisting of the Rope)   Douglas Hyde.

At the Large Concert Hall, Rotunda, Dublin:

21 March 1907:
*The Fiddler's House   Padraic Colum.
The Last Feast of the Fianna   Alice Milligan.

At the Abbey Theatre, Dublin:

13 December 1907:
Deirdre   George Russell.
*The Matchmakers   Seumas O'Kelly.

22 May 1908:
*The Miracle of the Corn   Padraic Colum.

Maeve	Edward Martyn.
The Enthusiast	Lewis Purcell.

24 November 1908:

The Turn of the Road	Rutherford Mayne.
*The Flame on the Hearth[6]	Seumas O'Kelly.

At the Large Concert Hall, Rotunda, Dublin:

29 April 1909:

*The Shuiler's Child	Seumas O'Kelly.
The Gomeril	Rutherford Mayne.

12 November 1909:

Deirdre (Gaelic)	Revd Thomas O'Kelly.

At the Molesworth Hall, Dublin:

10 February 1910:

The True-born Irishman	Charles Macklin.
*Expiation	Kathleen Fitzpatrick.

28 March 1910:

*The Spurious Sovereign	Gerald MacNamara.
*The Homecoming	Seumas O'Kelly.

12 February 1911:

The Storm	Alexander Ostrovsky

At the Hall, Hardwicke Street, Dublin:

17 November 1911:

*The Marriage of Julia Elizabeth	James Stephens.

18 and 19 December 1911:

---

[6]Later retitled *The Stranger*.

*A Bunch of Lavender	Jane Barlow.
*The Widow Dempsey's Funera	Watty Cox.

18, 19 and 20 April 1912:
Metempsychosis	Thomas MacDonagh.
The Reformers	Lewis Purcell.

2 and 3 May 1912:
Caitlin Ni Uallachain	W. B. Yeats
	(Revd Thomas O'Kelly).
An Gliocas	Pádraig Ó Séaghadha.

1 July 1912:
The Ordeal of David	Victor O'D. Power.

Players:
Catia Nic Cormac, Nora Fitzpatrick, U. Hogan, Betty King, Honor Lavelle, Constance Markievicz, Nelly O'Brian, Eileen O'Doherty, Sheela Hallissy, Maire Nic Shiubhlaigh, Charles Brady, Matthew Carolan, J. M. Carrie, Padraic Colum, G. Fitzgerald, Ian Gilbert, Joseph Goggin, A. H. Gordon, Tommy Gordon, Edward Keegan, Luke Kileen, Frank Lowrey, F. MacDonald, Thomas R. Madden, Jack Morrow, Austin Martin, Rutherford Mayne, J. Stuart Myles, George Nesbitt, Diarmuid O'Conaire, Seumas O'Conghaile, Seumas O'Sullivan, William Pearse, Ambrose Power, Eugene Sheehy, Prionsias Mac Siubhlaigh, James Stephens and Diarmuid Trench (and others).

19–24 April 1915:
Pagans	Thomas MacDonagh.
The Walls of Athens	Eimar O'Duffy.

28 June–4 July 1915:
Uncle Vanya	Anton Chekhov.

8–13 November 1915:
The Privilege of Place	Edward Martyn.

27 December 1915–1 January 1916[7]:
Bairbre Ruadh[8]   Padraic O Conaire.
The Phoenix on the Roof   Eimar O'Duffy.
Author! Author!   John MacDonagh.
The Swan Song   Anton Chekhov.

3–7 March 1916:
Easter   August Strindberg.

[7]This list is incomplete. I have been unable to secure the date of every performance of the company during this period.
[8]First produced at the Oireachtas, 1908.

Appendix VIII
Irish Theatre Productions, 1914–1916

(asterisk indicates first productions)

At 40 Upper O'Connell Street, Dublin:

2–7 November 1914:
The Dream Physician   Edward Martyn.

At The Hall, Hardwicke Street, Dublin:

4–9 January 1915:
Fe Bhrig na Mionn (The Troth)   Rutherford Mayne
                                   (trans. Liam O Domhnaill).

The Revolt   Auguste Villiers de l'Isle-Adam.
The Phoenix on the Roof   Eimar O'Duffy.
The Swan Song   Anton Chekhov.

12, 13, 15 and 16 February 1915:
The Dream Physician   Edward Martyn.

Acknowledgements

It's impossible to thank everyone who has given me help and encouragement with this project. The most deserving recipient of my gratitude is my mother, Gráinne Kenny. Without her aid and memories I might still be sitting on this book. Like Maire Nic Shiubhlaigh (pronounced 'nee hew-lee'), she is a strong, irrepressible, resilient woman with more accomplishments than I could ever hope to achieve. I love you, mum.

Also my beautiful wife, Gill, for her love and support over the years, and in particular for tolerating me endlessly babbling on about the Abbey and 1916.

My sisters, Niamh and Deirdre, have been part of this story all of their lives. This book is for them too, and their other halves, Rory Hickey and Martin Murphy.

And let's give a shout out to Ben and Amelie Lewis (the coolest kids in the world), Paul and Carmel Carroll, and Sophie and Dom Lewis, and Minnie, my writing companion.

I'm also grateful to my cousin, Kevin Stanley, and his family (Annie's grandchildren) for their assistance. And the Careys— Daisy Walker's grandchildren. They were more like brothers and sisters than cousins to us growing up. This is for Nóinín and Kathleen.

I'd like to thank Teresa Breathnach for all her invaluable help in bringing Matthew to life … and for falling so madly in love with him. Paul Horan deserves a special tip of the hat for unearthing the O'Hanrahan/Carlow connection for me. *Maith an fear*. Also, my thanks to Fearghall McGarry.

Extra special thanks goes to Mairéad Delaney at the Abbey for her tireless work and assistance digging out pictures. Thanks also to Fiach Mac Conghail and his crew for allowing us to use the J. B. Yeats portrait, and the other images in this book.

I can't praise the staff at the National Library highly enough. I'm a journalist, not a historian, and their quiet help and enthusiasm helped spur me on in my research. Many thanks. The papers I drew from are ms27,618-27,635, ms49,752/32, ms49,752/42, ms49,752/35 and ms49,752/36.

I will donate my 'ephemera' to the NLI when I have finished my next book, which is about Gipsy.

The other sources I used for my introduction are Ted and Maire's papers and books, Witness Statements from the Bureau of Military History, interviews with family members (including the gorgeous Julie Robinson), and a plethora of other odds and ends. I get countless emails every year from academics and Maire fans from all around the world. Thank you for the snippets and for keeping her memory alive.

Finally—and with heartfelt gratitude—I would like to thank the staff at New Island Books. Thank you Dan Bolger and Edwin Higel for seeing the importance of this book. Shauna Daly, you did a great job on the photo section! Justin Corfield, you deserve a medal for your patience with me and all the last-minute changes. You, sir, are quite possibly the best in the business.

And thanks, Dad. It's your birthday (10 February) as I type this. I hope you're enjoying a celestial pint.

dave@davekenny.com